White Man's Wicked Water

White Man's Wicked Water

The Alcohol Trade and Prohibition in Indian Country, 1802–1892

William E. Unrau

To Jeanne Gorham,
with very best wishes —
Bill Unrau

University Press of Kansas

Published by the University Press of Kansas (Lawrence, Kansas
66049), which was organized by the Kansas Board of Regents and is
operated and funded by Emporia State University, Fort Hays State
University, Kansas State University, Pittsburg State University,
the University of Kansas, and Wichita State University

Library of Congress Cataloging-in-Publication Data

Unrau, William E., 1929–
White man's wicked water: the alcohol trade and prohibition in Indian
country, 1802–1892 / William E. Unrau.
p.   cm.
Includes bibliographical references and index.
ISBN 0-7006-0779-X (alk. paper)
1. Indians of North America—Alcohol use—West (U.S.)   2. Indians
of North America—West (U.S.)—History—19th century.   3. Indians of
North America—West (U.S.)—Social conditions.   4. Liquor industry—
West (U.S.)—History—19th century.   5. Prohibition—West (U.S.)—
History—19th century.   6. West (U.S.)—History—19th century.
I. Title.
E78.W5U57   1996
362.29′2′0978—dc20   95-51317

British Library Cataloguing in Publication Data is available.

Printed in the United States of America

10 9 8 7 6 5 4 3 2 1

The paper used in this publication meets
the minimum requirements of the American National Standard
for Permanence of Paper for Printed Library Materials
Z39.48-1984.

*To the memory of my mother,
Margaret Epp Unrau—
teacher in Indian country*

CONTENTS

(A photo insert follows page 59.)

PREFACE

I first became interested in alcohol in Indian country as a fledgling graduate student at the University of Wyoming nearly forty years ago. During the course of my research on the relationship between Fort Larned and the Santa Fe Trail, I came across a sick report compiled by the surgeon general for that remote military post in western Kansas, covering the years 1870–1875. The report provided the mean strength of the officers and enlisted men stationed there and listed their afflictions over the four-year period: remittent and intermittent fevers, rheumatism, consumption, syphilis, gonorrhea, pneumonia, bronchitis, diarrhea, hernia, dysentery, gunshot wounds, and alcoholism. The data for 1872–1873 were of particular interest, for they indicated that 34 percent of the six officers and 110 enlisted men were alcoholics and that this "local disease" had been on the increase every year since medical statistics were first compiled at Fort Larned in 1868.[1]

That the situation at Fort Larned was no exception became apparent from reports from other military installations in Indian country—at Fort Laramie in 1864, for example, where more than half of Company E of the Eleventh Ohio Volunteer Cavalry headed for Deer Creek Station were drunk and firing at one another,[2] or at Fort Dodge in 1872, where the entire mail escort headed for Fort Supply were so intoxicated they could not ride their horses.[3] But what made the situation at Fort Larned especially intriguing was that in the mid-1860s it also served as official headquarters for the Kiowa-Comanche Indian Agency and other Plains tribes attracted to the area for annuity distributions by the federal government and commerce moving along the great wagon highway between Missouri and Santa Fe.

I was well aware of the federal prohibition against alcohol sales to Indians in Indian country since the early 1830s and, despite the military presence there, of the almost routine complaints of Indian agents that illicit alcohol was destroying the tribes more rapidly than gunpowder or the advance of white yeomen with the plow. I was tempted to seize upon an easy solution to the problem, but more thoughtful consideration suggested that drunkenness and disorder in the frontier military establishment were only symptomatic of larger forces underlying the deluge of alcohol in Indian country.

Subsequent research leading to the publication (with Craig Miner) of a study dealing with Indian removal from Kansas[4] underscored the devastating character and consequences of the land cession–annuity subsidy strategy for the white assault into Indian country, and, with few exceptions, a corresponding increase in alcohol consumption by those being dispossessed. A cursory search suggested also that the more restrictive Indian prohibition became in an increasingly vague region called Indian country, the greater the amount of alcohol consumed by Indians.

While there are numerous case studies dealing with Indians and alcohol in the American West, most are local and insular in nature, and for the most part ignore the judicial problems accompanying prohibition and enforcement within the framework of federal removal policy dating back to the days of Jefferson. The one exception is Otto Frovin Frederickson,[5] who half a century ago addressed what he called "The Liquor Question" among the Indian people of nineteenth-century Kansas. Often cited as the definitive work on government efforts to interdict the flow of alcohol west of Missouri, Frederickson's study contains a wealth of detail regarding trade violations but is deficient on prohibition as an integral part of federal Indian policy and especially the legal problems of Indian county, and blatantly ethnocentric regarding the Indians' supposed natural inclination to drunkenness.

Other than challenging this racist view and suggesting that the advent and proliferation of alcohol among Indians in Indian country are at bottom strong evidence of tribal accommodation to a pervasive aspect of white culture in the nineteenth century, this study offers no new theory regarding "problem" drinking among Indians, either then or now. Rather, the emphasis is on the relationship between Indian country as an evolving legal fiction and Indian drinking there, within the framework of a cumbersome prohibition code made all the more innocuous by the breakdown of the frontier judicial process and the lawless opportunism of liquor vendors who invaded Indian country with impunity.

Heavy drinking of whites amidst or in close proximity to Indians may have encouraged resentment and defiance among would-be native imbibers, and it is possible that individual or tribal drinking orgies were a form of protest against prohibition and the white onslaught against traditional Indianness. But in the absence of documentary evidence from the Indians' side of the ledger, a conclusion of this sort is more speculation than fact. The most that may be said is that, like their non-Indian mentors who were determined to reshape Indian culture on the white model, Indians in Indian country learned to savor the pleasures of the bottle and, like their white counterparts, occasionally drank to excess.

I am indebted to several people in the preparation of this study. Elliott West, Robin Room, Burton Smith, Patricia Prestwich, and Fred Woodward read all or parts of the manuscript, and to them I wish to express gratitude for their critical comments and suggestions for clarification or revision. Brian W. Dippie, James Duram, Kevin Ast, Barbara Beale, Craig Robbins, and Debbie Taylor provided valuable research assistance, and Ann Cummings—former graduate student at Wichita State University and now on the staff of the National Archives—warrants special thanks for her guidance in identifying obscure records dealing with Indians and alcohol in nineteenth-century America. And as in the past, I profited a great deal from discussions with Joe Herring on the nature and complexity of Indian/white relations in the trans-Missouri West.

Chapter 1

Setting the Standard

Theories regarding excessive consumption of alcohol by American Indians in the United States are legion. In scope they range from the destructive impact of federal Indian policy and the difficulty of sustaining Indianness in the face of white oppression, to genetic weakness, dysfunctional dependency behavior, or cumulative frustrations accompanying cultural marginality and transformation. A veritable flood of articles, books, and special studies on the subject have inundated libraries in recent decades. Yet the enormous amount of research has yet to provide a consensus regarding the paramount reason or reasons for chronic Indian inebriety. So long as Indians drink, the research—conclusive or otherwise—goes on.[1]

Some historians may ignore this quandary on the grounds that causality is the domain of the social scientist or, perhaps, the theologian. But historians are humanists, and humanistic inquiry at the least is concerned with violence and serenity, with death and survival, and ultimately, the extent to which well-being was realized through human action. Applied to widespread and often fatal consumption of alcohol by Indians in the face of an expansive, ethnocentric, and hard-drinking white society determined to reshape Indian culture in its own image, a view of this sort suggests that, whatever else may explain Indian accommodation to the potentially destructive commodity, it would be difficult to argue that white America played no role in Indians' turning to drink. After all, on the stalking ground of acculturation, most Indians adapted well to iron, the horse, gunpowder, and lawyers—so why not alcohol?[2]

Clearly, non-Indians drank heavily during the formative years of the American republic. One foreign observer was "perfectly astonished at the extent of intemperance," while another reported "general addiction to hard drinking." Whether Americans were simply regular tipplers and not outright drunkards, as one British traveler suggested, was challenged by a Scottish observer who concluded that because Americans were so "seasoned" from habitual heavy drinking they did not appear as intoxicated as in fact they often were.[3] Based on extended travel and residence in America, Englishman William Cobbett devoted several pages to Americans literally floundering in a sea of alcohol. Admitting he had "turned from the thought, as men do from thinking of any mortal disease that is at work in their frame," Cobbett lamented, "It is not covetousness; it is not niggardliness; it is not insincerity; it is not enviousness; it is not cowardice; above all things, it is DRINKING. . . . You cannot go into hardly any man's house, without being asked to drink wine, spirits, even IN THE MORNING. . . . Even little boys at, or under, TWELVE years of age, go into stores and tip off their DRAMS!"[4]

Domestic observers agreed with reports of such widespread consumption. Drunkenness was "everywhere prevalent," and the quantity of spirits consumed was "scandalous."[5] Besides 90 proof distilled whiskey, rum, gin, and brandy consumed with abandon at local taverns, at home "there was a continuous dabbling in spirits, grog, sling, toddy, flips, juleps, elixirs, &c., as if alcohol in one or other of its seductive disguises, had become a necessity of life."[6] Given an 1830 estimated annual consumption of over seven gallons of spirits, wine, cider, and beer for every adult (age fifteen or older) in the United States,[7] it is not surprising that frontier preachers and eastern literati alike decried the excess. Methodist circuit rider Peter Cartwright was saddened by a man who asserted that unless he drank with him "he would never hear me preach again,"[8] while in New England, in an essay extolling the virtues of water and milk over alcohol, Nathaniel Hawthorne averred that from the lowly town pump "must flow the stream that shall cleanse our earth of the vast portion of its crime and anguish which has gushed from the fiery fountains of the still."[9]

But Hawthorne's plea to the contrary, water and milk often were not preferable to distilled whiskey, which in the first third of the nineteenth century emerged as virtually the beverage of national choice. Clear, sparkling water—as opposed to the sediment-laden water from the Ohio, Mississippi, and other rivers, not to mention the high mineral content of water taken from most wells—was at a premium, and in most instances was considered lacking in nutrition and of little value in digesting the heavy diet of bread, meat, and potatoes consumed by the masses. Milk supplies were dependent on local, seasonal production, and when in short supply were necessarily reserved for children. Lack of refrigeration precluded storage; prices were erratic (sometimes higher than for an equal amount of whiskey), and the fear of fatal milk sickness caused by poison transmitted from cows was widespread. Whiskey, by contrast, provided no such hazards. It would not spoil. It seemed to stimulate digestion and certainly could be transported more profitably than the grain from which it was manufactured. But most important of all, for family stills and commercial distilleries alike, it provided a lucrative market for the burgeoning corn production of the trans-Appalachian West.[10] And ideologically, as whiskey displaced un-American gin, rum, and expensive foreign Madeira, its regular ingestion for many prompted feelings of patriotism and individual self-assurance during the nationalistic fervor following the War of 1812. Indeed, corn liquor took on the status of a cult. Queried one distiller critical of British, Irish, French, and Dutch habits of the glass, "[A]nd why should not our country have a national beverage?"[11]

Business and government alike promoted the regular consumption of alcohol. Contrary to the view that benevolence born of paternalism loomed large in the issuance of three or four jiggers of whiskey a day to Irish canallers,[12] the fact is that alcohol was an important element in keeping workers on the job. It was a component of real wages figured directly into labor costs or sold on credit in company stores. It provided a means of overcoming the dull and physically demanding spadework needed to put bread (and more whiskey) in workers' stomachs; and in anticipation of the regular arrival of the whiskey pail while on the job, it was a powerful incentive to keep workers from defecting from the grim reality of their day-to-day exertions. In short, whether by calculation or economic expediency, the chronic consumption of alcohol by laborers was encouraged by contractors.[13] The same can be said for boatmen employed by the major fur companies in the trans-Missouri West. Since federal law prohibited the sale of whiskey to Indians, special licenses granted by the Indian Office for boatmen consumption suggest just how crucial spirits were to the viability of the trade. Not a little of the alcohol eventually went to the Indians, of course, but that the boatmen expected and received their share is patently clear. In 1831, according to the commander at Fort Leavenworth, no less than 8,000 gallons of liquor went up the Missouri River. The following year one trader alone was granted a permit for 450 gallons of whiskey, and in 1833 the American

Fur Company was obliged to ship corn from distant Missouri in order to keep its "excellent quality" distillery at the mouth of the Yellowstone River in production.[14]

The government promoted alcohol consumption in other ways as well. During the American Revolution each soldier was allowed one gill (four ounces) of whiskey as part of his daily ration. General Washington also authorized each brigade to engage the services of a sutler who was allowed to sell unspecified quantities of spirits at fixed prices, but not after nine at night or the beating of reveilles, or during divine services on Sundays.[15] In practice, however, the federal "spirit ration" was superseded or more often augmented by the individual colonies. In 1776, for example, the Maryland Council of Safety authorized its troops to receive a daily ration of one-half pint of rum per man plus discretionary allowances for special occasions, while in that same year the Pennsylvania Assembly fixed the ration for Pennsylvania soldiers at one quart of small beer per man per day.[16] Even with these seemingly generous allowances, however, it was impossible to keep the soldier out of the private resorts that inevitably sprang up around military installations and fields of operations, and for the next century, in a dizzying fluctuation of regulations regarding the dangers, virtues, and amounts of alcohol to be dispensed, one thing was clear: alcohol consumption was a vital part of military life in the United States.

The legislative record and military regulations bear this out. On April 30, 1790, one year after the War Department was established, Congress reduced the daily ration of alcohol to half a gill of rum, brandy, or whiskey, and on March 3, 1799, eliminated the ration except for those who had enlisted prior to that date. But an important provision of the law allowed commanding officers to issue half a gill of spirits and more in the case of fatigue or extraordinary circumstances. Three years later, on March 16, 1802, Congress not only reinstated the spirit ration but doubled the amount to one full gill. And in response to Jefferson's belief, as well as that of former President Adams, that other forms of alcohol might better promote good health in the military, Congress allowed a malt liquor or low wine option equivalent to the amount of rum, whiskey, or brandy authorized two years earlier.[17]

During the Monroe administration Secretary of War John C. Calhoun voiced concerns over the spirit ration, mainly on disciplinary and medical grounds. The surgeon general, however, provided no strong support for eliminating the ration, and so Calhoun enlisted the aid of the Commissary of General Subsistence, whose lackadaisical response in 1820 was to issue a general circular providing for the substitution of money to those soldiers who opted not to accept the alcohol ration.[18] Few post commanders paid heed to the circular, and there the matter rested until 1829, when the House of Representatives directed the secretary of war to report on "what beneficial effects, if any, have risen . . . from the daily use of spirituous liquors by the Army, and whether the consequences . . . have not been, and will not be, injurious; and particularly of its influence upon the health, morals, and discipline of the soldiers."[19]

The final report presented by Secretary of War Peter B. Porter "deduced" four "propositions" drawn from studies carried out by army headquarters, the surgeon general, and the commanding general of subsistence,

1. The habitual use of ardent spirits, even in moderate quantities, was unfavorable to health; and the chances for health were generally greater for those who found it convenient to wholly abstain.
2. The use of one gill a day at proper times would not seriously impair the health of a man of active employment.
3. Sudden and total abandonment of the free use of alcohol will diminish a man's vigor, and probably injure rather than improve his health and constitution.
4. The evils of intemperance in the army arose not from the spirit ration but rather from excessive quantities procured by other means.[20]

The fourth proposition constituted the core of the report. Secretary Porter bemoaned the fact that too many confirmed drunkards were enlisted. Soldiers who purchased liquor without permission were severely punished, he emphasized, while the citizen who sold the liquor was not "obnoxious to the slightest punishment" under existing laws of the several states. Surgeon General James Lovell concurred. Emphasizing that the soldier could obtain ardent spirits from his ration, the sutler, or from the "host of hucksters who infest almost every military post," Lovell singled out the latter and especially civil court inaction as ultimately responsible for the evils of military inebriation. "The sin of intemperance which is laid at the door of the Army," he lamented, "belongs in truth to the community from which it is taken."[21]

Nothing resulted from the report, although Secretary Porter's suggestion that a monetary commutation for the spirit ration "might be advantageously adopted"[22] provided the groundwork for change in the future. That change came with the appointment of John H. Eaton as head of the War Department during the first Jackson administration in 1829. A strong supporter of the fledgling temperance movement, Eaton presented a blistering report to Congress in February 1830, in which he provided statistics indicating that the majority of desertions in the army were attributable to alcohol consumption. Congress took no action, but on the following November 30, citing the "pernicious effect" of alcohol on the health, morals,and discipline of the army, Secretary Eaton issued a department order abrogating the spirit ration and providing an allowance of money in lieu thereof to be issued by the Subsistence Department, computing the alcohol ration at the contract price of delivery.[23]

No period of sobriety in the army immediately ensued. As early as 1821, War Department regulations had turned the position of sutler from that of unofficial camp follower (similar to laundresses and blacksmiths) to that of official post sutler, with important duties for providing for the health and comfort of men in the ranks.[24] Having eliminated the spirit ration in favor of a monetary substitute, Secretary Eaton's 1830 order did nothing to end the sutler's authority to sell alcohol. In fact, with their newly awarded substitute money, thirsty recruits could now obtain their liquid repast from the sutler, who under the new regulations was allowed to sell twice the amount of the original ration to individual imbibers, the only requirements being that purchases had to be approved by commanding officers and not consumed prior to noon of each day. This proved unsatisfactory, and two years later, under order of Secretary of War Lewis Cass, the sutler's authority to dispense spirits was rescinded as well. But the fatigue ration remained—indeed thrived—as did the hosts of private dispensers who vied with one another "to sell their products at all hours of the night." Finally, on July 5, 1838, Congress substituted coffee and sugar for the fatigue ration, only to have the latter creep back into official use by the Revised Army Regulations of August 10, 1861.[25]

The fatigue ration meant whatever a company or regimental commander wished to have it mean, as is evident in the issuance of a barrel of whiskey to Captain Eugene F. Ware at Fort Kearney, in 1863, as he prepared to construct Fort Cottonwood near the confluence of the North and South Platte Rivers. Ware's practice was to provide his men with a gill of whiskey in the morning and another in the afternoon, which in his words "worked well." With army approval, the company of about seventy-five enlisted men eventually required seven more barrels (totaling 250 gallons) to complete the job.[26] And as evidence that officers consumed their share of fatigue alcohol, we have the words of Union Commander George McClellan on the occasion of reviewing the conviction of an officer for drunkenness in early 1862: "Would all the officers unite in setting the soldiers an example of total abstinence from intoxicating drinks, it would be equal to an addition of 50,000 to the armies of the United States." McClellan meant business, particularly after Senator Samuel C. Pomeroy of Kansas charged that one-third of all Union casualties in one campaign alone were "chargeable to the daily ration of whiskey and quinine," and on June 19, 1862, he ordered that the fatigue ration be replaced with hot coffee—an order that obviously meant little in Indian country west of Fort Kearney.[27]

In the post–Civil War years government policy focused on the sutler as the scapegoat for drunkenness and demoralization in the military, and on July 28, 1866, the office was abolished. Then, following several years of confusion involving certain temporary exceptions to the sutler's legal demise, Congress passed a law on July 15, 1870, authorizing the secretary of war to permit one or more private trading establishments at military posts not in the vicinity of towns or cities, for benefit of the military and nonmilitary alike. Officially, the post trader now returned to the status of camp follower, and efforts to regulate military drinking went down the drain. Officers and enlisted men had their clubrooms and drinking quarters, where in company with Indians, trappers, miners, emigrants, cowhands, desperados, entrepreneurs, gamblers, or government agents they could drink to their heart's content. A few efforts of questionable legality were made to enforce the 1862 prohibition, and in 1881 President Rutherford B. Hayes ordered the War Department to take "suitable steps" to prevent the sale of intoxicating liquors at military posts. But after a short period of control the government-sanctioned saloons were once again booming, certainly after the War Department, in response to the 1881 presidential order, ruled that beer and wine were not intoxicating liquors.[28]

During the better part of the nineteenth century, then, efforts to eliminate or control drinking in the military were compromised by policies and practices that, with few exceptions, deemed drinking as a standard of military life—as important to men of the ranks as to the farmer, the merchant, or the canaller. Such was the crux of Secretary of War Porter's report on alcohol to Congress in 1829:

> To render an army efficient, a rigor of discipline . . . becomes indispensable. Soldiers are aware of this, and cheerfully submit to it from its acknowledged necessity. But absolutely to deprive a citizen, because he is a soldier, of the necessities, or even comforts, which should belong equally to all . . . is not more justifiable in military than it would be in civil life. While it is impossible not to commend the object of those who would legislate from soldiers the use of ardent spirits, it is confidently believed that the subject should rest where it now is; leaving a broad discretion to . . . the officers of the Army, who best know the habits and wants of this class of men.[29]

With regard to Indian affairs, however, distinctions between military and civil were clouded. From the beginning, Indian administration was assigned to the War Department and so remained until relinquished to the newly created Interior Department in 1849. On September 11, 1789, Congress authorized territorial governors to serve as ex officio superintendents of Indian affairs, and, by subsequent intercourse acts, civilian agents were assigned to specific tribes, with responsibilities for residing among the Indians, encouraging allegiance to the United States, and "civilizing" them in the agricultural and domestic arts. These agents, many of them former military officers, were under the supervision of the superintendents and were directed to report through them to the secretary of war, who had final responsibility for implementing policies established by Congress and the executive branch.[30]

Preventing Indians from obtaining alcohol, which as policy began during the first Jefferson administration,[31] exacerbated not infrequent dissension between military and civilian administration of Indian affairs. Both camps, however, were involved in the distribution of alcohol in Indian country, while rationalizing their actions within the context of government policy or blaming others for the increasing inebriety of the tribes.

There is no question that agents and superintendents used alcohol in their dealings with the Indians. In September 1825, at the St. Peters Agency in Minnesota, Agent Lawrence Taliaferro authorized the distribution of fifteen kegs (150 gallons) of whiskey to the Chippewas "to do away with their present impression and the belief that they were poisoned by drinking mixed whiskey given to them by the [government] Commissioners at the late [August 19, 1825] treaty at Prairie du Chien."[32] One of these commissioners was Lewis Cass, then governor of Michigan Territory and ex officio head of the Michigan Superintendency, who two years later in a widely circulated periodical insisted, "Every practicable method has been adopted by the government of the United States, effectually to prevent this [liquor] traffic." Continued Cass,

> The inordinate indulgence of the Indians in spirituous liquors is one of the most deplorable consequences, which has resulted from their intercourse with civilized man. Human nature . . . presents no phenomenon like this. . . . But the Indians in *immediate contact with our settlements* [emphasis added], old and young, male and female, the chief and the warrior, all give themselves up to the most brutal intoxication whenever this mad water can be procured.[33]

Wherever it could be procured was no less significant, as Cass failed to note in his indictment of sources other than the military. Prior to the Prairie du Chien affair of 1825, the future secretary of war had ordered 662 gallons of whiskey for the Saginaw Chippewa treaty of 1819 and 932 gallons of whiskey for the Ottawa, Chippewa, and Potawatomi treaty at Chicago in 1821.[34] To the north, at the Sault Ste. Marie Agency, Cass's performance was matched by that of Agent Henry Rowe Schoolcraft, who in 1822 sought to wean the Indians of his agency away from the British at Drummond Island by "some of your father's milk [alcohol], that you may drink to his health,"[35] and to the south in Kansas Territory by Perry Fuller, who sold poisoned alcohol to Indians just prior to his appointment as Sauk and Fox agent in 1859.[36]

The military could complain of Indian agency involvement in the alcohol trade with Indians, as was the case in 1832 when the commander at Fort Crawford accused the Prairie du Chien subagent of being engaged in "this unlawful traffic,"[37] but it was the military who came under more regular fire for complicity and even encouragement of Indian drinking. While on winter leave in 1830, Agent Taliferro was appalled by the amount of whiskey consumed by the Indians at St. Peters and, more particularly, the failure of troops from nearby Fort Snelling to "put a stop to this greatest of all scourges among the Indians."[38] From Fort Leavenworth the following year, Agent John Dougherty reported that Indian drinking in the area was so extensive that "the day is not far distant when they [the Indians] will be reduced to the most object [sic] misery ever inflicted on the Land of Civilized Man."[39] Superintendent William Armstrong of the Western Superintendency advised the War Department in 1837 that at Fort Gibson "whiskey is as common . . . as in Arkansas and I consider it . . . a more corrupting influence among the [Cherokee and Choctaw] Indians than anything I know of";[40] and at Fort Riley in 1856, at Fort Lyon in 1862, and at Fort Dodge in 1868, the military sold alcohol to the Indians.[41]

Through lax enforcement of its own sanctions the government provided still other means whereby Indians obtained alcohol. By legislation passed in 1802 and amended in 1822,[42] alcohol was banned as an Indian trade item. Under pressure from the private sector, however, the executive branch granted permits allowing boatmen to consume whiskey in Indian country on the model of the military, that is, one gill per day. Employers of the boatmen were obliged to post bonds with the Indian Office, and strict accounting of consumption was required for what apparently was considered a necessary staple for those who toiled at the oar.[43]

The remoteness of most fur trade operations discouraged enforcement of the ban. Profits from the illegal trade were enormous, and chicanery on the part of both boatmen and their companies was commonplace. In 1831 St. Louis Superintendent William Clark was reliably informed that near the mouth of the Platte, Omaha Chief Big Elk brazenly transported eight gallon kegs of whiskey to his camp from a trade station of the American Fur Company nearby. The following year trader William Sublette was issued a permit for 450 gallons of whiskey even though he did not employ a single boatman. Indeed, reported Clark to officials in Washington, the illegal trade was so profitable that "very little of the liquor taken to the Indian country is actually used by the boatmen."[44]

Even so, the white populace residing closest to the Indians and the tribal lands they so greatly coveted played the dominant role in supplying the Indians. During the 1820s and 1830s, as Washington officialdom fine-tuned a policy that would result in the removal of thousands of eastern Indians to the area west and southwest of the Missouri River, hard-drinking white farmers and merchants in the trans-Appalachian West turned grain into alcohol and plied it among the Indians. Soon-to-be-removed tribes such as the Miamis, Ottawas, and Potawatomis—to name a few—were the victims, and even though the territorial legislatures of Michigan, Illinois, Louisiana, and Mississippi passed laws prohibiting sales to Indians,[45] the penalties were insignificant and enforcement an exception rather than the rule. The situation at Peoria, on the Illinois River, provides grim evidence of the alcohol trade that flourished from Michigan to the mouth of the Mississippi. In a letter to his superiors in 1824, Sauk and Fox Agent Thomas Forsyth explained,

> It is truly shameful that such quantities of whiskey are sold and traded with the Indians on this river. Almost every settler's house is a whiskey shop, and . . . when spoken to on the subject, the whiskey seller will say, well prove it and the Justice will fine me. . . . The information of whiskey selling to Indians I procure from the Indians themselves, therefore no proof can be had. It appears to me that nearly all the settlers from the mouth of the [Spoon] river up to this place sell whiskey to Indians.[46]

The passage of time and change of place did not alter matters, so long as the white man was there to set the standard. Twenty-five years later, at the confluence of the Missouri and Kansas Rivers and the gateway to the trans-Missouri West, an editor in the thriving hamlet of Kansas City wrote that the Indians in the vicinity of the settlements were well on the road to "civilization." They were lying, swearing, stealing, chewing tobacco, and "drinking whiskey equal to the white man."[47]

Chapter 2

Father's Milk East, Wicked Water West

Alcohol figured prominently in the European invasion of North America. It was endemic wherever the French, British, or Dutch established New World beachheads and deployed policies for cultural alteration and economic gain among the native people encountered there. Wilbur R. Jacobs has flatly charged the British with "using it extensively in all their dealings with the Indians."[1] In his monumental history of the fur trade Paul C. Phillips has described in great detail the Anglo-French use of alcohol among Indians dating back to the sixteenth century,[2] and Moravian missionary John Heckwelder's contention that Manhattan (Manahachtanienk) meant "the island where we all became intoxicated" in the Delaware language speaks strongly for the use of alcohol by the Dutch (and later British) as a trade item with the native population there.[3] As an instrument of revolutionary cultural change among American Indians in the seventeenth and eighteenth centuries, Francis Jennings has placed alcohol on a par with firearms, implements, cloth, missionaries, and epidemic disease; more recently, Peter C. Mancall has documented in great detail how alcohol was a prominent feature of colonial Indian policies as well as a profitable commodity in the development of free market capitalism in North America prior to the American Revolution. Indeed, because it often rendered more efficient the work of the trader, the missionary, or the government agent, alcohol constituted a particularly versatile weapon in the invader's arsenal. The Potawatomi experience preceding the French and Indian War provides a telling example. In 1742 a delegation of that nation journeyed to Montreal to protest accusations that some of their warriors had killed more than a score of Frenchmen in the Illinois country. The delegation was greatly agitated and used alcohol as a bargaining chip to secure an acquittal of the charges. New France Governor Charles de Beauharnois eventually absolved them of bad behavior and agreed to send brandy to their villages, so long as they promised "not to go and get milk [i.e., alcohol] from the English, which spoils your Hearts and Minds and Prevents you from paying your debts."[5] In the same vein, although years after the French and British had been expelled from the trans-Appalachian West, Thomas L. McKenney—then ranking official for the administration of United States Indian policy—reported at the Fond du Lac of Lake Superior Treaty of 1826 that the Chippewas "fully acknowledge[d] the authority and jurisdiction of the United States, and disclaim[ed] all connection with any foreign power," while thinking of "nothing but the arrival of the hour when the promised drink of whiskey is to be given, at the close of it all."[6]

Puritan clerics echoed Jesuit vilifications against supplying the "savages" with alcohol, largely on grounds that it encouraged "unruliness" and made it more difficult to convert the "heathen" to Christianity, and colonial officials from the Carolinas to Nova Scotia sought to regulate and even prohibit alcohol as a trade item. But the fact is that by the end of the American Revolution, most Indians east of the Mississippi River had access to or were well supplied with the nefarious commodity. As one recent study has indicated, "Alcohol was a profitable consumer good for the traders since there was a frequently recurring demand for it; whereas a woolen blanket might last for many months and a metal knife or copper pot for years, liquor was quickly consumed, creating a demand that perpetuated itself."[7]

The eastern Algonkians and splinter remnants of the Iroquois who fell victim to white expansion and numerous land cession treaties between the Revolution and the War of 1812 were well acquainted with alcohol prior to their removal to Indian country west of Missouri during the Jacksonian era. Regular consumption for some, in fact, dated back more than a century. In 1664, for example, the duke of York decreed that licenses be issued for "strong liquor" to the Delawares up to the amount of ten gallons, provided that the licensee would stand security for the Indians' good behavior. Since quantities of this magnitude were not sold to individuals in the New Netherland taverns, the obvious intent was to keep the Indians from getting drunk in the towns, thus confining inebriation to the countryside or tribal villages.[8]

During the Anglo-French conflict in the Great Lakes region, the tightening of the French supply of brandy—which dated back to Jacques Cartier's encounter with the Micmacs in 1535—prompted the Ottawas to turn to the English for a more regular supply in 1730.[9] According to Catholic missionaries in southern Michigan, the Miamis were "debauched" as early as 1721 and continued to suffer addiction seldom matched among Indians of the Old Northwest. A century later it was reported that sixty Miamis died of alcohol in the Fort Wayne area alone; one Miami woman was widowed three times by age twenty-five from alcohol that killed her husbands.[10] A prominent Miami leader pleaded that the government suppress the liquor trade that was devastating his people and the Potawatomis of the Wabash valley,[11] and following the Black Hawk War of 1832, Sauk and Fox Agent John Beach advised authorities in Washington that on the Wisconsin-Iowa frontier "two-thirds of the frontier population was engaged in trading with the Indians with whiskey as the bait."[12] Similarly, Sauk and Fox Agent Thomas Forsyth reported from Peoria in 1824, "It is truly shameful that such quantities of whiskey are sold and traded with the Indians on this [Illinois] river; almost every settler's house is a whiskey shop and will buy from the Indians the most trifling article for whiskey." His views were confirmed by an interpreter for the Potawatomis who reported from Fulton County, Illinois, that "nine-tenths of the inhabitants . . . of this place sell whiskey to Indians for any and all articles that they may have."[13]

In the South the situation was no better. As early as 1623, two hundred Chiskiack Indians in the lower Potomac valley died after drinking sack (a strong Spanish wine) following a treaty with the British.[14] The Cherokees were regularly supplied with rum by the early eighteenth century, and in 1819, in his travels down the Mississippi, naturalist Thomas Nuttall encountered a "store" near modern Memphis operated by Chickasaw mixed-bloods where, at two dollars a gallon, well-watered whiskey was sold "without restraint"; at a nearby encampment many Chickasaws were in a state of total intoxication.[15] The following year, at Doaks Stand in central Mississippi, each Choctaw was issued a daily ration of corn and beef plus "free access to alcohol" during the treaty proceedings there, with nine cents per ration going to William Eastin and Major William B. Lewis, close friends of the principal federal negotiator, General Andrew Jackson. Under the Doaks Stand accord the Choctaw agent was empowered to "confiscate all the whiskey which may be introduced into said nation." Yet the same treaty allowed the Choctaw chiefs to dispense alcohol as they saw fit, as well as unlimited sales at "public stands."[16] Sur-

veying the situation in a report to the War Department in 1830, Superintendent McKenney characterized the condition of the southern Indians, excluding the mixed-bloods, as "deplorable." As for the northern
Indians, apart from fishing and planting a few patches of corn, all they
did was "dance, paint, hunt, fight, get drunk when they can get liquor,
and starve."[17]

As the United States sought treaties of friendship, diplomatic attachment, and land cession during the early nineteenth century, Indians
repeatedly were manipulated into a childlike perception of themselves in
relation to the federal government. President Jefferson was certain that
the first inhabitants of the hemisphere could not make their way unas-
sisted in the face of advancing white civilization for the reason that "the
Indian could only be considered a child."[18] Likewise, Superintendent
McKenney was persuaded of the infantile character of the Indians when
he wrote, "Indians, I have found out, are only children, and can be properly managed, only by being treated as such. It requires care, and a knowledge of their character to guide them—but it can be guided."[19] What
emerged from such analysis was the belief, albeit tempered with not a little diplomatic realism, that the president of the United States was the
"Great Father" whose advice for and action on behalf of his children were
honorable and beyond repute. In fact, so durable was this belief that
toward the close of the nineteenth century Indian Commissioner Thomas
Jefferson Morgan could write, "[The Indians] are the wards of the Nation.
From time immemorial, the Indians have been taught to call the President of this mighty republic the "GREAT FATHER," and all communica-
tions from them to the Indian Office are addressed in this way. In their
speeches, they say they regard the President as their father, that they are
his children, and they look to him for protection, for justice, for succor,
for advice."[20] Moreover, it should be emphasized, presents were to be
given as a reward to Indians for dutiful acquiescence to their father's well-
intended intervention on their behalf: flour, pork, guns, ammunition,
plows, annuities, missionaries, schools, new lands for old, *and* alcohol—
an important ingredient of the parental way of life. Contrary to the view
of alcohol as a sinister, pejorative commodity during diplomatic encoun-
ters with Indians—that is, parleys where drunken tribal leaders staggered
to the treaty table to sign away their birthrights, only to regret their
actions once the effects of the alcohol wore off—there is better evidence

to suggest that alcohol was primarily used as a reward for negotiations well done or soon to be consummated.

So invigorating did the Indians find alcohol that they often referred to it as "milk" or, better yet, "our father's milk." In the form of a universal nutrient that sustained life at the very onset of human existence, the significance of the metaphor should not be lost as a vital part of the father-child relationship cultivated by government agents determined to coax their wards into submission. For the Chicago treaty with the Ottawas, Chippewas, and Potawatomis in 1821, the Michigan superintendent was authorized to purchase 350 barrels of flour, fifty barrels of port, and 932 gallons of whiskey. As surely was the case with the other commodities, and in line with the military spirit ration then in effect, there is every reason to believe that at least some of the whiskey was for non-Indian consumption and that this consumption took place for all the Indians to observe. By all accounts, however, the Indians were denied their whiskey until *after* the treaty had been signed.[21] At Fond du Lac in 1826, McKenney reported that each band of Chippewas was given a taste of whiskey upon arrival. During the course of the negotiations the Indians made repeated speeches in which they begged for some "milk," but again it was only after the document had been finalized that Superintendent Cass authorized a general distribution of whiskey for the Indians.[22] Indeed, so routine was alcohol as a childlike reward by the Great Father, that as early as 1801, when dealing with the Choctaws at Fort Adams on the Mississippi, federal commissioners James Wilkinson, Benjamin Hawkins, and Andrew Pickens were positively amazed when the Indians refused any alcohol whatsoever. Writing to Secretary of War Henry Dearborn, the commissioners reported, "It is a singular fact, perhaps without example, and therefore it is worthy of record, that this [Choctaw] council should not only reject a quantity of whiskey as a present to them, but should have requested that none be issued before, during, or after, the conference."[23] There is, perhaps, a no more vivid example of the government's use of alcohol as a paternalistic device than when, following St. Peters Agent Lawrence Taliaferro's issuance of 150 gallons of whiskey to ameliorate difficulties between the Eastern Sioux and Chippewas in 1825, St. Louis Superintendent William Clark chastised Agent Taliaferro not for issuing the whiskey itself but for allowing delivery to be made by a private trader rather than an official agent of the United States government.[24]

As early as the Jefferson administration, however, there was concern that too much alcohol impoverished the Indians and stood in the way of the government's trade houses (or factories) that were attempting to wean the Indians from private traders, as well as the British. In a poignant and at the same time deferential speech to President Jefferson, Little Turtle of the Miamis pleaded for assistance to stop the flow of alcohol that was devastating his people, saying,

> Father: The introduction of this poison has been prohibited in our camps but not in our towns, where many of our hunters, for this poison, dispose of not only their furs, &c. but frequently of their guns and blankets, and return to their families destitute. Your children are not wanting in industry; but it is this fatal poison which keeps them poor. Father: Your children have not that command over themselves, which you have, therefore, before anything can be done to advantage, this evil must be remedied. Father: When our white brothers came to this land, our forefathers were numerous and happy; but, since their intercourse with the white people, and owing to the introduction of this fatal poison, we have become less numerous and happy.[25]

Coming in the wake of the Choctaws' insistence that no alcohol be available when treating with federal commissioners, Little Turtle's speech loomed large in President Jefferson's determination, on the occasion of his request for renewal of the factory system of trade, to decry the "baneful effects" that alcohol had on the "morals, health, and existence" of the Indians. Some of the tribes earnestly desired prohibition of "ardent spirits," emphasized Jefferson, and Congress should consider "effectuating that desire . . . in the spirit of benevolence and liberality" toward the goal of "conciliating their friendship."[26]

Since no regulations regarding alcohol were attached to the several laws dealing with the Indian trade during the Washington and Adams administrations, Jefferson's initiative broke new ground. Even so, the consequent provision attached by Congress to the Intercourse Act of 1802 provided little in the way of control—it simply allowed the executive branch to "prevent or restrain the vending or distribution of spirituous liquors among all or any of the said Indian tribes" as it saw fit.[27] Territorial and Indian officials were advised of the new dispensation, but according to Indiana Territorial Governor William Henry Harrison a year after the new law went into effect, more whiskey was consumed by Indians in his jurisdiction than prior to the 1802 enactment.[28]

Between 1805 and 1815, a flurry of territorial laws providing modest fines and/or prison terms for selling to Indians in Indiana, Illinois, Michigan, Louisiana, and Mississippi proved difficult if not downright impossible to enforce,[29] due mainly to inaction or lack of commitment on the part of territorial courts that enjoyed little or no support for denying the Indians the very commodity so common in the daily regimen of non-Indians. Another federal law in 1815 prohibited the operation of distilleries in an ill-defined area called "Indian Country,"[30] but because alcohol in its most volatile, concentrated form could be transported substantial distances with considerable efficiency, this law too was ineffective in denying the Indians a regular supply. Thus it was that from such outposts as St. Louis in 1820 the newly organized Missouri Fur Company, with a loan of $29,910 from a Boston investment house, sent nearly eight hundred gallons of whiskey to one of its main trade camps as one of its initial actions of business.[31] And the farther west the white man proceeded, the more alcohol figured as a necessary staple in both private and government relations with the Indians.

The savior faire of Meriwether Lewis and William Clark with Indians on their celebrated journey up the Missouri River confirms this essential fact. On January 18, 1803, three months before Robert Livingston and James Monroe struck the dramatic bargain that led to United States acquisition of Louisiana from France, President Jefferson secured a congressional appropriation of twenty-five hundred dollars "for the purpose of extending the external commerce of the United States" beyond the Mississippi.[32] In what William H. Goetzmann has termed a calculated, "programmed" venture deemed essential to national security and expansion,[33] Jefferson's instructions to Lewis and Clark, while providing a degree of needed discretion, were nevertheless quite to the point: "In all your intercourse with the natives, treat them in the most friendly and conciliatory manner which their own conduct will permit." Thus in line with protocol for the successful conduct of Indian diplomacy dating back to the eighteenth century, nearly seven hundred dollars' worth of gifts were authorized for the journey: blue glass beads, brass buttons, knives, awls, fishhooks, brooches, kettles, tobacco, vermilion, ivory combs, scissors, and a wide variety of textiles.[34] And alcohol, for the detachment's daily spirit ration and nurturing the goodwill of the Indians.

In mid-May 1804 the Lewis and Clark expedition arrived at the Kickapoo villages on the Missouri River west of St. Louis. Here Captain Lewis recorded that the Kickapoos were given two quarts of whiskey for deer meat their hunters brought to camp. The expedition reached the mouth of the Kansas River on June 19, where a court-martial was held for John Collins and Hugh Hall for drawing whiskey from "the Said Barrel intended for the party" and for being drunk while on sentinel duty. Near the mouth of the Platte a month later, an Otoe party was welcomed with a bottle of whiskey; a council with the tribal leadership two weeks later concluded with additional spirits for the Indians. Since the Otoes begged for more, they were given an additional canister of whiskey the morning following the council. By August 31 the expedition reached the mouth of the James River, where a deputation of Yankton Sioux leaders begged for some "Powder, Ball, & a little Milk." Captain Lewis managed to put them off until nightfall, when a bottle of whiskey was given to one of the interpreters who camped that night on the opposite side of the river with one of the Yankton dignitaries and his son. A month later, just below the mouth of the Bad River near present-day Pierre, South Dakota, Black Buffalo, Buffalo Medicine, and Tortohongar of the Brulé-Tetons were each given some trade whiskey aboard the expedition's keelboat after they complained that other gifts given them were inadequate. They were "very fond" of the whiskey, observed Clark, and "sucked the bottle after it was out." Not until they reached the Arikara villages near the mouth of the Grand River did Lewis and Clark refrain from the use of alcohol in the conduct of Indian diplomacy, for like most of their Pawnee relatives to the south, the Arikaras made it be known that liquor made Indians act like fools and thus was unwelcome.[35]

Likewise, Lieutenant Zebulon M. Pike's abortive quest for the source of the Mississippi River, again under orders of Jefferson and the War Department, brought more government alcohol to Indian country. In eastern Sioux country, Pike reported in 1805 that the Indians who greeted him "had all been drinking" before he arrived. Among the presents Pike distributed was alcohol as an inducement for two Sioux chiefs to sign a peace accord with the United States, the first of its kind with any of the Sioux people, but which later was repudiated by both the

Indians and the federal government. Its rejection, however, was not because of "its libatious conception."[36]

Major Stephen H. Long's foray onto the central plains and the Rocky Mountains as part of the Yellowstone expedition of 1819-1820 provided additional insight regarding the extent to which alcohol had penetrated the vast region acquired from France in 1803. Dr. Edwin James, professional botanist attached to the expedition and Long's official chronicler, observed the "proneness to that most abominable and degrading vices, intoxication from the use of spirituous liquors" on the part of the Indians located immediately west of the Missouri River. Even a member of a Pawnee war party encountered at the main Kansa village near present-day Manhattan, Kansas, "fell on his knees, and laid his hands convulsively upon his breast and stomach, crying out, with a voice and manner of earnest supplication, 'Whiskey, whiskey.' " Yet in fairness, wrote James, the actions of drunken Indians were no less "ridiculous and puerile as those of *civilized* [emphasis added] drunkards." Continued James, "[C]hiefs, warriors, and common men, roll indiscriminately on the earth together, or dance, caper, laugh, cry, shout, fight, or hug and kiss, and rub each other with their hands, in the most affectionate or stupid manner. . . . Whiskey, which is the only spirituous liquor they are acquainted with, is furnished to them freely by the traders; and the existing law of the United States, prohibiting the sale of it to the natives . . . is readily evaded."[37]

The expeditions of Lewis and Clark, Pike, and Long indicated that the Indians of the trans-Mississippi West were no less conversant with alcohol than their counterparts east of the Mississippi, and that they viewed the commodity as an important prerequisite to the conduct of diplomacy with their new Great Father in distant Washington. From the Kickapoo villages west of St. Louis to Arikara country on the upper Missouri, the Otoes, Missourias, Iowas, Osages, Kansas, Omahas, Pawnees, Poncas, and Yankton and Teton Sioux had all been introduced to alcohol by the nineteenth century. Even so little as a spoonful of milk offered by their father's emissaries confirmed that what the private traders had provided for some time was an acceptable, indeed a vital, ingredient of the invader's culture.

In comparison with the amount provided by the private sector, the government's distribution of spirits to the western Indians was insignificant. The establishment of Fort Osage as the westernmost federal trade

factory near the mouth of the Kansas River in 1808 and a federal prohibition in 1815 against the erection of distilleries in Indian country[38]
were evidence that the government was serious about interdicting the
westward flow of alcohol. In fact quite the opposite was the case. Alcohol continued to flow up the Missouri River past Fort Osage, prompting
Upper Missouri Agent Benjamin O'Fallon to propose special search and
seizure detachments for the government factory there. "During the season of Trade," he wrote to the War Department in 1819, "the [Indians]
are kept in a constant state of confusion by the dozens of [whiskey]
traders."[39] Whiskey moved overland as well. In 1824, before a justice of
the peace in Chariton County, Missouri (some sixty miles northeast of
Fort Osage), John McCorkle testified that in 1821 he and four other
teamsters were hired by W. James Neofs to drive five wagonloads of
whiskey from Chariton to the Indian camps at Council Bluffs on the
Missouri. His complaint was not about hauling alcohol to the Indians
but rather that en route to Council Bluffs the wagons were plundered by
a party of Otoe Indians, resulting in a substantial property loss to his
employer.[40]

The flow of whiskey into Indian country was accomplished in other
ways. Since the fur companies, particularly large ones such as John Jacob
Astor's American Fur Company and others based in St. Louis, insisted
that their boatmen required whiskey as part of their daily regimen, permits were issued by the Indian Office in St. Louis based on the number
of imbibers and the amount of time they would be absent in Indian
country. Permit holders were required to post bond against any alcohol
that might be sold or given to Indians contrary to the law of 1802. Given
the remoteness and vast extent of Indian country, it is not surprising that
disregard of these regulations was commonplace. Boatmen lists were
padded, and one trader was allowed a 450-gallon ration even though he
took all of his merchandise overland and employed not a single boatman. While the commander at Fort Leavenworth asserted that the
amount of whiskey transported up the Missouri River in 1831 was twice
the amount certified for legal consumption, an Indian agent went further by declaring that only one of every hundred gallons of whiskey in
Indian country that same year was actually covered by boatmen permits
issued by Indian Superintendent William Clark.[41]

The demise of the government's factory system of trade by House

vote on May 4, 1822,[42] only added to the flow of alcohol in Indian country, although legislative action two days later suggested that the government's intent was otherwise. On May 6, in an amendment to the
Intercourse Act of 1802, War Department officials and the Indian Office
were authorized to search for and seize ardent spirits in the possession of
traders operating in Indian country. Mere "suspicion or information" was
adequate justification for instigating searches, and all goods were to be
confiscated, that is, alcoholic and nonalcoholic, with one half for the
use of the informant and the other half for the government. Under the
new law also the bonds of licensed traders apprehended could be put in
suit.[43]

The finesse with which the American Fur Company was able to
evade this new attempt at liquor control, principally on grounds that
rigid enforcement made it impossible for American companies to compete with the British across the northern border, has been well documented.[44] But smaller operators were no less defiant. While lamenting
the dismissal of fellow missionary Peter Clyde for drunkenness and the
failure of a fledgling temperance society at the Baptist Indian Mission at
Fort Wayne in 1822,[45] the Reverend Isaac McCoy complained bitterly
about licensed traders who "as regularly laid in ardent spirits, as part of
their annual stock to carry to their store-houses, as they did blankets,
calicoes, or any other article."[46] And in a letter to Secretary of War John
C. Calhoun from Detroit three years later, Colonel Joshua Snelling confirmed the blatant disregard of the 1822 law:

> I have taken a house about three miles from town and in passing to
> and from it, I had daily opportunities of seeing the road literally
> strewed with the bodies of [Indian] men, women, and children in the
> last stages of brutal intoxication. . . . I was informed by a person of
> veracity, that one man (a Mr. _____) had purchased this season
> above three hundred blankets for whiskey; they cost him, on an aver-
> age, about seventy-five cents each. I passed this man's door daily; it
> was always surrounded by Indians, and many were passing in and out
> with kegs on their backs.[47]

Snelling acknowledged that whiskey was available from the British
at Malden, but he was quick to point out that a "fruitful source of com-

plaint" was against those traders who obtained their supplies from St. Louis.[48]

The experience of the Baptist temperance society at Fort Wayne provides important insight as to why the 1822 law failed. The society was formed on June 12, 1822, as "The Humane Abolition Society of Fort Wayne"; its preamble spoke at length about the wretched consequences of providing Indians with liquor in violation of the "good laws of the United States." Some traders joined the society, but one who refused was soon apprehended for selling liquor to the Indians, "with proof positive, which made him liable to fines in three offenses." Members of the society took their evidence to court at Winchester, some eighty miles from Fort Wayne, where "the proper civil officials" took no action. "There it *ended*," according to McCoy, and, finding it impracticable to induce the enforcement of federal law, the society disbanded and "matters returned to run in their former channels."[49]

Ironically, the abortive Fort Wayne temperance experiment was in dire contrast to a native effort to interdict Indian drinking in the 1820s, indicating that at least some Indian leaders were aware of the suffering wrought by the white man's milk. The movement was led by Kenekuk of the Vermillion band of Kickapoos in Illinois Territory. As a young man Kenekuk had killed one of his uncles during a drunken rage and for that reason was banished by his own people. While doing odd jobs as a means of survival in the white settlements nearby, the future "Kickapoo Prophet" came under the influence of a white missionary who instructed Kenekuk in the rudiments of Christian theology and advised him that if he took these "good teachings" to his own people, they would forgive him for the murder of his uncle. The syncretic religion Kenekuk developed, which preserved important Kickapoo traditions and utilized prayer sticks as substitutes for the written word, focused on the sin of alcohol and how the indulgent faced nothing but eternal damnation in the "burning pits of hell." Only those who renounced their sins in public and submitted to whippings as physical proof that God had cleansed them could gain absolution.[50]

The result was a dramatic decrease in alcohol consumption and a return to agrarian prosperity that became the envy of the Vermillion band's white neighbors. Indeed, so successful were Kenekuk's teachings that the band's displacement from Illinois to the trans-Missouri West was deferred for more than a decade. Other bands of Kickapoos were less fortunate, however, although they too were beginning to suspect that the white man's milk had gone sour. Following the Treaty of Castor Hill (1832), which provided for removal of the northern Kickapoos from central Missouri to a new location in future Kansas,[51] a tribal spokesman let it be known that his people were concerned about the whiskey merchants operating in and around Fort Leavenworth, near the promised land. "We are afraid of the wicked water brought us by our white friends," he told United States Commissioner E. A. Ellsworth. "We wish to get out of its reach by land or water."[52] To which Commissioner Ellsworth responded,

> You have made two objections to your present situation. The scarcity of game and the introduction of the wicked water. In regard to the first, it is obvious that the game you want will soon be gone, when all the other Indians shall come over [the Missouri River]. Your Great Father is going to help you. . . . The wicked water of which you speak has been carried two hundred miles further into the country. Your Great Father was very sorry when the wicked water was brought into the country; but he will stop it, and will punish the wicked men who brought it by Judges sent to try them.[53]

Chapter 3

Respite and Resolve

On May 28, 1830, President Andrew Jackson signed into law the Indian Removal Act, authorizing the chief executive to designate lands west of the Mississippi not included in any territory or state to which Indian title had been extinguished as a permanent home for Indians who agreed to relinquish their lands in the East. Compensation for ceded lands and improvements were guaranteed, as were financial aid and assistance for the emigration itself. During the first year also, the government agreed to provide support for tribal adjustment to the new lands in the West.[1]

The most critically acclaimed studies of this important juncture in Indian policy and administration generally focus on the plight of the southern Indians, particularly the Cherokees and Choctaws; on state versus national authority regarding constitutional jurisdiction over the status of Indians in the American body politic; and especially on the debate between politically adroit Jacksonian expansionists and their no less skillful opponents, the American Board of Commissioners for Foreign Missions.[2] By contrast, much less attention has been given to the thousands of Indians of the Old Northwest who in the years immediately following the War of 1812 were also exploited by white yeomen and speculators, in terms of both land intrusion and illicit alcohol. A writer in a Mississippi newspaper could complain that the main activities of the Choctaws were "loafing and drinking,"[3] but his carping was mild in comparison with what was being reported in the North and, as removal policy was being fine-tuned in Congress, by Indian Office personnel in the West.

In a letter transmitted by Green Bay Agent Henry B. Brevoort, for example, the Senate Committee on Indian Affairs was told that leaders of the Stockbridge tribe deplored the evil of liquor among their ranks. Several years before the Indian Removal Act was passed they had been forced to leave Ohio for Wisconsin but had been unable to escape the ravages of alcohol. "It is an *evil* we wished to flee from," they wrote in

1827, "and we came into this distant clime with the hope of finding a resting place. . . . But we are sadly disappointed in this. We hope that some effectual measures will be adopted to stop it. . . . [B]elieve us, on the success of this depends the interest and survival of thousands."[4]

Three years later, while the removal debate was intensifying in Washington, the Indian Office was informed that as white settlers occupied land near the Miami domain in Indiana, the Indians "learned to imbibe all the vices of the lower white population. . . . They seek intoxication with avidity and spend a great portion of their time in dissipation . . . and are a poor, degraded set of human beings who are rapidly decreasing in their numbers." Armed with such evidence, an executive commission with instructions to negotiate a removal treaty warned the Miamis, "If you continue here where you now are . . . and let the white people feed you whiskey and bring among you bad habits, in a little while where will be the Miami Nation? They will all be swept off." But there was hope, according to the commission: "Situated as you are, your Great Father cannot prevent his white people from coming among you. He wants to place you in a land where he can take care of you [and] protect you against all your enemies, whether red men or white."[5]

In short, destructive native drinking was the inevitable, indeed the uncontrollable, consequence of white contact that could be eradicated only by removal to an environment where the evil did not exist. Such environment was in the West, a pristine Indian Canaan west of the Mississippi or more likely the Missouri, where the adage "Stranger, will you drink or fight?"[6] presumably had not yet achieved prophetic fulfillment. That virtually every argument in favor of removal assumed this to be the case is thus less surprising than failure by the opposition to take notice of evidence to the contrary, and to exploit the alcohol issue as a major obstacle to Indian improvement in the West. To be sure, it was widely known that fur companies used it on occasion, mainly to compete with the British. But the extent of the traffic in ardent spirits was ignored. Prevailing sentiment had it that Indian drinking was amenable to control by law, and in any case, alcohol seemed not to present a significant obstacle to land acquisition in the East and saving the Indians in the West.

In the West, however, the view was otherwise. In a strongly worded letter sent from Fort Leavenworth to Superintendent Clark in St. Louis, Upper Missouri Agent John Dougherty stated that unless something were done to halt the flow of alcohol beyond the Missouri, the day was not distant when the Indians would be reduced to the most abject misery ever inflicted on mortal man. "Liquor flows as freely here as the Missouri," he reported. "For God's sake, for the sake of humanity, exert yourself to have this article stopped in this country." More than twenty-two hundred packs of buffalo robes had been purchased that season alone with whiskey priced at a dollar a gallon on the St. Louis market, but more than thirty dollars a gallon in Indian country.[7]

In view of such enormous profits, even the novice vendor could take comfort in the vague and uncertain definitions of Indian country, which generally held that it was actual reservation land not ceded to the federal government by treaty or legislative decree, and in loopholes in the 1822 search and seizure law. The law was directed at licensed traders in Indian country. But what of nonlicensed white citizens—for example, trappers, missionaries, squatters, or merchants ostensibly headed for Mexico or the Pacific Northwest—on or adjacent to Indian land in the Fort Leavenworth area west of the Missouri River? Could they sell their own, presumably legal, alcohol to Indians in Indian country? Or, as more often was the case, could they sell to Indians who of their own volition sought them out on these non-Indian "island" settlements in Indian country?[8] And what of the Indians themselves? Could they engage in the alcohol trade with other Indians in Indian country?

These problems were exacerbated by some of the very treaties then constituting the basis for establishing the locus of Indian country. In June 1825 major land cession treaties were negotiated with the Kansa and Osage tribes whose domains lay mainly west of Missouri and Arkansas. Superintendent Clark, principal government negotiator, informed the War Department that the cessions were more than adequate "to provide residences for other tribes in different States, who may be willing to remove west, in pursuance of gradual removal and collection of Indians," and that the cessions conformed strictly with instructions received from Washington. The diminished Osage reservation commenced about twenty-five miles west of the Missouri state line, and the Kansa reservation about double that distance. Both were situated "sufficient to prevent the stock of the two parties [Indians and whites] from intermixing [and] render the access to ardent spirits more difficult." The treaties also included provisions granting 640-acre tracts to each of the sixty-three mixed-bloods of the two tribes, provisions deemed essential for tribal approval of the treaties. "It may not be amiss to observe," added Clark cautiously, "that more than half of the reservations for individuals are out of the State and Territorial limits."[9] His concern, no doubt, was whether or not these tracts were legally a part of Indian country for purposes of enforcing Indian alcohol laws then in effect. And because land speculators and other government officials soon took the view that the mixed-blood tracts were fee-simple grants to individuals beyond the control of their respective tribes, and thus not a legal part of Indian country, Clark's concern certainly was no idle speculation. A federal statute of 1862 and the Kansas Supreme Court in 1864 eventually confirmed this,[10] while, in the meantime, profit-hungry liquor traders applauded the uncertainty surrounding both the Kansa and the Osage tracts.

The first major test of the 1822 law came not in Kansa and Osage country but at Fort Wayne hundreds of miles to the northeast, among the Miamis who eventually would be moved to the trans-Missouri West. In 1824 Indian Agent John Tipton seized trade goods consigned by the American Fur Company for the Indians there because he found alcohol as part of the shipment. Tipton quickly libeled the goods in the District Court of the United States for the District of Ohio, which prompted John Jacob Astor to instigate a personal vendetta against Tipton in letters to the War Department, charging that the agent was more interested in injuring the company than in fulfilling the duties of his office. Tipton, however, held his ground, and the Ohio court upheld his action in 1825. Astor then appealed to the Supreme Court on a writ of error, claiming there was no evidence whatsoever that the alcohol was intended for sale to Indians.[11] He also dispatched a strongly worded letter to Missouri Senator Thomas H. Benton and the Senate Committee on Indian Affairs, in which he complained bitterly of the Hudson Bay people flooding the market with cheap woolens and "giving Spirituous liquors to the Indians." His company, said Astor, "the only respectable one of any capital now existing in the country," was unable to compete with the British and, in the absence of government protection and cooperation, would be obliged to suspend operations. "I take the liberty to call on you now for your good aid," he wrote Benton, "and I ask it on account of the many young and enterprising men engaged in the trade."[12] As it turned out, Astor's lobbying was unnecessary, for in 1829 the Supreme Court overruled the Ohio court on grounds that an improper charge had been given the jury regarding the meaning of "Indian country."[13]

Astor, of course, was anything but sympathetic to competition afforded by the smaller fur companies and individual operators. He could complain mightily about their use of alcohol in the Indian trade, just as he did with the British. But rather than exonerate him from providing Indians with alcohol, failure of his conviction on a technicality had the effect of confirming the cloudy character of Indian country and, more importantly, the difficulty of interdicting the Indian alcohol trade with the statutory arsenal then in place. Certainly the liquor vendors now had much less to fear from the judicial process, as was apparent from Colonel Mathew Arbuckle's abortive attempt to bring the liquor-trading firm of William DuVal and Peter A. Carnes to justice in Arkansas Territory soon after Astor had been cleared by the Supreme Court.[14] For those sincerely interested in the Indians' welfare, the situation was frustrating in the extreme. "Our government," lamented Baptist missionary and government surveyor Isaac McCoy in 1827, "has made laws forbidding the introduction of ardent spirits into [Indian] county; but it has no power, in the present posture of affairs, to enforce their observance. The evils of intemperance have not been . . . lessened by all the laws made to repress it."[15]

There were still other means of evading prosecution for taking alcohol into the Indian country west of Missouri. Following the independence of Mexico in 1821, a burgeoning mercantile trade developed between several communities near the mouth of the Kansas River and the upper Rio Grande settlements centered around Santa Fe. With profits as high as 600 percent in 1824, pressure mounted for federal protection in the form of treaties with the Indians, as well as a formal survey to the international boundary at the Arkansas River. Under the guidance of Senator Benton, Congress authorized a thirty-thousand-dollar appropriation on March 3, 1825, and in mid-August of that same year Commissioners Benjamin H. Reeves, George C. Sibley, and Thomas Mathers negotiated supplemental agreements to the Kansa and Osage land cession treaties concluded three months earlier.[16]

As opposed to the cessions secured by Clark with the Kansa and Osage leadership in St. Louis, Reeves, Sibley, and Mathers dealt with whomever they could find to carry out the government directive of March 3. Osage agreement was secured at Council Grove on August 10; six days later, on the Santa Fe Trail at Running Turkey Creek in present McPherson County, Kansas, a Kansa hunting party accepted the government proposal.[17] In both instances the signers were paid five hundred dollars for the government's right to mark a road across their land, where, on all occasions, they would "render such friendly assistance as may be in their power, to any citizens of the United States or the Mexican Republic, as they may at any time happen to meet or fall in with on the road aforesaid." Contrary to the treaties of three months earlier, nothing was said regarding ceding the land in question. In fact, Article 1 of both treaties specifically emphasized that the respective tribal concessions applied to "any of the territory owned or claimed by the said Kansa [and Osage] Nations." Taken in conjunction with questionable federal authority on the mixed-blood tracts and the earlier treaties that authorized an immediate gift of nine hundred cattle, nine hundred hogs, fifteen hundred domestic fowl, and thirteen yoke of oxen—ostensibly to encourage agricultural pursuits but in fact more easily sold to white traders—and an annuity of $210,000 for the twenty-year period written into the treaties, the two tribes now enjoyed significant buying power for the purchase of alcohol that soon moved freely on the Santa Fe Trail.[18]

The availability of this alcohol was increasingly dependent on the grain and distillery business in Missouri. In the late eighteenth century the principal source of distilled alcohol for the Missouri region was New Orleans. But mounting difficulties over American navigation of the Mississippi and the declining power of Spain over control of Louisiana that led to transfer of that vast region back to France in 1800 prompted St. Louis entrepreneurs to seek their own means of production. Thus in 1799, with a grant of more than a thousand acres of land from Carlos Dehault Delassus, Spanish lieutenant governor of Louisiana, Auguste Chouteau constructed a commercial distillery in St. Louis.[19] Timber from the tract was used to fuel Chouteau's boilers, and the land cleared of trees was placed in corn production to provide the minimum of one bushel for every two gallons of alcohol produced. That the enterprise was successful from the start can be seen in the twelve distilleries operating in the St. Louis area by 1810. By 1821 the Murphy and Nagle distillery alone was producing three hundred gallons of pure grain alcohol per day.[20]

As noted earlier,[21] a federal statute of 1815 prohibited the operation of distilleries in Indian country, which proved no problem for the St. Louis distillers operating on land ceded by the Great and Little Osages in 1808.[22] But as the corn culture moved up the Missouri River west of St. Louis,[23] potential distillers were obliged to proceed with care until additional cessions could be secured. Happily for their cause, the government cleared title to the land north of the Missouri River in a treaty with the Sauk and Fox and Iowas in August 1824, and to the remaining Indian land south of the Missouri through the Osage treaty of June 1825.[24]

By then several communities had been established only a few miles from the western Missouri state line. Liberty, county seat of Clay County, was laid out in 1822 and within three years had no less than six dramshops—because, in the words of one local historian, "our first settlers loved their toddy."[25] But the distillery established there in 1824 by Cyrus Curtis, early town trustee and respected businessman, apparently provided alcohol for persons other than travelers and local white residents. As early as 1817, Curtis obtained a license from Superintendent Clark to trade with the Kansas, Osages, Otoes, and Omahas at their villages on the Missouri River, and in 1822 he and his partner Michael Ely posted a twenty-five-hundred-dollar bond for renewal of their license to trade with the same tribes. The dramatic increase in the Santa Fe trade led Curtis and Ely to expand their operations to include a trading post just across the Missouri River in Westport.[26]

As local corn production increased and talk of Indian removal to the region west of Missouri became commonplace, others entered into the profitable distilling business, including David Dailey, who constructed a gristmill and distillery at Blue Springs between Independence and Westport,[27] and James Hyatt McGee, who arrived at Chouteau's Landing from Liberty in 1828. With a government contract to provide flour for the Shawnees then being removed from southeastern Missouri to a new reservation on the Kansas River west of Missouri,[28] McGee emerged as one of the more prominent distillers in the Kansas City area. He established a sawmill, gristmill, and distillery on O.K. Creek, and eventually accumulated a thousand-acre estate at a location he renamed Westport Landing. Merchandising and town development were also his forte, and with the help of his sons Allen and Milton, McGee soon was heavily involved in the Santa Fe trade. Allen, one of Kansas City's "leading businessmen," was put in charge of the mill and distillery, and "was always a favorite with the Indians," apparently because "he became familiar with their habits and modes of living and knew how best to deal with them." Milton, a future mayor of Kansas City, was "flamboyant, reckless, intensely colorful, and fiercely independent," and had most of his family inheritance attached by the government for selling whiskey to Indians in Indian country, after which he fled to California to avoid prosecution. In fact the entire McGee family was involved in the alcohol trade, as reported by Fort Leavenworth Indian Agent Richard Cummins in 1843. "This family," wrote Cummins to the Indian Office in Washington, "have been selling whiskey to the Indians ever since I became Indian Agent [in 1830]."[29]

The area at the mouth of the Kansas River, what in 1824 former Fort Osage factor and Santa Fe Trail surveyor George C. Sibley termed "The Garden of Missouri . . . which it is presumable the God of Nature designed for the use of civilized man,"[30] was not the only source of alcohol for Indian country. In October 1829, when Bvt. Major Bennet Riley and two hundred men of the Sixth U.S. Infantry met Mexican Colonel José A. Viscarra on the Santa Fe Trail some four hundred miles southwest of Westport Landing, much of the alcohol consumed by over five hundred Mexicans, Americans, and "Indians of several tribes" during the two-day meeting was of American (and most likely Missouri) manufacture. That Riley's detachment carried a substantial supply of alcohol is evident in his having issued "an extra ration" to his men on July 4 at the Cimarron Crossing. But when Viscarra served an elaborate dinner for the American detachment on the evening of October 13, the alcohol consumed was of Mexican origin—most likely from the Taos region.[31]

In 1824 Thomas Long Smith, native of Kentucky, traveled from Missouri to Santa Fe with the Alexander La Grande caravan and then moved to Taos, where with the assistance of James Baird and Samuel Chambers he constructed the first major distillery on the upper Rio Grande. Utilizing corn grown by the Pueblos of that region, as well as grain from his own fields, Smith's distillery produced what came to be known as *aguadiénte de Taos* (Taos Lightning)—a high-proof alcohol that eventually became a staple of the Santa Fe trade.[32] Others soon joined Smith in the distilling business at that distant outpost of northeastern Mexico. On February 13, 1826, William Workman wrote his brother David in Franklin, informing him that he had just purchased a large quantity of corn and wheat, and requesting that David ship him two eighty-gallon stills for a distillery he and Mathew Kinkaid were planning to erect at Taos.[33] By 1830 it was reported that the Arapahoes were buying Mexican whiskey from John Gant on the upper Arkansas, and by the mid-1830s, at Bent's Old Fort on the American side of that river, William Bent entered the Indian alcohol trade in order to compete with the Mexican whiskey merchants who were diverting the Cheyenne trade away from his post. Bent insisted that he "was strongly opposed" to Indians having alcohol, but in fact it became an important part of his operations.[34] Because trading alcohol "often endangered the trader's life" and brought an end to all "legitimate business," Bent's practice was to take the alcohol directly to the Indians:

> Two or three times a year, therefore, after many visits from the chiefs, asking for liquor . . . a lot of liquor would be sent out to a camp. A trader coming into the village deposited the kegs, of various sizes, at the lodge of the chief. The Indians then came to the lodge and offered what they had to trade, and each man was assigned a keg of a certain size, according to the number of robes or the horses or mules he had offered to trade. Each Indian then tied to his keg a piece of cloth or a string to mark it as his, and it was left in the chief's lodge, unopened, for the present. When the trade had been completed the trader left the village, and not until he had gone some distance did the chief permit the Indians to take their kegs of liquor and open them."[35]

Such demand for the *aguadiénte de Taos*, plus rumors that the United States government might further legislate against alcohol and thus cut into the profits of the Missouri distilleries, prompted the construction of still another commercial distillery on the upper Rio Grande. In 1832 Simeon Turley of Arrow Rock, Missouri, moved to Arroyo Hondo a few miles north of Taos, where he constructed a two-story mill and large distillery. Turley also entered into the Santa Fe trade, built a store at Pueblo near the mouth of Fountain Creek on the Arkansas, and soon emerged as a major supplier of alcohol for the overland trade and Indians of the trans-Missouri West.[36]

Thus by the early 1830s, facilities for the production of alcohol were booming on both borders of the region traversed by the Santa Fe Trail, with the Taos distillers dominating the High Plains region and their Missouri counterparts supplying the lower Kansas and Platte valleys, as well as Sioux country to the northwest. With whiskey worth twenty-five cents a gallon on the St. Louis retail market in the early 1830s, thirty-four dollars a gallon at Fort Leavenworth, and up to sixty-four dollars for the same quantity at the mouth of the Yellowstone, the profits were obviously immense.[37]

Not surprisingly, then, Indians with annuity dollars consequent to the government's removal program and abetted by guarantees for safe passage along the Santa Fe Trail dating back to 1825 moved into the alcohol trade as middlemen in areas where white sellers were less than welcome. Writing to Secretary of War Cass in the fall of 1832, Osage Subagent Paul L. Chouteau reported that the Osages were well supplied with whiskey in the remote Neosho valley southwest of Kansas City. "I take the liberty of informing you that the Kansas Indians have been in the habit of introducing whiskey among the Osages, sometimes a horse for a bottle or two," wrote Chouteau. "But I have not interfered in this traffic since I believe that U.S. Indian Agents generally do not interfere when liquor is introduced into Indian Country by Indians." Because the trade encouraged the Osages to steal horses from the Cherokees, Creeks, Shawnees, and Delawares to obtain whiskey purchased by the Kansas in western Missouri, Chouteau's question to Cass was: "Has an Indian countryman the privilege of introducing liquor in Indian Country?"[38]

In Washington, Cass was then involved with the more pressing problem of Cherokee removal to Indian country, while in St. Louis it was left to Superintendent Clark to deal with violations of the alcohol laws of 1802 and 1822. In what might best be described as an angry and frustrating letter to Cass, Clark wrote,

> In obedience to a resolution of the Senate of the 2nd of March last, and in answer to several enquiries accompanying your letter of the

9th of September (both requiring information relative to the Fur Trade and the Inland Trade to Mexico), I have the honor to state that I had at an early date communicated the same to the Indian Agents within this Superintendency, and to individuals engaged in the Fur Trade or acquainted with the subject of your enquiries. . . . The several laws regarding Trade & Intercourse with the Indian Tribes prohibit the selling, bartering, or giving spirituous liquors to Indians. By special authority vested in the Superintendent of Indian Affairs by the President of the United States, the former is empowered to grant permits to traders, to take into Indian Country, *whiskey for the use of boatmen*, . . . and taking bond that it is not to be sold, bartered, exchanged, or given to Indians. . . . Within the few days past, however, I have received information on this subject and from such a source as to place the matter beyond a doubt, and to convince me that the privilege of taking whiskey for the use of the Boatmen has been abused: that instead thereof and for the purpose specified, *alcohol* has been taken which it seems (after being reduced) has been furnished to the Indians by the *gallon keg*! . . . As these Traders have evinced so little good faith—such disrespect for the government as to violate its most immanent laws & so little humanity toward the Indians themselves, as to disregard the most sacred provision for their protection, I shall conceive it my bounden duty to recommend the total & entire prohibition of this article in the Indian Country, under any pretense, or for any purpose whatsoever.[39]

Having vented his wrath to Cass, Clark reaffirmed his position in a letter to Elbert Herring, only recently appointed by President Jackson[40] as head clerk of the office that soon would become the Commissioner of Indian Affairs. Were his views too strong? Would evils result from the Indians' failure to obtain alcohol? But more to the point, would the traders be inconvenienced by total prohibition? To the novice Herring, who believed that "isolation [i.e., removal] from corrupt white elements" was the ultimate weapon to stop the whiskey vendors,[41] Clark came down hard on the traders, many of them licensed by his very own office and obviously scornful of the regulatory legislation then in effect. "I will observe that I am not aware of any evil which could possibly result to the Indians for the want of it [alcohol]," he wrote Herring. "On the contrary,

I have ever been of the opinion that a more pernicious article could not be introduced among them, as it is well known that not an Indian could be found among a thousand, who would not (after a first drink) sell his horse, his gun, or his last blanket for another drink—or even commit a murder to gratify his passion for spirits. If the Traders should suffer personal inconveniences from the want of it, it is certainly a consequence of their own seeking."[42]

Here it is important to emphasize that Superintendent Clark, veteran federal official with at least as much experience with the problem as anyone then in the Indian service, accompanied his call for more stringent legislation with a reminder of the Indians' insatiable passion for alcohol, while at the same time disregarding—other than the "personal inconveniences" some merchants might experience—the market forces encouraging tribal consumption. Yet Clark's brief but firm comments regarding the native passion for drink were by no means unique and, in fact, conformed well with many of his white contemporaries. "Their love of liquor is really inconceivable; . . . It is a regular tarantula to them [for] as soon as they are bitten by it, all their blood flames in their veins, and they are crazy for more," wrote the Jesuit Father Pierre-Jean DeSmet on the basis of nearly four decades of missionary toil among Indians of the trans-Missouri West.[43] "Among other nations, civilized or barbarous, excessive ebriety is an individual characteristic, sometimes indulged and sometimes avoided," observed Michigan Indian Superintendent Lewis Cass in 1827. "But the Indians . . . old and young, male and female, the chief and the warrior, all give themselves up to the most brutal intoxication. . . . Human nature in all its vast variety of aspects," he lamented, "presents no phenomenon like this."[44] And like most foreign travelers who visited Indian country in the 1820s and 1830s, the English geologist George W. Featherstonhaugh was persuaded that because of their "inordinate passion" for spirits, the Indians "have no other ambition than that of passing through life in a perpetual state of delirium."[45] The consequence of this deficiency, as Bernard Sheehan has observed, was that the white man's "social lubricant" in the hands of a primitive people had "proved itself a poison of startling efficacy" and was contributing mightily to the social disintegration of a once noble race.[46] The solution, then, was not to *regulate* the wicked water, as in the past, but to *remove it absolutely* from the natives' grasp. Hopefully, under firm

federal fiat, frontier farmers, distillers, and traders, as well as the overland vendors from Missouri to Santa Fe and from Fort Leavenworth to
the mouth of the Yellowstone, would come to their senses and support
this well-intentioned, philanthropic cause.

The legislative enactment came on July 9, 1832. As part of the federal statute that created the office of Commissioner of Indian Affairs, it
was decreed that "no ardent spirits shall be hereafter introduced, under
any pretence, into the Indian country."[47] What little formal debate that
did take place centered on the heavy workload of the Indian Office and
the large number of licenses issued to date—ninety-eight by 1830—suggesting, in light of the prohibition clause, that violations were commonplace and that the traders could no longer be trusted with alcohol
in Indian country.[48] No new penalties were then attached to the prohibition, nor was any definition of Indian country provided in the 1832
law, for these issues were then being debated in a sweeping attempt to
restate and reorganize the essentials of federal Indian affairs and policy,
and to consider the creation of a western territory for those Indians who
had already emigrated west or shortly would be experiencing the force
of the removal hammer.[49]

Following a "considerable and violent" House debate in the spring of
1834, a proposal to organize an Indian territory in the West was postponed
indefinitely,[50] and it was left to another bill to provide what in effect was
a substitute for the failed Indian territory bill. Section 1 of "An Act to regulate trade and intercourse with the Indian tribes, and to preserve peace
on the frontier," passed June 30, 1834,[51] simply stated, "That all that part
of the United States west of the Mississippi, and not within the states of
Missouri and Louisiana, or the Territory of Arkansas, and, also, that part
of the United States east of the Mississippi River, and not within any state
to which the Indian title has not been extinguished, for the purpose of this
act, be taken and deemed to be Indian country." Excluding Arkansas,
which became a state two years later, no new states were immediately contemplated west of the Mississippi, so that in the view of the resident Indians or those soon to be placed there—and for that matter, in the opinion
of most government officials—the vast region west to Mexico and the
Oregon country was recognized as "permanent Indian country."

With the boundaries of Indian country thus delineated, Section 20
of the same act authorized penalties for violation of the 1832 prohibi-

tion under four categories: those who sold, exchanged, gave, bartered, or disposed of spirituous liquors or wine were subject to forfeiture and a fine of five hundred dollars; those who introduced or attempted to introduce, forfeiture and a three-hundred-dollar fine; government agents and/or military officials who had "reason to suspect" that whites or Indians were "about to introduce, or have introduced" could seize liquor or wine, keeping half for themselves, with the other half to be held libel in the proper court; and any person in the service of the United States or any Indian were authorized "to take and destroy any ardent spirits or wine found in the Indian country, excepting military supplies as mentioned in this section."[52]

Respite had given way to resolve, and with the goverment's plan to relocate thousands of Indians well under way, there was optimism and hope that the wicked water in Indian country would soon be a thing of the past. In 1835, for example, Commissioner Herring reported that the exclusion of liquor "wherever possible" had resulted in "much good" and was contributing to the advancement of civilization.[53] But a speech made by a Shawnee chief on the eastern border of Indian country soon after the prohibition law went into effect suggested otherwise:

> We know the whiskey is bad. But a few days ago, when our agent had read to us his instructions from our great father, our young men went to Independence [Missouri] where they met some white traders in whiskey who said there was no law against Indians taking whiskey into their country, and nobody said so except their Agent and bad men at the Fort [Leavenworth]. The white men told our young men to take some whiskey even to Mr. [Agent] Cummin's house and they would not be punished. If the whites should put them into jail, they would go and let them out again. We are sorry my father that this is so—we have no laws and our great Father does not put into execution those he makes himself.[54]

To which Henry Ellsworth, member of the Stokes Commission, whose task it was to expedite Indian removal, explained,

> In a prosecution on the frontier of Missouri under a state law which prohibits the sale to an Indian, a witness testified that he saw the

Trader draw the whiskey from the Cask and pour it—into the jug of an Indian who carried the same away. To be more sure the witness tasted a little that remained in the measure. Upon cross examination the witness was asked if he tasted any in the jug? He replied no, but that the jug was filled from the measure. The criminal was acquitted. . . . Last July [1834], three persons were brought by Lieutenant [?] Nichols to Independence for trial, for violating the intercourse law. One of the Commissioners happened to be passing through Independence at the time—2 barrels of whiskey were found in the possession of the criminals. . . . The criminals were defended by able Counsellors, one a distinguished advocate from St. Louis—all were acquitted.[55]

Agreeable, but unimpressed with such legal detail, a Delaware warrior simply insisted that the problem be understood from a broader perspective,

My father, what you say is true. Whiskey is bad for our people. We see it every day, but the whites first gave us whiskey. We did not once love it. The white man said it was good and our young men took it. . . . We cannot keep our young men from going into the states. The traders along the [Missouri] line have "a heap" of whiskey. Our men drink some and bring some home. We have no law and it is a difficult thing to stop. But we know it is a bad thing.[56]

Chapter 4

Annuities and Alcohol in Indian Country

Between 1825, when a band of Shawnees accepted a reservation immediately west of Missouri, and 1847, when the last of the emigrant Miamis
arrived on a reservation just south of the Shawnees, the federal government moved some seventy thousand Indians to Indian country west of
Missouri and Arkansas—sixty thousand Cherokees, Choctaws, Chickasaws, Seminoles, and Creeks to future Oklahoma, and ten thousand
Algonkian-speaking people to future Kansas. This massive uprooting,
with all its bureaucratic snarl, profiteering, suffering, and human casualties, finds its place in most textbooks (as well as the more specialized
studies) dealing with Indian-white relations in the United States. Yet
alcohol as a part of that tragedy too often receives little more than a
passing, albeit remorseful, nod.

At the time, the plan for native improvement did not escape public
attention. In 1844 a writer in a popular journal was persuaded that the
Indians had finally been placed beyond "the wasting influences" that
had debauched them in the East. It was possible that they might "content themselves with imitating things they do not fully understand or
appreciate" and thus suffer a temporary setback. Still, there was reason
for optimism. As the first residents of the hemisphere established roots
in "a fertile and salubrious" Indian country, the benevolent powers of
nature would prevail and native civilization would thereby be improved.
"From the tree that bears blossoms," it was insisted, "we expect fruit."
Here, according to further explication, the metaphor sprang from the
writer's assumption that native councils operating under "constitutional
fixity" would of necessity develop into congressional bodies and "enlarge
the authority of the chiefs and sagamores into something like presidential dimensions."[1] But the movement to organize Indian country into a
western territory, which might have established the groundwork for such
a development without nature's assistance, had failed in Congress,[2] and

the metaphor as well might have been the wicked water, which having blossomed well in the East would bear bountiful fruit in the West.

Everywhere, it seemed, alcohol was available. Alongside contractors who submitted inflated or fraudulent claims for supplying the Indians,[3] the whiskey vendors made the most of removal. As the Lewiston Shawnees made preparations for their final departure from Ohio in the spring of 1833, for example, Special Agent James B. Gardiner reported directly to Secretary of War Cass, "Among the many men who are in the habit of trading with the Indians, cupidity usurps indomitable sway over feeling of moral obligation, and the destructive use of ardent spirits is brought to bear on the hapless creatures."[4] Later that fall, from Richmond, Indiana, Gardiner wrote, "Many are sick . . . in consequence of the officious interference of the whites, and beastly use of ardent spirits, which it is impossible to keep from them, as we pass through the settlements."[5] The situation was no better in the South, where the superintendent of Choctaw removal in Mississippi informed his superiors that "whiskey was plentiful throughout the country, and many whites are detaining the Indians."[6] And, as a warning that matters would not improve once the Indians reached Indian country, two Kickapoos who refused to purchase whiskey were killed and all the horses of their fellow emigrants were stolen by a gang of whiskey merchants in northwestern Missouri.[7]

Not to be outdone by their counterparts in the East and on the rivers and roads to Indian country, alcohol vendors in the West were more than ready for the Indians. From the mouth of the Platte in the North to the Red River in the South—a distance of over five hundred miles—the boundary of Indian country became literally inundated with whiskey dispensed by prominent merchants and small-time hucksters whose principal customers were Indians. In 1838 Captain John Stuart of the Seventh U.S. Infantry wrote from Fort Coffee that along the western boundary of Arkansas there were no less than fifty and more likely as many as seventy "whiskey shops" selling to Indians. The Cherokees themselves viewed Section 20 of the 1834 law as useless, oppressive, and in fact an affront to their liberties as a civilized people. Proudly insisting that they drank "like white men" and sold whiskey to other Indians, they complained further,

Those Indians that wish to introduce spirits have all the white men on the line, from the Red River to Missouri to help them, which is true as holy writ, for all who have whiskey will sell it to the Indians, and those who have not the article, will not attempt to prevent the sale of it. . . . The people of [Arkansas] sell whiskey to the Indians of all classes and tribes, and when some of the most savage of them become riotous . . . the whites pretend to be awfully alarmed for their own safety.[8]

While Stuart and the Cherokees had reason to argue otherwise, Bellevue, far to the north, was then termed the "whiskey capital" of Indian country. Located on the west bank of the Missouri River near the mouth of the Platte, and thus in Indian country as defined by the 1834 law, Bellevue was a fur trade center and, more importantly, the principal destination for alcohol shipped by steamer up the Missouri River from distilleries in St. Louis. Amazed and distressed at the arrival of a major consignment of pure alcohol at Bellevue in 1838, the Presbyterian missionary John Dunbar confided to one of his associates, "Intemperance reigns here like a mighty flood. . . . How the Indians get their whiskey, right in the face of the severe laws of the United States against selling it to them, others know better than I." The Iowas and Omahas were regular customers, noted Dunbar, and the Otoes—who traveled up to two hundred miles to obtain whiskey at Bellevue—were starving and "have been drunk most of the past winter."[9] A year later, the Catholic missionary Father Pierre-Jean DeSmet provided a more detailed account of the situation at Bellevue. In his journal he wrote:

May 12 [1839]. Two Potawatomies killed on the river in a drunken frolic. May 27.Three Potawatomies drowned in the Missouri, supposed to be drunk. . . . May 30. Arrival of the steamer *Wilmington* with provisions. . . . Fifty large cannons have been landed, ready charged with the most murderous grape shot, each containing thirty gallons of whiskey, brandy, rum or alcohol. . . . A squaw offered her little boy four years old, to the crew of the boat for a few bottles of whiskey. . . . May 31. Drinking all day. . . . Four dollars a bottle! . . . Aug. 8. Arrival of the *St. Peters's* with the annuities. . . . Aug. 19. Annuities $90,000. Divided to the Indians. . . . Aug. 20. Since the day of payment, drunkards are seen and heard in all places. Liquor is rolled out to the Indians by whole barrels; sold by white men even in the presence of the agent. Wagon loads of the abominable stuff arrive daily from the settlements, and along with it the very dregs of our white neighbors. . . . Two more noses bit off, and a score of mutilations have taken place. One has been murdered. Two women are dangerously ill of bad usage.[10]

And as evidence that the market for alcohol was truly big business, Isaac McCoy reported two years later that eight thousand gallons of whiskey were headed toward Bellevue and points west in one shipment alone, again from the St. Louis suppliers. To interdict the traffic, he advised officials in Washington, would require "all the dragoons in the United States Army."[11]

Even so, the area surrounding the mouth of the Kansas challenged Bellevue as the premier conduit for moving whiskey into Indian country. Several factors dictated this less than laudatory distinction. For one thing, the Missouri-Kansas confluence became a primary supply and overland departure point for Santa Fe and the Oregon country. Located at a northern turn of the Missouri River, Liberty, Westport, Blue Springs, Independence, and the several towns comprising future Kansas City were, prior to the transcontinental railroad era, in a strategic location for supplying consumer goods for overland travel and trade to the upper Rio Grande and the valley of the Willamette. A day's travel west of Kansas City, the two trails forked in a mighty Y: the Oregon Trail turned northwest to the Marysville crossing of the Blue and then on to the Platte, through South Pass, and eventually to Oregon or California. The other headed southwest to the big bend of the Arkansas, and by way of Raton Pass or the Cimarron Desert to the commercial emporiums of northern Mexico. Both were major arteries of international travel whose patrons transported, consumed, or traded alcohol in ignorance, but more often defiance, of the 1832 and 1834 laws.[12]

Due also to the location of more than a dozen emigrant reservations within a hundred-mile radius west of Kansas City, the confluence of the Missouri and the Kansas was a central gateway to the Indian West. Immediately west of Kansas City were the Shawnee, Delaware, and Wyandot reserves. Directly north were the Kickapoo, Iowa, Sauk and Fox of Missouri, and Otoe-Missouria reservations. South, along the Missouri border, were the Wea, Piankashaw, Peoria, Kaskaskia, Miami, New York, and Cherokee Neutral lands, and due west of the Miami reservation were the Ottawas, Chippewas, Potawatomis, and the Sauks and Foxes of the Mississippi. Still farther west were the Osages and the Kansas, whose recently diminished reservations extended onto the High Plains but who for commercial reasons (including the alcohol market) resided near the eastern borders of their respective reserves.[13]

Despite the location of Fort Leavenworth less than thirty miles from Kansas City, according to reports from Indian Office personnel, the Indians were able to obtain whiskey "with absolute impunity." Directly across the river from Leavenworth, vendors at the frontier hamlet of Weston openly supplied the Indians and the military. On the Indian country side of the river, operating in the very shadow of the only federal military installation between Bellevue and Fort Gibson, a motley group of "whiskey squatters" challenged the Weston whiskey merchants for control of the Indian-military trade. It was, reported Upper Missouri Agent John Dougherty, an extremely profitable business, with no less than eight and perhaps as many as ten border distillers buying local corn and fueling their boilers to accommodate the thousands of Indians residing directly to the west.[14]

Liberty, with half a dozen dramshops and seven "groceries" that sold more whiskey than coffee or sugar, prided itself with profits derived from the local Indian trade. "Indians across the river drew annuities," recalled an early settler, "so that the trade was safe and almost without exception on a cash basis."[15] Not to be outdone, nearby Westport literally teemed with Indians seeking spirits and a good time:

Sacs and Foxes, with shaved heads and painted faces; Shawnees and Delawares fluttering in calico frocks and turbans; Wyandottes dressed like white men, and a few wretched Kanzas wrapped in old blankets, were strolling about the streets or lounging in and out of the [whiskey] shops and houses. . . . Ponies, furs, and annuity moneys were received by the early traders . . . and as there was at that time no temperance orders among these buyers and sellers, a little bad whiskey was also sold by the large and small.[16]

It was, in fact, big business. Manufacturing in Missouri began with flour mills, ropewalks, meatpacking plants, and distilleries. With the westward advance of farming along the Missouri River and onto the upland prairie country, grain production increased greatly, and by 1840 supported sixty-four steam flour mills, 636 gristmills, and numerous distilleries that turned out half a million gallons of whiskey annually. Beer production thrived as well. With a total of 172,570 barrels by 1850, Missouri proudly claimed fifth ranking of all the states in the nation. And while the bulk of alcohol was retailed in the St. Louis area, Kansas City certainly sold its fair share. With not more than fifteen hundred permanent residents and whiskey sales totaling $135,000 in 1857, a local merchant warned that excessive drunkenness witnessed daily on the streets of Kansas City would surely lead to violence, lynchings, and civil disorder.[17]

Government payment to Indians, however, was the bottom-line attraction for the Kansas City merchants. By 1845, total monetary obligations sanctioned by treaties with the removal Indians—including the Five Civilized Tribes west of Arkansas—amounted to $26,983,068.[18] While some of these funds were held in trust and invested by the government for so-called educational, agricultural, and moral improvement, most were issued as annuities in the form of hard specie that could be used as tribal leaders saw fit. Based on land cession treaties dating back to the early 1800s, the yearly payment to the tribes located west of Missouri alone came to just over a million dollars.[19] Leading the list were the Miamis, who under the treaties of 1838 and 1840 were owed $885,000 by the goverment, to be paid in ten and twenty annual installments, respectively. The Shawnee take was $829,000, as provided by the 1854 treaty and earlier agreements dating back to 1817, and the Ottawas were awarded $93,200 in 1833, to be distributed over a period of twenty years. The Wyandots accepted a perpetual annuity of $17,500, as did the Delawares at the rate of $1,000 a year in 1829. By the treaties of 1825, the Osages and Kansas received $100,000 and $60,500, respectively, to provide reservation land for the emigrant tribes, and an 1832 award to the Kickapoos came to $113,000. A series of treaties between 1837 and 1854 guaranteed the Sauks and Foxes $205,400, plus 5 percent interest on an additional corpus of $800,000, and with comparable annuities going to the Potawatomis, Piankashaws, Weas, Peorias, and Kaskaskias, it is not difficult to understand why merchants at the mouth of the Kansas River provided the Indians with almost limitless credit and pursued the alcohol trade in defiance of federal law.[20]

Whiskey vendors with an eye for legal detail were encouraged by loopholes in the government's anti-alcohol code. Unlike previous laws that contemplated the regulation of alcohol exclusively in Indian country, Section 20 of the 1834 law added "to an Indian" as a modifier to the phrase "in the Indian country" regarding the illegality of alcohol transactions with Indians.[21] But what of Indians who left Indian country and purchased alcohol at locations not designated Indian country? What if a party of Shawnees traveled only a few miles from their Indian country reservation to Westport across the Missouri line, purchased a barrel of whiskey, and there consumed the contents? Section 20 levied fines against persons (including Indians) who introduced or attempted to introduce alcohol into Indian country but was silent on Indians' obtaining and consuming alcohol in Missouri or Arkansas, or, for that matter, in the nation's capital while on official business with their Great Father.

On the plains the overland traders continued to view the Santa Fe Trail as outside the authority of the 1832 and 1834 laws. Nearly all the troubles and domestic afflictions of the Plains tribes were attributable to excessive use of alcohol, according to Central Superintendent David D. Mitchell in 1843.[22] Agents in the field reported that numerous merchants were openly operating "traveling groceries" on the trail, claiming that the intercourse laws did not apply to them. Only occasionally would the military come to the assistance of an agent attempting to arrest traders, reported Fort Leavenworth Agent Richard Cummins, with the result that the majority of agents were being "laughed at" and were afraid to call on the military for fear they would be "worsted in the end." The only corrective Cummins could recommend was that the Indian commissioner counteract "wrong impressions" by publishing in the St. Louis and Independence papers an explanation of the law and stern warnings to active or potential offenders.[23] Others believed that the only means of controlling the Santa Fe whiskey merchants was to establish a major military post on or near the border between the United States and Mexico.[24] Yet the construction of Fort Larned in 1859, Fort Zarah in 1864, and Fort Dodge in 1865—all along the Santa Fe Trail—did not diminish the alcohol trade in the least. Indeed, as late as 1866, from his agency headquarters at Fort Zarah, Kiowa-Comanche Agent Jesse H. Leavenworth wrote the Indian Office,

> A man of the name Dietz . . . has established a ranch in the Fort
> . . . and being plentifully supplied with whiskey has supplied the Indi-
> ans with all they wanted. I have taken the ground that this place and
> west of here is 'Indian Country.' Am I right? If so, I wish it *distinctly*
> stated. I do not want a suit commenced against me unless I am in the
> right. I did not destroy any property but simply made the parties
> leave the country with all their effects.[25]

At Fort Zarah also it was reported that Upper Arkansas Indian Agent I. C. Taylor was "constantly drunk" while pursuing his official duties and that he sold whiskey to the Indians from his residence on the fort's grounds. At nearby Fort Larned a post commander was dishonorably discharged for "habitual drunkenness"; at Fort Dodge a detachment of enlisted men sent out to intercept and destroy an illicit whiskey train from Mexico in 1868 ended up getting so drunk that several of their own ranks were killed in the melee that followed. Even at the much larger, more permanent, and presumably more disciplined Fort Riley, officers sold whiskey to the Indians on a regular basis. On what clearly was an outrageous interpretation of Indian alcohol law, sales of this sort were rationalized on grounds that military installations technically were not in Indian country, or worse, that because annuity funds used by the Indians to purchase alcohol were issued by civilian Indian agents, the military had no responsibility for the consequences. Even so, annuities were not the only culprit. In fact alcohol was readily available for sale to Indians at most federal military posts west of the Missouri.[26]

No less important sources of alcohol were at least half a dozen whiskey stations along the Santa Fe Trail between the mouth of the Kansas and Fort Larned. At "110 mile crossing" just south of Topeka and within four miles of the Sauk and Fox reservation, for example, was Fry McGee's "doggerie." Forty miles west, at Council Grove, a local judge dispensed whiskey from his cellar to thirsty Indians and Santa Fe Trail travelers alike. His principal competitor was J. L. French, who operated a "wayside grocery" adjacent to the Kansa reservation. Less than a day's travel farther west was Thomas Wise's hotel and tavern at Lost Springs, where on one occasion Wise was trapped on the roof of his establishment for half a day by Indians who demanded whiskey. Twenty miles still farther west at Cottonwood Crossing was the Moore ranch, where, according to the establishment's ledgers, "Red Jacket Bitters, Hostetters, Ginger Brandy, cognac, sweet wine, and whiskey galore" were available at "highly inflated prices." At Cow Creek Crossing, just east of the great bend of the Arkansas, Asabel Beach and his son Abijah operated a federally chartered toll bridge, post office, and grocery that sold sugar, bacon, flour, and whiskey. And less than a mile from the notorious Dietz operation at Fort Zarah, there was the Walnut Creek Crossing whiskey ranch first operated by William Allison of Independence in the 1840s and then by a Mr. Peacock until an irate Kiowa party led by Chief Satank cracked open Peacock's skull, cut out his tongue, and thrust it into the cleft of his head—apparently for whiskey transactions gone awry. Even so, the obviously profitable alcohol conduit at Walnut Creek remained in operation. Following Peacock's death it was taken over by the no less notorious and opportunistic Charlie Rath and, in the late 1850s, by a more businesslike firm headed by William Griffenstein. Griffenstein, who was awarded several federal contracts for supplying the Kiowa-Comanche Agency in the mid-1860s and who subsequently became one of the principal founders and developers of Wichita, enjoyed a "good" business at Walnut Creek well into the Civil War period.[27]

Prior to first-time annuities awarded the Cheyennes and Arapahoes (among numerous other tribes) by the Fort Laramie Treaty of 1851 and to the Kiowas and Comanches by the Fort Atkinson Treaty of 1853,[28] the Plains tribes relied mainly on skins and robes to obtain alcohol. But after these dates specie awarded by the federal government became the preferred medium of exchange for both the Indians and the dealers. Thus it was that in 1868 Chief Big Mouth of the Arapahoes purchased eighteen bottles of whiskey at Fort Dodge and Pah-up-pah-lop secured five gallons at Fort Larned. Trail trader J. L. Butterfield advised Central Superintendent Thomas Murphy that such easy transactions would bring "real trouble" in the spring, but the "really horrible thing about all this is that if they [the Indians] have the robes they can get all the whiskey they want from any military post."[29] Confirming what Fort Leavenworth Agent Richard W. Cummins had complained of more than a decade ear-

lier, Central Superintendent Alfred Cumming was advised in 1858 that
"regulations of the Indian Department may be trampled upon by lawless
violators and the Indian agent may in vain call upon the military branch
of the government for succors."[30] And once the annuities were spent,
the natives could always revert back to more traditional methods of
barter at civilian establishments, as was reported by a Council Grove
paper in 1861:

> A fat brave with his unctuous better-half, and a pack of buffalo robes,
> all piled upon the back of a small pony, is no uncommon spectacle.
> Being a man of business, the Indian immediately proceeds to the
> store to trade, and by a series of signs and grunts, manifests his desire
> to buy something. His first demand is always whiskey. Business trans-
> actions complete, the two leave for camp, with a degree of compla-
> cency that is natural to nothing but the Indian.[31]

Thus in the years following passage of the 1834 law defining the limits of Indian country with unfettered clarity, a combination of whiskey
ranchers, overland traders, and military personnel stationed at posts
along the commercial highway between the mouth of the Kansas and
the Mexican boundary provided the Indians with an ample supply of
alcohol—all in violation of Section 20 of the 1834 law. On the Oregon
Trail west of Missouri and Iowa the situation was no better. White emigrants headed across Indian country for Oregon or the California mines
brought with them a plentiful supply of alcohol for daily consumption
and, not to be outdone by vendors operating to the south, engaged in a
brisk alcohol trade on grounds that they "knew no better than to sell it
to the Indians."[32]

Omnipresent annuity funds in concert with land cession treaties prerequisite to the implementation of federal removal policy in the West
constituted still another avenue for providing Indians with alcohol and
evading the 1834 law. Although other Indians indigenous to the trans-
Missouri West were involved in the whiskey trade with fellow tribesmen
(e.g., the Iowas, Otoes, Missourias, and Osages), the Kansa nation clearly
was at the forefront of the intertribal alcohol traffic on the Missouri border. Indeed, so widespread and pervasive was their network of operations
that one federal official termed them "the moral ulcer in the body

politic"; another described their villages west of Kansas City simply as "dens of whiskey smugglers."[33]

These condemnations aside, the Kansas in fact exploited an important loophole for engaging in the alcohol trade without violating the boundaries of Indian country written into the 1834 law. As recognized by agents of the federal government in 1825, the Kansa domain included the entire Kansas River drainage from the mouth of the Kansas to sources of the Smoky Hill on the high plains of eastern Colorado, roughly the northern half of present Kansas. To accommodate the removal Indians it was essential that a land cession be negotiated for their benefit, and because the area immediately west of Missouri was preferred, Superintendent William Clark secured a Kansa land cession from the Nebraska line south to a point some fifty miles south of Kansas City and west to the site of modern Topeka—what after 1825 would include the removal reservations for the Kickapoos, Delawares, Wyandots, and Shawnees, as well as portions of the Ottawa, Miami, Peoria, Wea, Piankashaw, Kaskaskia, and Sauk and Fox reserves in Indian country.[34]

For this cession the Kansas drove a hard bargain. In addition to two thousand dollars worth of merchandise, three hundred head of cattle, five hundred hogs, five hundred domestic fowls, three yoke of oxen, sundry agricultural implements, and a thirty-five-hundred-dollar annuity for twenty years, Chief White Plume and eleven other tribal dignitaries insisted that the government grant one-mile-square (640-acre) individual reservations to each of the twenty-three half-bloods of the Kansa nation, to be located along the north side of the Kansas River adjacent to the diminished tribal reservation and extending twenty-three miles east toward the Missouri border.[35]

Superintendent Clark insisted that these fee-simple reservations granted to select individuals would have a salutory effect on the tribe as a whole and on the government's civilization program in general: "Reserves of this kind have been heretofore made in behalf of such persons, and in my opinion have a good effect in promoting civilization, as their attachment is created for a fixed residence and an idea of separate property is imparted without which it is vain to think of improving the minds and morals of the Indian or making any progress in the work of civilization."[36] Having thus extolled the virtues of individual land ownership, Clark was less optimistic regarding contacts between the Kansa nation

as a whole and the hard-drinking white farmers and merchants of western Missouri: "Experience having convinced me of the necessity of preventing a White and Indian population from remaining in immediate
contact with each other and the Indians themselves being fully sensible
of the inconvenience of such neighborhoods . . . it has been stipulated
that the [main] Kansa reservation be about fifty miles west of Missouri, to
prevent the stocks of the two parties from intermixing."[37]

Four months after the treaty was negotiated, Clark bluntly defended
this buffer zone on grounds that there "could be no control over [white]
citizens on the borders of the settlements." With annuities in hand it was
easy for the Indians to cross over to Missouri, purchase all the spirits they
wanted, and return to their villages to consume alcohol as the white man
did.[38] Clark's hope, of course, was that by moving the Indians farther west
such transactions would be discouraged. Yet the 1825 buffer zone became
the very locus where Clark's efforts at control fell victim to removal policy until the 1834 boundaries of Indian country—which Clark helped
draft—went into effect. Here it was that the emigrant tribes were placed
and here also it was that the Kansa mixed-bloods engaged in the whiskey
trade without violating the 1834 law, for the simple reason that the 640-
acre reservations granted in 1825 for the advance of civilization and tribal
improvement were not legally a part of Indian country.

Frustrated by the loophole written into the 1825 treaty, agents in the
field lamented that it was "utterly beyond their power" to intervene in
the Kansa whiskey traffic,[39] and in 1837 Isaac McCoy reported that the
twenty Osage mixed-bloods who in 1825 had been granted fee-simple
reservations similar to the Kansas were openly engaging in the alcohol
trade as well.[40] In fact, few Indians actually resided among the "dens of
whiskey smugglers" that cropped up on the Kansa and Osage mixed-
blood tracts and, so long as they shared in the profits, were content to
allow non-Indian dealers such as John Sibille to conduct the trade without fear of fines or loss of personal property, as happened in 1842 when
a federal magistrate in Platte City, Missouri, refused to take action under
the 1834 law after Sibille and his men had been arrested for having fifty-
five gallons of whiskey in their possession on the Kansa lands.[41] Indeed,
so defiant were the traders and so judicially secure were their operations
that St. Louis Indian Superintendent David D. Mitchell concluded in
1849 that the only recourse was for the government to buy back the

mixed-blood reservations at the $1.25-an-acre minimum, as Isaac McCoy had suggested more than a decade earlier.[42] By midcentury, however, the market value of the tracts had appreciated substantially, and with the Kansas mixed-blood tracts worth well over a quarter of a million dollars, no action was taken on Mitchell's request.[43]

Chief White Plume, principal signer of the 1825 treaty, died of whiskey consumption and exposure in 1838; Fool Chief, one of his successors, was killed in a drunken brawl while on a begging trip to Missouri.[44] Superintendent Mitchell estimated in September 1841 that at least 120 Indians west of Arkansas and Missouri had died of alcohol during the past twelve months,[45] and from the area west of Iowa missionary William Hamilton reported that sixty members of the Iowa and Sauk and Fox nations had been killed by fellow tribesmen during "drunken sprees."[46] Summing up the unfolding demographic tragedy in 1842, Mitchell informed authorities in Washington that no less than 500 adult Indian males had died at the hands of the bottle over the past two years, and that alcohol was "as destructive and more constant than disease" in the depopulation of the western Indians. Annuities in the form of merchandise occasionally had positive results, said Mitchell, "but whenever money is around it soon finds its way into the hands of the whiskey dealers, who swarm like birds of evil omen around the place where annuities are paid."[47] The movement of federal troops across the plains occasioned by the outbreak of the Mexican War in 1846 only exacerbated the situation,[48] and, the 1834 law notwithstanding, Indian country by the mid-forties had become a fiction—an enormously profitable sanctuary for bootleggers and a place of premature death for Indians.

Uncontrollable passion and moral deficiency were recurrent themes regarding the abandon with which the Indians consumed alcohol. Because the native ardor for alcohol was as strong as the determination to indulge in it at all hazards, Lewis Cass insisted that Indian drunkenness presented a phenomenon unprecedented in the history of humanity. "Elsewhere habitual drunkards have paroxysms of intoxication followed by sobriety," said Cass, "but as long as the stimulus can be obtained, an Indian abandons himself totally to its indulgence, with the recklessness of desperation."[49] Federal removal commissioners Montfort Stokes, John F. Schermerhorn, and Henry Ellsworth described Indian drinking in the West as "the living fountain of depravity." Alcohol immediately excited the demonic side of Indians, they wrote in 1834, and "with every baneful passion excited and every moral barrier prostrated," the natives presented a "loathsome spectacle" wholly beyond any conception of civilized life.[50] And a decade later, Indian Commissioner T. Hartley Crawford attributed excessive consumption to moral deficiency,[51] a view shared by his successor William Medill, who discerned a native "weakness" for alcohol in the face of the white man's greed.[52]

Appraisals of this sort by government officials responsible for the formulation and administration of Indian policy were matched by frontier newspaper commentators who concurred with the deficiency view of Indian drinking. Not atypical was the comment of a Missouri editor who, while conceding that a few Indians had made "rude" advances toward civilization, nevertheless concluded that the majority "indulge in their natural indolence and seek every means and opportunity to obtain whiskey, which they always drink to excess."[53] At Council Grove on the Santa Fe Trail the local paper agreed. "We have resided close to these delectable children of the prairies, for lo! these sixteen years," reported the editor. The government had provided the local Kaws (formerly the Kansa) with daily sustenance and implements for tilling the soil, "all of which have been sold for whiskey, and still the Indians are more fierce and fond of rapine, and murder, and the chase than ever before."[54] With such pessimistic reporting certain foreign observers concurred. Swedish traveler Carl David Arfwedson reported in 1832 that the Indians were being ruined "by an inordinate passion for strong liquors," and the German historian Friedrich von Raumer wrote in 1844 that while the white man deserved to be censured for defrauding the tribes, "the Indians' passion for liquor was their own fault."[55] In the same vein more recently— this time by a professional historian—it has been asserted that liquor vended by dissolute white peddlers "combined with a lack of inhibition in these undisciplined barbarians made their drinking revels so brutal and terrible as to defy adequate description."[56]

Others, however, took issue with such analysis. The Reverend Isaac McCoy, iconoclast Baptist missionary and government surveyor of removal reservations who spent years in Indian country, addressed the issue in letters to the Indian Office and the president of the United States in 1842. Responding to the assertion that Indians had a natural propensity toward alcohol, and disillusioned after Congress on purely partisan grounds had refused to establish a western Indian territory where Indian people might have exercised more political power and where the judicial arm of the national government might have been more effective in controlling the liquor traffic,[57] McCoy inveighed mightily against the proponents of native deficiency. By 1842, wrote McCoy, no less than thirty thousand gallons of whiskey were being transported into Indian country annually; fighting, maimings, and killings were routine occurrences at treaty talks and annuity distributions; tribal indebtedness to the whiskey peddlers was absolutely shocking; indolence and starvation were commonplace. "How many white men under the discouragement of real misfortune," asked McCoy, "have abandoned themselves to drink?" Contrary to the belief that Indians were intractable slaves to their savage passions and thus unable to control their drinking, McCoy rejoined: "The natives are apt scholars, and the white men who furnish them liquor are well-qualified teachers."[58] And when searching out the very root of the problem, even Commissioner Crawford could agree:

> Worse for the red man . . . is the traffic in whiskey, to which our citizens lend themselves, from the most contemptible and sordid motives. Outraging every principle of morals, all law, and the dictates of humanity, they deliberately place the instrument of destruction in his hand, and persuade him to use it, brutalizing him, and making victims of his wife and children, that they may fraudulently pick his pocket and strip his back of the blanket that covers it.[59]

A close friend of President Jackson and a strong supporter of Indian removal, Crawford was adamantly opposed to any formal territory in the West that might eventually result in Indian statehood. Rather, he advocated the return to a modified government factory system, where high-quality goods at the several Indian agencies would be available on a regular basis, to be sold only to Indians for their cash annuities. He also favored working through tribal leaders as a means of controlling the liquor traffic that was inevitable so long as white people occupied the borders of Indian country.[60] But old fears of monopoly and excessive government regulation, agitated by pressure exercised by the Indian trade lobby, prompted Congress to reject Crawford's recommendations,[61] and during the tenure of his successor, stiffer penalties, scapegoats for failed federal policy, and particular disregard for the legal quagmire of Indian country that encouraged illicit sales became orders of the day.

William Medill became Indian commissioner in the year of Texas annexation and settlement of the Oregon controversy, and served through the turbulent years of the Mexican War that saw a dramatic increase in whiskey consumption in Indian country.[62] A purely political appointee and one possessed of no prior knowledge of Indian affairs, Medill was convinced that Indians were innately inferior and, if pampered too much, would deteriorate into lazy, wretched, intemperate outcasts of society.[63] As others before him,[64] Medill sought out scapegoats by complaining that annuities paid to tribal leaders inevitably fell into the hands of the whiskey traders.[65] Clearly, there was an awareness in high places that annuities were central to the alcohol trade.

As early as 1836 Senator John C. Calhoun of South Carolina assured his fellow solons that so long as annuities flowed into the hands of the Indians "it was the easiest thing in the world to keep them quiet."[66] Ten years later, however, with the collective payment to the tribes exceeding a million dollars annually, federal agents and superintendents throughout Indian country were in agreement that the annuity-alcohol system was ravaging the Indians. Reporting from St. Louis in 1846, Superintendent Harvey flatly declared that the government was unable to prevent Indians from obtaining alcohol, either in the states or in Indian country.[67] The subagent at Council Bluffs dismissed the intercourse law as a "dead letter." To expect an agent to stop the trade was preposterous, he inveighed. "What can you do by 'moral suasion,' even among the whites, where strong passions and base appetites are to be restrained? And how much less among a rude people, such as the unlettered, untaught Indians!"[68] State officials on the border joined in the outcry. "Our system of 'trade and intercourse' with Indian tribes is rapidly destroying them," advised the governor of Iowa to officials in Washington. "They are the victims of fraud and intemperance, superinduced by the large sums paid them annually by the government, without proper guards to protect them against the superior cunning and avarice of unprincipled white men."[69]

One suggested "reform" was to insert stipulations in future treaties prohibiting the payment of annuities to satisfy debts incurred for alcohol obtained on credit from white traders—much like articles that were included in future treaties requiring withholding annuities to individual Indians who consumed alcohol or engaged in the trade[70]—but the governor of Wisconsin Territory reminded Medill that such regulations ran the risk of impeding the negotiation of future land cession treaties because of the "controlling influence" the mixed-bloods and white traders had over the Indians.[71] Commissioner Crawford called for amended Indian lives and better Indian morals, what he called "the lever to which I have always looked for lifting the red man out of the mire";[72] in a similar vein, Superintendent Harvey suggested that "the only hope is in the moral improvement of the Indians, which can be effected only through Christianity and education."[73]

Excluding a letter written by McCoy to President Polk, requesting a strong supplement to the Indian code that would clearly define the boundaries and internal extent of Indian country,[74] no one in the Indian Office or Congress raised the demanding issue that this vast region reserved exclusively for Indians in 1834 was being overrun, in fact disassembled, by a host of merchants, grain farmers, clandestine distillers, overland traders, frontier soldiers, and western emigrants caught up in the spirit of national expansion, in the enormous economic potential Indian country held for squatter invasion and corporate speculation, and, of course, the easy profits that could be had by exchanging locally produced alcohol for annuities guaranteed by federal law. Indeed, in the long and dreary history of federal subsidy to western expansion, one would be hard-pressed to discover a more dependable and profitable means toward that objective.

Some action, of course, was mandatory, if for no other reason than to placate public complaint, reaffirm that the government's civilization program was not floundering, and to vindicate the Great Father's desire to prohibit Indian drinking dating back to 1802. Claiming that his judgment represented the "overwhelming recommendation" of federal agents and subagents throughout the length and breadth of Indian country, Commissioner Medill called for imprisonment of liquor law violators and a dramatic change in the annuity distribution system in Indian country.[75] And no less surprisingly, a Congress more concerned with the war with Mexico than with alcohol consumption and Indian mortality in Indian country accepted his nostrums without debate.

In the first significant revision of the Indian alcohol code since the Trade and Intercourse Act of 1834, Section 2 of the statute of March 3, 1847, stated that

> any person who shall sell, exchange or barter, give, or dispose of any *sirituous* [sic] liquor or wine to an Indian, *in the Indian country* [emphasis added], or who shall introduce, or attempt to introduce, any *sirituous* [sic] liquor or wine *in the Indian country* [emphasis added], except as may be necessary for the officers of the United States and the troops of the service . . . such person, on conviction thereof before the proper District Court of the United States, shall in the former case be subject to imprisonment for a period not exceeding two years, and in the latter case not exceeding one year, as shall be proscribed by the court, according to the extent and criminality of the offence. And in all prosecutions arising under this section, and under the twentieth section of the act to regulate trade and intercourse with the Indian tribes, and to preserve peace on the frontiers, approved June thirtieth, eighteen hundred and thirty-four, to which this is an amendment, Indians shall be competent witnesses.[76]

Thus, for the first time, offenders convicted of vending alcohol to Indians at a specified location were to be given substantial prison sentences, and for the first time also, the testimony of an Indian was to be recognized as that of a competent human being. Section 3 of the statute required that

> all annuities or other moneys, and all goods, stipulated by treaty to be paid or furnished to any Indian tribe, shall, at the discretion of the President or Secretary of War, *instead of being paid over to the chiefs* [emphasis added], . . . be divided and paid over to the heads of families and other individuals entitled to participate therein, or, with the consent of the tribe, be applied to such purposes as will best promote the happiness and prosperity of the members thereof.[77]

It was further provided that no annuities were to be distributed to Indians under the influence of intoxicating liquor, nor if there was reason to believe that any sort of intoxicating liquor was within convenient reach of the Indians. Finally, annuities were to be withheld if the chiefs and/or headmen of the tribe failed to "pledge themselves to use all their influence and to make all proper exertions to prevent the introduction and sale of liquor in their country."[78]

While the boundaries and geographical extent of Indian country as stipulated in 1834 were reaffirmed by the 1847 law, not one word was said regarding the transport of alcohol into Indian country via the overland trails that traversed it from east to west. Writing to Superintendent Harvey less than a year after the 1847 law went into effect, Agent Richard W. Cummins reported that a large portion of the Santa Fe Trail commerce soon to leave Missouri was in whiskey. The traders insisted that the trail was a public highway and thus exempt from the 1847 law; other vendors entertained the same view, including army sutlers stationed along the trail. In fact, reported Cummins, it was the Indians' complaint that any and all vendors claimed to be overland traders until they were well into Indian country, at which point they went wherever they desired. "If I am aiming to do too much, as some of the traders say I am," offered Cummins in an obviously apologetic manner, "it will be a very easy matter for you or the [Indian] Dept. to stop me."[79]

On April 13 Secretary of War William L. Marcy issued a detailed directive for implementing the 1847 law. Explicit instructions were provided concerning fines, imprisonment, seizure of property, destruction of distilleries, revocation of trade licenses, removal of agents from office, and even a directive requiring that Indian leaders who refused to cooperate in the enforcement of the new law would have their individual annuity payments withheld.[80] Three months later Marcy wrote a strong letter to the governors of Arkansas, Missouri, and Iowa, soliciting their aid in halting the liquor traffic.[81] But not a word of explanation or clarification was provided regarding whether or not areas such as overland commercial highways, fee-simple grants to individual Indians, federal military reservations, Indian trust lands, or lands not specifically granted by treaty as tribal reservations *within* Indian country were excluded under the new law. The implication, then, was that the boundaries originally designated in the 1834 statute remained inviolate.

That year also one of the first cases under the new law was heard in a Missouri federal court. The case against Abraham Potter for selling whiskey to Indians in Indian country was filed on July 2, 1847, continued to March 1853, for reasons not recorded, then to October 1853, at which time it was again continued because "the defendant could not be found." The Potter case was finally dismissed in July 1854 on grounds that "the witnesses have all disappeared."[82]

"Sharp Trade." Southern Cheyennes trading whiskey for buffalo robes with the Kiowas at their Pawnee river village west of Fort Larned in the spring of 1869. From *Harper's New Monthly Magazine* 39 (1869): 25.

"Treaty Makers." Oil on canvas. By an unknown artist, c. 1840. Courtesy National Museum of the American Indian, Smithsonian Institution, New York.

"Father Ignacio Moved by the Spirit." Catholic priest doing a jig in a roadhouse between Taos and Santa Fe with the assistance of a bottle of *aguadiénte de Taos*—the "Taos Lightning"— produced by distillers in New Mexico and traded in Indian country along the Santa Fe Trail. From *Harper's New Monthly Magazine* 47 (1854): 581.

"Home for the Boys." Cosy setting leading to violence following the consumption of "ardent" spirits by non-Indians in an Indian country bar. From *Harper's New Monthly Magazine* 59 (1865): 5.

"Effect of the Climate in California." Alcohol arrives in California, which became a part of Indian country by the Treaty of Guadalupe Hidalgo (1848) ending the Mexican-American War. From *Harper's New Monthly Magazine* 24 (1861–1862): 300.

"A Question of Title." One way miners and squatters dealt with conflicting land titles in Indian country. From *Harper's New Monthly Magazine* 22 (1861): 154.

"Whiskey Still in Ravine." Camouflage was of the essence when producing alcohol contrary to the law. From *Harper's New Monthly Magazine* 59 (1865): 516.

"The Stage." Passing time on a stage express crossing Indian country in 1861. From *Harper's New Monthly Magazine* 22 (1861): 152.

"Cowboys." Texas cowboys relaxing on the trail to Indian country. From *Harper's New Monthly Magazine* 59 (1879): 708.

"Bull Eagle Drinking the Fire-Water." Bull Eagle (Tahtunga-mobellu), chief and esteemed medicine man of the Sioux, drinking with agents of the American Fur Company on the upper Missouri, c. 1843. From Rufus B. Sage, *Wild Scenes in Kansas and Nebraska, the Rocky Mountains, Oregon, California, New Mexico, Texas, and the Grand Prairies, or Notes by the Way, During an Excursion of Three Years, with a Description of the Countries Passed Through, Including Their Geography, Geology, Resources, Present Condition, and The Different Nations Inhabiting Them*. Philadelphia: G. D. Miller, Publisher, 1855.

"Prairie Schooners at the Dock." Freighters on the Santa Fe Trail pausing for refreshment at a saloon west of Council Grove. From *Harper's New Monthly Magazine* 61 (1880): 187.

"Fritz Durien and His Warehouse Treasury." Kansas bootlegger Fritz Durien revealing the subfloor "Treasury" in which he stored his illicit merchandise. Early twentieth-century photograph. Courtesy of the Kansas State Historical Society.

"Fritz Durien and His Dog." Durien was a notorious bootlegger in the Topeka vicinity in the late nineteenth and early twentieth centuries, and is here shown with his dog, a bottle of his merchandise, and an Indian statue—the latter symbolic, perhaps, of a valued clientele. Early twentieth-century photograph. Courtesy of the Kansas State Historical Society.

"St. Joe Brewery." The massive brewery at St. Joseph, Missouri, on the eastern border of Indian country. Early twentieth-century photograph. Courtesy of the Kansas State Historical Society.

"Winthrop, Missouri, across from Atchison, Kansas." Saloons on the Missouri side of the Missouri River, on the eastern border of Indian country. Late nineteenth-century photograph. Courtesy of the Kansas State Historical Society.

"View of Tavern at Arrow Rock." This historic tavern was located on the Santa Fe Trail in Missouri and was constructed in 1830. Courtesy of the Kansas State Historical Society.

Annuities and merchandise being distributed to Indians by agents of the United States Office of Indian Affairs, 1882. From *Harper's Weekly*, 11 February 1882.

"Praised be Moses, the keg is saved!" From *Harper's New Monthly Magazine* 23 (1861–1862): 596.

"Modern Idolatry." Spirituous idolatries of national origin in the United States, c. 1861. From *Harper's New Monthly Magazine* 23 (1861): 141.

"Modern Idolatry." Preferred idolatries of the West by comparison with other regions of the United States, c. 1861. From *Harper's New Monthly Magazine* 23 (1861): 142.

George Catlin's paintings of Wi-jun-jon (The Pigeon's Egg Head), distinguished Assiniboine warrior, before and after he visited Washington. Catlin met Wi-jun-jon in St. Louis, in 1832, and again upon the warrior's return to the upper Yellowstone country later that year. His new costume included a beaver hat, stiff collar with lace, fine blue broadcloth laced with gold, an umbrella, and two bottles of whiskey stuffed in his pockets. He quickly fell into disgrace with his own people, who deplored his lies, his claim to political eminence, and his swaggering about "with keg under his arm, whistling Yankee Doodle." From George Catlin, *North American Indians, Being Letters and Notes on Their Manners, Customs, and Conditions, Written during Eight Years' Travel amongst the Wildest Tribes of Indians in North America, 1832–1839.* Vol. 2. Edinburgh: John Grant, 1926. The quoted phrase is on p. 225.

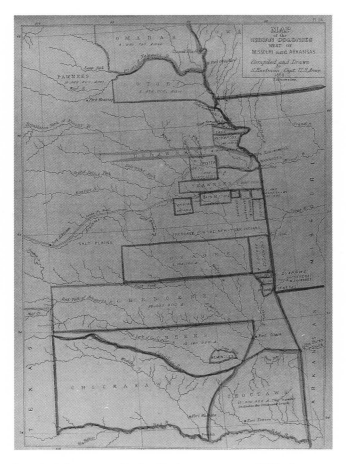

Detail of the eastern flank of Indian country in 1853, showing the several emigrant reservations established under the federal government's removal policy dating back to the mid-1820s. This map appears similar to the map Indian Commissioner George W. Manypenny prepared at Missouri Senator Thomas Hart Benton's request in 1853, and which Benton edited for distribution to potential non-Indian settlers in Indian country that same year. "Map of the Indian Colonies West of Missouri and Arkansas, Compiled by Seth Eastman, Capt. U.S. Army, 1853." Courtesy Ablah Library, Department of Special Collections, Wichita State University.

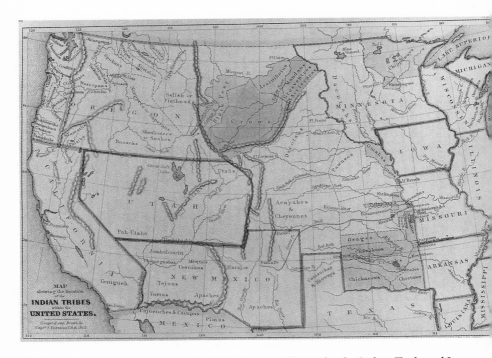

Location of the various tribes in Indian Country in 1852. Under the Indian Trade and Intercou Act of 1834 Indian Country extended west only to the western boundary of the Louisiana Purchase as determined by the Adams-Onnis Treaty with Spain (1819). Following the Oregon Settlement with Britain (1846) and the treaty ending the Mexican-America War (1848), the boundary was the Pacific coast of the United States. "Map showing the location of the Indian Tribes within the United States. Compiled and Drawn by Capt. Seth Eastman, U.S.A., 1852." Courtesy Ablah Library, Department of Special Collections, Wichita State University.

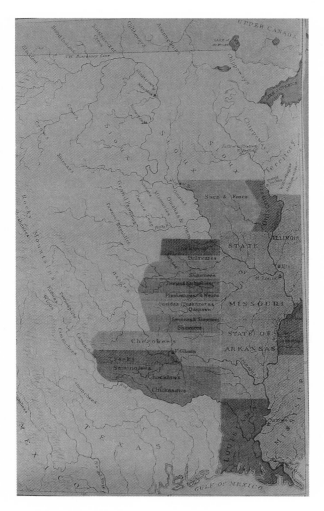

Indian country as depicted by George Catlin in 1840, six years after passage of Indian Trade and Intercourse Act of 1834. The boundaries of the emigrant reservations west of Arkansas, Missouri, and the Mississippi River are approximations and do not conform with the legal boundaries as described in the various removal treaties. From George Catlin, *North American Indians, Being Letters and Notes on Their Manners, Customs, and Conditions, Written during Eight Years' Travel amongst the Wildest Tribes of Indians in North America, 1832–1839*. Vol. 2. Edinburgh: John Grant, 1926.

"Unnaturalized." The Indian in his natural state. Engraving by Henry Worrall of Topeka, Kansas, who by the early 1870s was widely viewed as a caricaturist of considerable accomplishment. From W. E. Webb, *Buffalo Land: An Authentic Account of the Discoveries, Adventures, and Mishaps of a Scientific and Sporting Party in the Wild West; with Graphic Description of the Country; the Red Man, Savage and Civilized; Hunting Buffalo, Antelope, Elk, and Wild Turkey; etc; etc*. Philadelphia: E. Hannaford & Co., 1872. Courtesy of Ablah Library, Department of Special Collections, Wichita State University.

"Naturalized." The Indian following acceptance of the White Man's Wicked Water. Engraving by Henry Worrall.

"The Pipe of Peace—The Professor's Dilemma." A Cheyenne party headed by Chief White Eagle (also known as Medicine Wolf) calling on the scientific leader of a white hunting party from the East to smoke the pipe following a drinking bout in Hays, Kansas, in the early 1870s. From W. E. Webb, *Buffalo Land: An Authentic Account of the Discoveries, Adventures, and Mishaps of a Scientific and Sporting Party in the Wild West; with Graphic Descriptions of the Country; the Red Man, Savage and Civilized; Hunting Buffalo, Antelope, Elk, and Wild Turkey; etc; etc.* Philadelphia: E. Hannaford & Co., 1872. Courtesy of Ablah Library, Department of Special Collections, Wichita State University.

Chapter 5

Courting Disaster

The Potter case was no exception. Mole Pettijohn and Simpson Vassar, arrested for vending alcohol to American Indians west of Missouri in August 1849, had their case continued to the 1851 term of the federal circuit court in Missouri and then dismissed for the reason that persons "important" to the proceedings "had left for parts unknown." Less fortunate but certainly not greatly inconvenienced were Samuel C. Roby, found guilty in 1848 of selling to Indians and fined $1.00 plus costs, or Charles Hempstead, found guilty of a similar offense that same year and fined $26.17—the value of his broken-down oxen, his wagon, and some corn and bacon in his possession at the time of his arrest.[1] Since the 1847 law augmented by previous regulatory statutes called for fines of up to $300 and prison sentences of up to two years, it is obvious that lenient sentencing was the order of the day.

The Roby case illustrates well why the whiskey vendors had little to fear from the courts. A longtime employee of the prominent Kansas City family of James Hyatt McGee,[2] Samuel C. Roby was denied renewal of his Indian Office trade license in 1843 on grounds he had vended illegal alcohol to the Delawares and Shawnees for more than a decade. Since the early 1830s his employers had been involved in the Indian alcohol trade west of Missouri, and in 1843 Fort Leavenworth Agent Cummins obtained a financial judgment against James H. McGee's son Milton in a Missouri court for selling whiskey to Indians. While the younger McGee left his wife in the care of relatives and fled to California to recoup his losses and mend his personal reputation, Roby moved up the ranks in the McGees' alcohol enterprise. According to Cummins, Roby was also guilty of stealing a large quantity of gold consigned to unidentified merchants in Santa Fe.[3]

But Cummins's actions did not deter Roby, for the simple reason that profits in the Indian alcohol trade were enormous. Eschewing the Delaware and Shawnee trade because of its location too close to the Fort

Leavenworth Agency, Roby moved deeper into Indian country and became a supplier for the Ottawas on their reservation some fifty miles southwest of Kansas City. Here, on April 16, 1846, Roby was once again arrested, this time for "swindling and selling brandy to the Ottawas," based on the testimony of Jotham Meeker, Baptist missionary to the Ottawas since 1837. An avowed foe of anything alcoholic, Meeker had helped organize an Ottawa Temperance Society and in 1838 proudly reported that the Ottawas had "unanimously decided that they forthwith quit the practice of drinking whiskey." In fact, Christian confession and formal association with the local Baptist Church were prerequisites to membership in the temperance society, and it was inevitable that backsliding would take place, particularly after Roby arrived on the scene with a large consignment of alcohol from the McGee warehouse in Kansas City. The 1842 Ottawa annuity payment was made on October 8, and within a week Meeker recorded that "the Indians around us are constantly drinking." It was then that the frustrated missionary filed a formal complaint with the Indian Office at Fort Leavenworth.[4]

Even so, it was not until the spring of 1848 that Meeker and Ottawa witnesses Pahtee and Thomas Wolf were subpoenaed to appear before a grand jury in St. Louis. Here, and later at Jefferson City, selected entries recorded by Meeker in his private journal describe well the tribulations (and expenses) of those who would testify against the whiskey traders.

April 8: Thomas [Wolf], Pahtee, and I give testimony before the Grand Jury, and are to appear before the U.S. Ct. Court the 10th. . . . Write to the [Baptist] Ex. Com. for $105.25 [assistance].

April 10: Secure passage to Westport for Thos. [Wolf] and Pahtee. . . . Attend at Court, hoping to be discharged today, but one of the jurors absent, nothing can be done till tomorrow.

April 11: Attend the Court at 10. It being announced that the grand jury could not rest until 5, Maj. [Thomas] Harvey interceded with the U.S. Dist. Attorney to make a motion that we be discharged. We then, Thomas, Pahtee, and I were bound over, on a penalty of $500 to appear before the U.S. Circuit Court at Jefferson City, on the first day of September next, to attend the trial between the U.S. and S. C. Roby after which we are discharged and receive . . . for our services total $52.25.

July 10: Learn that Mr. Roby has been imprisoned at Jefferson City
. . . [and] that he had given bail for his appearance . . . and is now
closing his business in Westport—that he is issuing various threats
against, &c., &c

July 13: Learn that Ashtonkwut [an Ottawa leader] . . . is oppos-
ing us with all his might—and that Roby, too, has just returned from
the East to Westport, that he has sent for all of the Ottawas, except
the Church members, that he is threatening to prosecute Pahtee and
me for perjury, &c., &c.

August 10: In Westport—do some business—have considerable
talk with M. McGee, who has lately been threatening to whip me,
kill me, &c., on account of my witnessing against Roby.

September 4: Visit the U.S. District Attorney [in Jefferson City].
. . . Have considerable talk with Roby, who tries hard to get us to
favor him in the trial. . . . Attend the court in the afternoon. Our
trial is taken up, and is to be disposed of on tomorrow.

September 5: Attend the court at 9 A.M. and continue until about
6 P.M. Am employed as interpreter for Pahtee and Thomas [Wolf],
and as a witness on Roby's trial. He is found guilty, fined $1, and
imprisoned one hour, paying about $350 costs. We receive for our
services $31 each.[5]

Meeker returned to his mission in Indian country, where in the summer of 1849 he reported that "spiritual sloth" was increasing among the
Ottawas. "They are becoming every year more and more civilized, and
are endeavoring to imitate the whites," he lamented.[6] Three years later
the local Indian agent contacted the commanding officer at Fort Leavenworth, requesting military assistance to protect him from a gang of
Indian whiskey traders. "You have the power and means to punish
them," he wrote, "and if these traders go unpunished no means of life is
secure who lives here."[7] But the vendors in this case were Osage Indians, and the plea for assistance was ignored. Just prior to his death in
January 1855, missionary Meeker reported that the Ottawas were virtually surrounded by white squatters, most of whom were running whiskey
shops on the very boundaries of the reservation. That the government's
prosecution of Roby had accomplished nothing was vividly confirmed
in a grief-stricken letter composed by Meeker's widow soon after her hus-

band's death: "Some of the Indians are now living on roots. I fear they will die of hunger. . . . The white people who are settling around us are some of the worst in the world, and are standing ready to injure the Indians in every possible way in their power."[8]

So long as Indians were the victims, the federal courts in Missouri and other states adjacent to Indian country displayed little concern. If, on the other hand, whites involved in the liquor trade suffered privation or bodily harm, it was quite another matter. An Indian in a drunken stupor could maim or even kill another Indian without fear of federal (or state) reprisal; a similar assault by an Indian against a white man was quite another matter. The case of *United States v. See See Sah Mah & Eschatiah* (1850)[9] provides poignant evidence of this, as well as the drinking habits of jurors who judged native behavior following passage of the more stringent statute of 1847.

See See Sah Mah and Eschatiah were Sauk and Fox Indians who were charged with "willfully, feloniously, and of their malice aforethought" killing, while under the influence of alcohol on April 2, 1847,[10] one Lorris Colburn. According to the grand jury convened at Independence, Missouri, on September 12, 1850, the deceased Colburn was a Missouri resident engaged in the Santa Fe trade. The arresting official was Osage Agent Charles N. Handy, and the incident had taken place on the Santa Fe Trail just north of the Sauk and Fox reservation in Indian country. Both Indians, it was alleged, had confessed to the crime.[11]

The case went before the federal circuit court in Jefferson City on January 8, 1851, and was concluded eight days later. Following pleas of not guilty by the defendants, attorneys Blair and Brown for the defense argued that the charges against Eschatiah be dismissed on grounds that the testimony of the Sauk and Fox woman Pequa was inadmissible because she was the wife of Eschatiah. They further argued that the indictment in general was deficient in substance, that See See Sah Mah was of unsound mind and thus incompetent to stand trial, that his confession obtained *prior* to the grand jury hearing "was made under such circumstances of terror and affright as would exclude it from a jury," and that it conflicted with the testimony provided by government interpreter John Goodell at the Independence hearing. The jury, however, speedily found both defendants guilty of murder in the first degree. Attorneys for the defendants immediately filed a motion asking that the verdict against Eschatiah be set aside because the court erred in allowing Pequa to testify against her spouse. This was summarily granted, if for no other reason than its conspicuous illegality, whereupon an astonishing motion to quash the verdict against See See Sah Mah was filed on grounds of an affidavit obtained by attorneys for the defense from the court bailiff *after* the case had gone to trial. Obviously based on olfactory evidence unavoidably obtained by Blair and Brown during the trial proceedings, and indicative that Indians on trial for murder while under the influence of alcohol required judgment by non-Indians unable to serve as jurors without a daily dosage of alcohol, the affidavit read as follows:

> James B. Wray, being sworn upon his oath says that he had charge of the Jury in the case of the United States against See See Sah Mah and Eschatiah at the present term of Court as bailiff, that by direction of William D. Kerr, Deputy Marshal, he furnished said Jury with whiskey three times a day, that is in the morning and just before dinner, and before supper. The quantity furnished at each time was about one pint and a half, he thinks not much more, that of that quantity each of the Jurors and himself drank the said whiskey, that the Jury while under his charge had no other spirits . . . except on Wednesday morning before breakfast, he permitted them to take their dram at the Bar of the Hotel, he not being prepared to furnish them at their room as had previously been done.[12]

Under oath Deputy Marshal Kerr admitted he had authorized the daily alcohol distribution, but to the defense argument that such consumption—nearly two hundred ounces of whiskey during the course of the trial—constituted improper conduct and precluded the jury from arriving at a rational verdict, affiant Wray testified that the amount of liquor furnished "was not sufficient to impair the faculties of the jurors." The court immediately accepted Wray's assertion and overruled the defense motion for a mistrial. On the technicality of Pequa's illegal testimony the charge against Eschatiah was dismissed and he was allowed to go free. But the verdict against See See Sah Mah was allowed to stand, and his sentence to be "hung by the neck until he be dead" took place on March 14, 1851, on the Jefferson City gallows.[13]

Local juries sitting in judgment of Indian alcohol law violations and violence were thus unsympathetic to basic Indian rights. While the federal law of 1847 allowed Indians to have their say in court as competent witnesses, there is no evidence that See See Sah Mah or his attorneys were allowed to respond to the libatious conduct of the jury that convicted him. Missouri law (like that of other states bordering on Indian country) ostensibly was committed to the interdiction of the Indian alcohol trade; in fact it disallowed Indian testimony in such judicial proceedings.[14] Indeed, far more important than federal law dictated from distant Washington and administered by generally unpopular federal bureaucrats, state law was what most Missourians understood and respected. Moreover, profits consequent to the trade bordering on Indian country dictated that juries impaneled to judge the actions of local liquor merchants were reluctant (or certainly lenient, as in the cases of Potter, Hempstead, and Roby) to convict fellow white citizens whose livelihood could very well depend on the trade. That See See Sah Mah went to the gallows for killing a whiskey trader—righteous or otherwise—was part of the game.

There is no disputing that certain traders, sometimes in collusion with the very federal authorities who granted them their licenses, sought to prevent Indians from making statements or testifying against liquor violations under federal law. Writing to Acting Commissioner of Indian Affairs Charles E. Mix in July 1851, Delaware trader W. George Ewing Jr. reported that while attending an annuity distribution at Council Grove, an "educated" mixed-blood Indian and a "respected" white citizen of western Missouri were shocked to observe Indians openly purchasing whiskey at a store operated by the Westport firm of Albert G. Boone and R. G. Bernard. They called the infraction to the attention of Sauk and Fox Agent John R. Chenault, but Chenault refused to take action "on grounds that the courts would not listen to him or any other Indian." Boone and Bernard were also in collusion with Osage Agent Henry Harvey, reported Ewing, who demanded that the matter be investigated by St. Louis Superintendent David D. Mitchell. Mitchell's clerk concurred with Ewing's contention that "the laws of Congress expressly provided for the admissibility and credibility of the testimony of Indians open to the charge of selling or giving liquor." But there the matter was allowed to rest. Significantly, it was Chenault who only a few days prior to the Council Grove incident had approved a trade license for Boone and Bernard with the Potawatomies, and it was fellow agent Harvey who had certified the same company to serve as government trader for the Osages. Despite Ewing's letter to Washington, Chenault continued as Sauk and Fox Agent for two more years, while the end of Harvey's tenure as government Indian agent a few months later was the consequence of an administrative shift of the Osage Agency to the Southern Superintendency, not his involvement in the liquor trade. Chenault and Harvey were not formally charged by the Indian Office; nor were Boone and Bernard, who continued to operate their Council Grove store through one of their local agents, Seth M. Hays. In fact, their business operations continued to expand. One year later, Chenault awarded still another trade license to Boone and Bernard, this time for the Sauk and Fox Indians of his own agency.[15]

Potter, Roby, Pettijohn, Boone and Bernard, and the McGees were in fact small fish in comparison with the American Fur Company operating on the Missouri from Bellevue northwest to the mouth of the Yellowstone. Always careful to articulate the view that it was bad policy for Indians to have alcohol and that the government's efforts to halt the trade deserved unwavering trader support, the American Fur Company nevertheless used alcohol in response to challenges posed by its competitors. Such was the case in 1841 when Pierre Chouteau, ubiquitous company official and spokesman, requested that the Indian Office appoint a special "roving agent" to interdict the liquor supply and bring order out of chaos on the upper Missouri. The Indian Office itself had evidence that more than a hundred Indians had died in drunken brawls in the Sioux country the past year and that whole villages were in danger of starving if the trade continued.[16]

Superintendent Mitchell's insistence that an itinerant inspector would be ineffective unless supported by a large and expensive detachment of troops prompted Chouteau to respond, indeed, to threaten,

> Contrary to our well founded expectations, the government as yet has taken no measures to prevent this violation of the laws in regard to the introduction of liquor into Indian Country. . . . We were honest in our intention, when we judged ourselves and our agents to cooperate with the officers of the government. . . . But if no steps are

taken and the Country is left open to every peddler and licensed trader to take what liquor he pleases, we will be compelled into self-deference to pursue the excuse we may view as best calculated to protect us in trade from our opponents.[17]

Commissioner Crawford finally relented, and in July 1842 appointed Andrew Drips as special agent to travel through the upper Missouri country for the purpose of suppressing the whiskey trade. Drips, who counted Chouteau as a personal friend and who was widely known as a company man (i.e., friend of the American Fur Company), was instructed to be absolutely objective in his mission. Nevertheless, he notified company officials in advance of his coming and eagerly accepted food, shelter, and companionship from old acquaintances at these wilderness outposts. After a year in the field, he wrote to Indian Office officials from Fort Pierre near the mouth of Bad River, "Since my arrival, I have not been able to lay my hands on any liquor, although I have no doubt but there is plenty in this section of the country."[18]

So there was, but Chouteau and the American Fur Company had determined to place their alcohol in hiding, with the hope that Drips would focus on the opposition and uncover illicit spirits in the hands of the company's competitors. In this he failed, although his presence did slow the flow of alcohol up the Missouri, causing the Indians to raise their prices for robes and furs and prompting complaints to the government from the traders. Not unexpectedly, then, Drips was relieved of his position in 1846, and it was left to others to try to bring the company to its knees.[19]

That task was left to a company attorney, James Arrott Jr., who in the summer of 1843 dispatched a blistering indictment to the secretary of war, charging that for years the American Fur Company through its various partnerships had conveyed alcohol to Indian country, that it had stored alcohol there, and that it had sold alcohol to the Indians over an extended period of time. Superintendent Crawford, to whom the charges were referred, vacillated on the matter of a formal investigation until June 1846, when a preliminary investigation of Arrott's charges resulted in District Attorney John Ganntt's filing twelve suits in the United States Circuit Court for the District of Missouri, asking twenty-five thousand dollars in judgment against the trade bonds of sundry American Fur Company partners and agents, plus the recovery of at least forty-three hundred gallons of illegal company alcohol transported to Indian country.[20]

While Chouteau and his associates exerted political pressure on the Indian Office to call off Ganntt and his clerks, the suits were continued time and time again due to legal technicalities reminiscent of the Potter, Pettijohn, and Vassar cases. Witnesses for the prosecution routinely failed to appear in court; several, it was alleged, died between 1846 and 1848, while others were sent by American Fur Company officials to new assignments far beyond the reach of court summons.[21] By the summer of 1848, Missouri Senator Thomas Hart Benton—a dedicated supporter of the company—had assured Chouteau that "no further trouble" was anticipated.[22] Ganntt himself was under fire from company advocates for judicial zeal "far beyond the discharge of any official duty" and for "feelings of personal hostility" toward Chouteau and his associates. Such strategy was followed by a letter from Chouteau to Indian Commissioner William Medill, on December 5, 1848, in which it was admitted that a few "obnoxious" company employees *may* have violated the federal liquor laws but certainly *not* under company orders, and another Chouteau letter to Ganntt a month later, offering five thousand dollars plus court costs as a reasonable settlement to the recovery of company bonds dating back to 1843. Ganntt tried to hold out for seventy-five hundred dollars plus costs, but fearful that he was losing control of the cases, he finally acquiesced to the five-thousand-dollar figure that in the meantime had been accepted as a reasonable compromise by Secretary of War William L. Marcy. The twelve cases were thus settled in the April 1848 term of the circuit court, followed by a letter from Chouteau to Ganntt in which Ganntt was applauded for his "sense of duty" in the matter. Chouteau also conveyed his hope that the suits had created "no unpleasant feelings" between the court and the company. Whether Ganntt was so inclined is doubtful, but in any case, judicial tranquility once again returned to St. Louis, and less than a year later the American Fur Company license for the upper Missouri Indian trade was renewed. On May 17, 1849, the company's steamboat *Martha* was ready on the big wharf in St. Louis for departure to Indian country. Its forty-thousand-dollar cargo included sixty gallons of pure alcohol approved by Superintendent Mitchell to fight cholera among the Indians.[23]

The defeat suffered by the government at the hands of one of the most affluent and powerful traders in the business can hardly be overstated. Coming on the heels of the 1847 law, which, ironically, Chouteau and his associates supported as part of their strategy to work out a compromise with Ganntt[24] and which was heralded as the beginning of a new era in stemming the tide of alcohol in Indian country,[25] the failure to hold the American Fur Company accountable was far-reaching. From the Choctaw and Cherokee country bordering on Texas and Arkansas to the mouth of the Yellowstone, and from the emigrant reserves of future eastern Kansas to the Cheyenne and Arapaho country west of the one-hundredth meridian, less affluent and certainly less politically connected vendors took great comfort in District Attorney Ganntt's ringing defeat.

That part of the 1847 law requiring payment of annuities to heads of families as opposed to tribal leaders prompted an investigation of a different sort regarding trader defiance of the Indian alcohol statutes. An important instance involved the Sauk and Fox Agency, whose certified traders in 1847 were Pierre Chouteau, Jr., & Co. (through Phelps & Co., their resident Sauk and Fox jobber); Willson A. and John B. Scott; W. G. and G. W. Ewing; and John Whistler and Robert A. Kinzie. A War Department investigation in September 1847 revealed that Sauk and Fox Agent Robert Beach went to St. Louis in August 1847 for the federal annuity money to be distributed to his wards. Beach left for Indian country with express orders not to make the payment until he had received a letter of instructions regarding new distribution policies under the law passed the previous March 3. The letter arrived at Westport on September 15, left there the next day, and on September 17 "fell into the hands" of William D. Harris, an employee of the Ewings, who suppressed it with the connivance of the other Sauk and Fox traders. On September 20, and contrary to the 1847 law, Agent Beach was induced by the chiefs—themselves under heavy pressure because of their faltering credit line with the traders—to make the payment following the procedure prior to 1847. According to the investigation, the Sauks paid Chouteau & Co. $10,000 and Kinzie $6,000, while the heads of families received only $11. The Foxes paid $21,000 to the Ewings, $9,000 to the Scotts, and to the heads of families only $3 each. Alcohol figured heavily in all these transactions. Superintendent Harvey testified that

Pierre Chouteau, Jr., & Co. received a lump payment of $45,000 because the company had underwritten and furnished the other traders with "the goods." Nevertheless, only the Ewing trade license was canceled, indicating once again the deference granted by the Indian Office to major operators in the Indian trade.[26]

Despite these setbacks, guarded optimism in the Indian Office seemed to suggest that the 1847 law was having some effect in Indian country. But such analysis soon flew in the face of Indian Commissioner Orlando Brown's 1849 report to the secretary of the interior that "all congressional legislation had failed to put a stop to the inhuman traffic of this article. . . . [T]he fiend-like and mercenary wretches who engage in it, in defiance of law, human and divine, find ample opportunities for introducing liquor into Indian country, and to vend it to the Indians at profits so enormous as to stimulate them to encounter a considerable risk in doing so."[27] Brown's recommendations that Indians who got drunk should be severely punished and that rewards should be given to Indians who assisted the government's anti-alcohol program[28] were evidence that the 1847 law was not working; in fact they complemented the view of Commissioner Medill, who a year earlier had applauded the more "civilized" tribes for enacting laws of their own for restricting the whiskey traffic in the face of the government's inconsequential regulations.[29]

Responding to widespread idleness, senseless acts of violence, and high mortality rates among their own ranks, and urged on by reports of non-Indian temperance societies that were substituting individual moral suasion as a means of curtailing consumption in favor of self-imposed community sanctions,[30] a few tribes (with the help of a few missionaries or an occasional government agent) sought to establish temperance societies and regulatory codes of their own.

A case in point is that of the Ottawas, who prior to the removal from Ohio to Indian country were notoriously intemperate. With the encouragement of Baptist missionary Jotham Meeker, they formed their own temperance society in 1839. The society enjoyed some initial success, but backsliding was not uncommon, as reported by Meeker in the early 1840s. Then, in 1848, the chiefs and principal men of the tribe induced the Ottawas in general council to accept a tribal law requiring fines, followed by forfeiture of annuities for a second offense, and, as a last resort, "delivery of offenders over to the severity of the white man's laws." Although Meeker admitted that "a person now and then strolls abroad to indulge his appetite for strong drink," he proudly reported in 1853 that the Ottawas were the only tribe in Indian country to register an increase in population.[31] It should be emphasized, however, that the Ottawas were annuity-poor in comparison with the other emigrant tribes and thus of little interest to the whiskey merchants. Moreover, their reservation was a considerable distance from the Missouri border and the main source of supply. All of this changed abruptly in September 1854. Responding to rumors that Indian Commissioner George Many-penny was planning a land cession treaty that would provide the Ottawas with a model educational facility, individual allotments, and especially high-dollar annuities, Meeker reported that their reservation was immediately surrounded by white squatters and whiskey shops, and within days the fledgling temperance movement was inundated in a sea of alcohol.[32] "Notwithstanding the severe laws which the Ottawa people have against drunkenness," lamented their agent, "they were filched of their earnings [and] . . . will continue to get drunk so long as the means are within their reach."[33]

More successful were the Vermillion Kickapoos, who under the leadership of Kenekuk banned the use of alcohol through syncretic religious institutions and practices developed in Illinois prior to their removal to Indian country in 1833. Chief Kenekuk, a reformed drunkard known also as "the Kickapoo Prophet," demanded total abstinence from his followers because of his belief that alcohol threatened the very existence of his people. Under his teachings, which included the use of prayer sticks and public whippings as evidence of repentance by those who had used alcohol, Kenekuk achieved a remarkable record in driving away the whiskey vendors and promoting a near-self-sufficient, indeed profitable, agricultural economy. Certainly his small community thrived in comparison with the nearby Prairie band Kickapoos and Potawatomis, and although a few of the younger men indulged in an "occasional frolic," the small Vermillion band continued to reject alcohol even after Kenekuk's death in 1852. A dramatic exception to the general rule in Indian country, the most comprehensive study of Kenekuk and the Vermillion band has concluded that their achievement was less the result of government policy and restrictions than a delicate blend of native and nonnative socioreligious practices, conceived and enforced by a charismatic Indian leader.[34]

Certainly the temperance societies or signed pledges to abstain from alcohol for a set period of time by the Cherokees, Choctaws, Chickasaws, Creeks, Osages, Wyandots, Delawares, Potawatomis, and Miamis during the years 1836–1847 were much less successful. The Cherokee Temperance Society organized in 1836, for example, claimed to have obtained two thousand pledges by 1844, and reports in the interval suggest that consumption did decline. This, however, was only temporary. That same year, 144 Creeks "signed the pledge" with comparable results. Self-help efforts among the Delawares, Potawatomis, Miamis, and Wyandots were even less successful, although a small minority in each tribe apparently were able to refrain from drinking for short periods of time.[35] On August 1, 1842, the Osages adopted a code prohibiting the sale but not the introduction of ardent spirits in their country under penalty of multiple lashes to offenders. Their agent's doubts regarding the action proved well founded, for a month later the Osages were consuming "more whiskey than they had ever done since they were a people," due in no small measure to a large steam distillery in nearby Missouri that made "five to seven bunches [of alcohol] a day . . . and furnished at least one hundred retailers to the Indians." In fact the very tribal leaders who were obliged to enforce the code were among the most chronic offenders, reported Agent Robert Calloway, and when Calloway dispatched a handpicked troop of Osage deputies to destroy some 250 gallons of alcohol in nearby Jasper County, Missouri, certain white citizens petitioned President Tyler to have Calloway removed for having destroyed their personal property and for frightening some women and children in the vicinity of the new distillery. Fortunately, a more sympathetic group of white citizens supported Calloway's action with a petition in his favor, and the beleaguered agent was able to retain his position until his appointment expired in 1844. The distillery, however, remained in operation and the Osages continued to drink.[36]

On the southern flank of Indian country, temperance societies flourished sporadically among the Choctaws. Reports to Western Superintendent William Armstrong at Fort Coffee in 1843, for example, indicated that drunkenness was not as frequent as in the years of removal a decade earlier, and that some of the most influential men in the nation had taken up the temperance banner.[37] Particularly effective in apprehending whiskey vendors were the Choctaw Light Horse—mounted detachments of Choctaw deputies deployed by the various district chiefs and speakers to hunt down and destroy alcohol brought onto the reservation. Noting that their work was dangerous and their pay inadequate, Armstrong nonetheless emphasized that "they cheerfully turn out, and have done more to prevent the introduction of ardent spirits in the Choctaw Nation than all the troops of the Government."[38] And like the alcohol-saturated region due west of Missouri, the Choctaws' efforts to promote temperance was not sustained by the influence and example of the white population residing in or adjacent to their country.[39]

During the early postremoval years, Arkansas vendors were the principal providers of alcohol for the southern part of Indian country. By the early 1840s, however, traders from Texas were providing well over half the amount of alcohol consumed by the Choctaws and Chickasaws, and Texas alcohol was available north of the Arkansas River in the Creek and Cherokee lands as early as 1838. With intelligence in 1843 that a large distillery was being constructed on the south bank of the Red River, government agents and spokesmen for various missionary societies urgently requested that the Republic of Texas be prohibited from selling alcohol in Indian country.[40] Nothing came of the matter, mainly due to diplomatic problems related to Texas independence, and the situation only worsened in the years following Texas statehood in 1845 and passage of the 1847 Indian alcohol law. In 1848 Western Superintendent Samuel E. Rutherford was informed that more Texas whiskey was being brought into Indian country than for several years past. "All up and down the Red River, on the Texas side, you will find whiskey shops," reported Agent A. M. M. Upshaw. "One of those whiskey dealers will take an Indian's new plough for a gallon of whiskey, without the least ruffle of conscience."[41] And well they might, for having retained title to their unappropriated lands as one condition of statehood, Texans were anything but sympathetic to federal Indian laws which the federal government itself admitted were unenforceable in Texas.

Of this the temperance-minded leaders of the Choctaw and Chickasaw nations were painfully aware. Faced with a dramatic increase in alcohol consumption by midcentury, they penned an eloquent memorial to the Texas legislature in 1851, that in part read as follows:

> Comparing our present and former numeration, we may well ask, what has caused so great a diminution of our numbers? To this we readily find answer: 'Tis the *"fire water,"* dealt out to us by our white brethren. . . . *Our laws have long prohibited the introduction and sale of ardent spirits . . . and many are the bottles, and jugs, and kegs which bite the dust* in consequences thereof. . . . We come, now, to you for help; and can you refuse? We want your help in a great and glorious cause, the cause of TEMPERANCE . . . . As much as we might wish that no place for the sale of ardent spirits might be found throughout your border, we leave the accomplishment of an end so desirable and important to our brethren, the citizens of your great and prosperous State. . . . The mode of suppression, we do not dictate. A favorable hearing, on your part, of this our petition, and corresponding legislation, will give great strength and success to every good work among us. That wisdom may guide your deliberations; and that prosperity of your State may be the crowning result of all your labors . . . and that we may realize the speedy accomplishment of our petition, we, your petitioners, feel bound in duty ever to pray.[42]

But Texas ignored the pleas of tribal leaders, who noted also that Wisconsin, Ohio, and Iowa had passed legislation prohibiting alcohol sales to Indians within their boundaries.[43] So had Arkansas and Missouri, but with little success. Even after the 1847 law went into effect, Commissioner Medill was of the opinion that unless the states would absolutely restrain their citizens from peddling liquor along the borders of Indian country, the traffic would never be brought under control. But his words ignored what had happened in Missouri since 1806, when the territorial legislature passed a law prohibiting sales to Indians under penalty of fines up to $150 or imprisonment up to thirty days. In 1839 Missouri reduced the fine to $100 while increasing imprisonment of convicted offenders up to six months, but Indians—except the Osages and Kansas, presumably because of their attractive annuities and close proximity to Missouri—were not allowed in the state without a permit from their agent. Prison sentences were reduced to thirty days in 1845, and the Osages and Kansas were finally brought under authority of the revised law.[44] Even so, the "Missouri system" was a farce. Explaining how it worked in practice, Osage Agent John M. Richardson reported in 1847 that the Osages traded twenty-four thousand dollars worth of their annuity goods to the Comanches for fifteen hundred mules worth sixty thousand dollars on the open market. Upon returning to their reservation, they traded a third of the mules for five hundred gallons of Missouri whiskey at forty dollars a gallon. "The ensuing drunken reveries made the region unsafe for whites and Indians alike," wrote Richardson. Although the Osages suffered both physically and financially, "the men who sold the whiskey went untouched because Missouri law does not allow Indians to serve as competent witnesses against whites."[45]

Increasingly confident that the federal government's ability to secure convictions under the 1847 statute was waning, enterprising vendors made the most of Indian middlemen as a more efficient means of supplying the Osages in defiance of Missouri law. Writing to Commissioner Medill in May 1848, the Osage subagent reported that a group of white bootleggers was contemplating the establishment of a trading house at the very doorstep of his agency headquarters in Indian country, and that very little could be done to thwart the action. As "heretofore had been the case," thus indicating that the scheme had worked well elsewhere, whiskey smuggled across the border by the bootleggers was to be distributed by an Osage mixed-blood and his black slave to native buyers in a manner that, according to the subagent, "would baffle all attempts" to thwart it. The Indian mixed-blood might be arrested and even indicted for appearance in a Missouri court, but the disallowance of his testimony (like that of his black slave) was tantamount to viewing him as a nonperson and thus beyond the purview of the state's prohibitory law. Unless federal law were evoked, which following the American Fur Company debacle was unlikely, this means of dispensing alcohol in Indian country posed no great threat of arrest or legal accountability.[46]

In the Pueblo country only recently acquired from Mexico by the Treaty of Guadalupe Hidalgo, efforts to halt the trade were no less successful. After Congress extended jurisdiction of the Trade and Intercourse Act of 1834 to the Mexican Cession in 1851, New Mexico territorial governor and ex officio Superintendent of Indian Affairs James S. Calhoun ordered Colonel James H. Carleton to put the whiskey merchants out of business in this remote region of Indian country. Accordingly, Colonel Carleton confiscated a large consignment of alcohol intended for sale to the Indians, only to suffer a suit filed against him by the traders for illegal seizure of their personal property. A district court jury found Carleton guilty and fined him five hundred dollars on grounds that the existence of Indian country in New Mexico Territory was a fiction. As a remedy to this blatant defiance of the congressional statute of 1851, Calhoun's successor David Meriwether determined to establish "definite reservations" for the Indians as a means of enforcing the federal alcohol code, and following the formal establishment of the Office of Surveyor General for the Territory of New Mexico in July 1854—which was empowered to grant land to non-Indian squatters in the territory—proceeded to negotiate formal land settlement treaties with the New Mexico Indians. But pressure from the squatters and land-jobbers, who argued that Meriwether had been too generous to the Indians, prompted the Senate to turn down the treaties and keep the land question in limbo. More and more land was occupied illegally, and in the absence of any further declaration regarding the legality of Indian country in New Mexico, continued encroachments and the traffic in arms and liquor finally led to violence, a situation that existed until the government's "peace policy" was inaugurated after the Civil War.[47]

By midcentury, then, Indian country as a strictly geographical locus where vending alcohol to Indians could be prevented was troublesome in the extreme. As in Missouri, Iowa, Arkansas, and New Mexico, one of the first acts following the creation of Minnesota Territory in 1849 was passage of a law for the suppression of ardent spirits among the Indians. "Still," reported Territorial Governor Alexander Ramsey, "in all communities will be found sordid wretches, sufficiently depraved to attempt, for filthy lucre, to elude the laws which prohibit their sale." Ramsey's complaint, of course, had a familiar ring. But Ramsey went further by proposing a new weapon for enforcing Indian prohibition in that amorphous entity called Indian country. Decrying a shocking increase in consumption among the Chippewas and Sioux that came with the steady white advance up the Minnesota, Crow, and St. Croix Rivers, he advised the Indian Office in Washington,

In a communication addressed to the Department, of the date April 16, 1850, I suggested the propriety of Congress extending the operation of the Trade and Intercourse Laws, over the public lands, contiguous to Indian territory [country], which have not become subject to private entry. As [non-Indian] individuals residing in these lands are technically trespassers, and as the fee is in the government, this kind of jurisdiction could with great propriety and utility be exercised. It is while in the transition state, after the extinction of the aboriginal title, and prior to the settlement of a white population sufficiently restrained by moral principle, that territory thus situated, without law, is made the theater of the Indian whiskey trade. A jurisdiction of this nature is essential to the safety of the Indian, and its extent must be determined by those who are called to exercise it.[48]

Ramsey's recommendation, which in effect would have expanded the geographical limits of Indian country, struck at a very sensitive aspect of the Indian alcohol trade. Yet it said nothing regarding a more rigorous enforcement in Indian country as originally defined in 1834, nor did it address the problem of enforcement on ceded land in Indian country adjacent to the ever-shrinking reservations being created by the government's emerging policy of tribal concentration. Indian Commissioner Luke Lea's response was to chastise the Hudson Bay Company for its continuing alcohol trade with the Indians across the international border, to call for better military enforcement of federal alcohol laws then in effect, and to emphasize that in a recent land cession treaty with the Mdewakanton and Wahpakoota Sioux (1851) the government had extended the full force of the laws "prohibiting the introduction and sale of spirituous liquors in Indian country . . . *throughout the territory hereby ceded* [emphasis added] . . . lying in Minnesota until otherwise directed by Congress or the President of the United States."[49]

Commissioner Lea himself had traveled to Minnesota to negotiate the Mdewakanton and Wahpakoota treaty of 1851. He personally observed the tense relationships between the Indians and whites, and his cautionary inclusion of Article 6 requiring explicit extension of Indian prohibition into the ceded territory amounted to uncertainty regarding whether in fact such territory (or any similar territory in Indian country) was a part of Indian country until extinguished by private entries under the public domain laws then in effect. Even so, and at a time of increasing white invasion of the mining West and mounting political pressure for additional land cession treaties to accommodate transcontinental railroad development, Commissioner Lea was content with the annuity system of trade, even to the point of allowing payments directly to the traders and personally intervening on their behalf in controversial license renewals. And, in contrast to his predecessors, he expressed no concern regarding the ubiquitous alcohol problem among the Indians. Indeed, it was his view that "the system is fastened upon us, and its attendant evils must be endured."[50]

And so they were, as the government moved toward a policy of tribal concentration in the trans-Missouri West. Intact still was the alcohol code dating back to the days of Jefferson, Jackson, and Polk, with its attendant difficulties of enforcement, and intact also was Indian country, an increasingly blurred region where enforcement was supposed to take place. But as early as 1835—one year after the boundaries of Indian country had been legally delineated—a warning bell regarding its inviolability had been sounded in a federal circuit court in distant Ohio. In *United States v. Cisna* (1835), dealing not with alcohol but with the theft of a horse from an Indian on the Wyandot reservation, the court ordered that the defendant be handed over to the state for prosecution on grounds that where the country adjacent to an Indian reservation had become so densely settled by non-Indians as to render it impracticable to execute the intercourse laws, such laws were obsolete and federal jurisdiction ceased; that it was immaterial whether the intercourse laws were expressly repealed or rendered inoperative by force of circumstances; and that it might be presumed, from the circumstances, that the United States intended by lack of enforcement to abrogate the law.[51] It was a bad omen for alcohol interdiction in Indian country, where on the eve of the Kansas-Nebraska Act of 1854 the "wicked water" continued to flow.

Chapter 6

Alcohol and Indian Country

Since the original indictment in *United States v. Cisna* was filed prior to the Trade and Intercourse Act of 1834, the legislative guideline was the Intercourse Act of 1802,[1] which in the circuit court's view did not prevent trade and intercourse with Indians living on lands surrounded by citizens of the United States within the "ordinary jurisdiction" of the individual states. "Stores and taverns are kept within the reservation by the Indians or those connected with them," said the court, "and are as much resorted to for trade and other purposes by the surrounding white populations, as similar establishments in any other part of the country." Moreover, the Wyandots had made rapid progress in the "arts of civilization," and many enjoyed the "comforts of life [including alcohol] in as high a degree as many of their white neighbors." Congress, it was conceded, derived the power to punish the offense from its delegated power to regulate commerce with the Indian tribes, and the Intercourse Act of 1802 did in fact require licenses for white traders to enter Indian reservations. But, countered the court, "if a tribe of Indians is so situated as to render the exercise of this power wholly impracticable, must it not of necessity cease?" In the court's opinion, then, the twelve-mile-square Wyandot reservation was no longer a part of Indian country, and Ohio's laws "afforded a more ample protection" to the Wyandots than the laws of the federal government.[2]

Accompanying their transmittal of the Trade and Intercourse Act of 1834 for consideration by the Committee of the Whole, the report of the House Committee on Indian Affairs emphasized that the boundaries of Indian country had become blurred. Calling attention to the multiplicity of treaties then in effect (including twelve Wyandot treaties dating back to 1789),[3] the committee cautioned that "it is now somewhat difficult to ascertain what, at a given period, was the boundary or extent of Indian country." To resolve the uncertainty and in fact constituting one of the most important features of the act, the committee directed

attention to the geographical exactness of Indian country under the proposed law:

> This act is intended to apply to the whole [emphasis added] of Indian
> country, as defined in the first section. On the west side of the Mis-
> sissippi its limits can only be changed by legislative act; on the east
> side it will continue to embrace only those sections of country not
> within any State to which the Indian title shall not be extinguished.
> The effect of the extinguishment of the Indian title to any portion
> of it will be the exclusion of such portion from Indian country. The
> limits of the Indian country will thus be rendered at all times obvi-
> ous and *certain* [emphasis added].[4]

In its final form, then, Missouri, Louisiana, and Arkansas Territory were
excluded, but otherwise the entire area west of the Mississippi was indis-
putably Indian country following passage of the 1834 act.[5]

Other than handing the defendant over to Ohio for prosecution, the
decision in *Cisna* was of little interest to the tribe as a whole. Pressure
for complete Wyandot removal was then intensifying, and whether or
not their twelve-mile-square reservation was a legal part of Indian country in Ohio seemed unimportant, which in fact it soon was. By the
treaties of 1836 and 1842,[6] the Wyandots relinquished claim to their
Ohio lands in favor of a new reservation west of Missouri, where their
lands would be secure under the Trade and Intercourse Act of 1834.
Even so, the importance of *United States v. Cisna* was apparent nearly
three decades later, when in *McCracken v. Todd* (1862)[7] the Kansas
Supreme Court cited *Cisna* as critical to its ruling that non-Indian settlement on the Delaware reserve west of Missouri prior to cession by
treaty was no violation of Indian country under federal law, including
the 1834 act. Certainly the wording in *McCracken* had a familiar ring:

> [P]eople came from all parts of the country, a portion settled upon
> the lands [of the Delawares], and continued in possession of them up
> to the time of sale by the United States in 1856. . . . The federal gov-
> ernment suffered them to remain there without molestation, and
> made no attempt to remove them, allowed them to retain the
> improvements they had made on the land, etc., etc. . . . It was imma-

terial whether the intercourse laws were expressly repealed or *rendered inoperative by the force of circumstances*; that it might be presumed, from circumstances, that the United States intended to abrogate the law.[8]

Even though the *Cisna* ruling and its corroboration in Kansas twenty-seven years later made no mention of alcohol sales to Indians as such, the implication was clear. Despite the several laws prohibiting the sale of alcohol to Indians in Indian country, the prosecution of an offender might founder simply on grounds as to *where* the sale took place, even though the sale of alcohol to an Indian was indisputable. Thus the *place* of an infraction was at least as important as the infraction itself. And in the interval between *Cisna* and *McCracken*, the "force of circumstance" argument postulated in *Cisna* became an ever more popular dictum as squatters, land-jobbers, and whiskey vendors invaded Indian country west of Missouri with little fear of expulsion.

For more than a generation historians have debated the background and intent of the Kansas-Nebraska Act signed by President Franklin Pierce on May 30, 1854. While the majority of studies focused on sectionalism, slavery, the Senate debate leading to actual passage of the act, and the motives of those who sought territorial status for transcontinental railroad development west of Missouri and Iowa,[9] only a handful of historians called attention to the act's impact on Indian people.[10] Excluding occasional references to ubiquitous Indian drinking in Indian country, however, even these studies fail to consider how the opening of the Kansas-Nebraska Territory exacerbated the difficulty of enforcing the Indian prohibition code.

For this the evidence is substantial. In a last-minute rider attached to the Indian Appropriation Act of March 3, 1853, proponents of white expansion into Indian country badgered Congress into providing fifty thousand dollars "to enter into negotiations with the Indian tribes west of Missouri and Iowa for the purpose of securing the assent of said tribes to the settlement of citizens of the United States upon the lands claimed by said Indians, and for the purpose of extinguishing the title of said lands."[11] It was, of course, a frontal attack on the integrity of Indian country dating back to the 1834 law. But before any land cessions could be finalized and nearly a year before passage of the Kansas-Nebraska Act, an acrimonious debate ensued between Missouri Senator Thomas Hart Benton and George W. Manypenny, appointed commissioner of Indian affairs on March 28, 1853, over whether a large part of Indian country was not already open to white settlement.

With the support of Willard P. Hall, Missouri representative in Congress, and Abelard Guthrie, an ambitious Wyandot-Shawnee mixed-blood who viewed himself as a territorial delegate should all or part of Indian country be politically organized,[12] Benton sent an outline map of Indian country to the Indian Office in Washington, requesting that the Pawnee, Kansa, and Osage cessions dating back to the mid-1820s, as well as the emigrant reservations as they stood in 1853, be located on the map. In his cover letter he emphasized that the details of individual cessions were not to be included, only "an outline of the whole." Clerks in the Indian Office complied as best they could and returned the map to Benton as requested. Benton then had copies lithographed by the Juls. Hutawa firm of St. Louis, with the caption "Official Map of the Indian Reservations in Nebraska Territory, drawn by the Commissioner of Indian Affairs at the request of Col. Benton, and published to show the public lands in the Territory subject to settlement" added to the original, and proceeded to distribute the edited version to sundry persons interested in establishing land claims in Indian country.[13]

Meanwhile, the Missouri senator gave speeches in the border country, announcing that his discovery boded well for immediate white settlement west of Missouri. Emphasizing that "new intelligence" he had received from the Indian Office was absolutely "astonishing," Benton boomed forth, "[T]he fact seems to be that this whole country from the Missouri [River] to the Rocky Mountains, with the exception of a few Indian reservations—covering only about one fourth of the ground—is now open to settlement! It already belongs to the United States, and there is no law to prevent the immediate occupation and settlement of the [Indian] country!"[14]

Commissioner Manypenny was in Indian country when he first saw a copy of the Benton map. He was understandably furious, and in a letter to the public printed in an Independence newspaper categorically denounced the map as a fraud "well calculated to deceive the reader." In fact, said Manypenny, "he had never prepared a map for any such purpose." The Indian country west of Missouri was closed to white settlement, and the maps prepared under the direction of Benton should be withdrawn from circulation. Manypenny was right, for until July 22, 1854, when Congress extended preemption privileges to squatters on unsurveyed land in Kansas Territory, Indian country was totally closed to white settlement. Even after the July 22 decree, and until Manypenny could arrange additional cession treaties, more than half of the area west to Council Grove—some fifteen million acres amounting to nearly 30 percent of Kansas Territory west to the Continental Divide—was Indian property in the form of reservations, diminished reservations, trust lands, and allotments in various stages of enrollment.[15]

No retraction came from Benton and his supporters. In fact, when Manypenny gave orders for the military at Fort Leavenworth to evict squatters on the Delaware reserve, Abelard Guthrie fired back, "Now where is the law investing the Commissioner with such powers? Is this fellow insane?"[16] Contemptuous of Indian rights and urged on by the question of slavery in the territories, non-Indians overran the eastern flank of Indian country, thus providing much evidence for the *McCracken* case eight years later.[17] And with this invading horde— whether pro- or antislavery—came alcohol, much more alcohol than ever before.

In 1857, in the small but growing Indian country hamlet of White Cloud north of Fort Leavenworth, an irate editor, fearful that inebriated Indians might endanger the well-being of his community, reported that over a hundred Sauk Indians had procured as much whiskey as they wanted from "a small town below here" and became so drunk that many could not even ride their horses. "These poor creatures have heretofore been harmless creatures," he wrote, "but sad experience has taught that these apparently inoffensive beings may sometime be driven or tempted to great atrocities." Enforce the law prohibiting sales to Indians, demanded the White Cloud editor, or "the people of the West know how to redress grievance which the law is inadequate to reach."[18] While he acknowledged no comparable consumption by local whites (which surely was possible, given the supply of spirits available there), other observers were more candid regarding non-Indian drinking. A writer in a Kansas City paper charged that a class of whites were no less suscepti- ble to the evils of alcohol than Indians, and that their dissipation was endangering public morals:

One great drawback to the growth and prosperity of the country, in this meridian, is the state of public morals—for which we may consider ourselves indebted to a few unprincipled creatures in the shape of men, who, for the sake of a little money, will not hesitate to introduce the deadly poison among a class of persons proverbially weak in controlling the appetite for strong drink. In this way do the morals of a whole community become corrupted—the daily routine of the people sinking into idleness, profanity and dissipation, with drunkenness and debauchery at all times, ready to greet the stranger in search of a future home.[19]

The message in both instances was clear. Unprincipled vendors, with no sense of public responsibility or personal morality, preyed on people unable to control their passion for hard drink: in White Cloud, poor and harmless Indians; in Kansas City, dissolute whites. In both instances also, the implied message was that the community at large frowned on and indeed refrained from such loathsome activity. Such analysis, however, was at odds with a more forthright appraisal of border country drinking, as reported by a correspondent from St. Louis to the *Salem Register* in Massachusetts and printed in a newspaper deep in the heart of Indian country. For New Englanders determined to journey beyond the mountains, whether to fight the slavocracy or simply seek economic gain, a St. Louis reporter spared no words regarding unrestrained imbibing in that distant land:

There is one thing which fixes a deep and lasting impression upon the mind of a New England man as he crosses the Alleghenies. At home, he has been accustomed to the idea that even to be a moderate drinker is disreputable, while in the West he finds almost every man a "free drinker;" whiskey and poor New York brandy are as common a beverage as coffee or tea. In this city, drinking saloons are more numerous than the stores of any other department of trade. Lager beer saloons stand out in bold relief at every turn; Germans and natives alike imbibe a beverage which a modern Solon has decided not to be intoxicating. This practice of whiskey and lager beer drinking is the great curse of the West. More men have been ruined by it than all other causes combined. It is confined to no class—the

merchant and clerk, the lawyer and client, the editor and the professor—all alike visit the fashionable saloons and drink to excess. A
strictly temperate man is an anomaly. This state of things is brought
about by a variety of causes, not the least of which is the fact that a
young man, coming here, feels that in order to be a true Westerner,
he must adopt the free and easy way, and drink whenever asked,
throw off all restraint and "go it blind," for the sake of being a "clever
fellow," which means in these times, a natural fool.[20]

And natural fools they indeed were, particularly in that part of Kansas
Territory where most of the emigrant Indians resided. At Tecumseh just
east of Topeka, for example, one of the first buildings erected was a tavern, to be followed by a "magnificent saloon" costing no less than eight
thousand dollars.[21] In nearby Lecompton, territorial capital in 1857, a
local resident reported meeting three wagons arriving in town, one loaded
with eight barrels of flour and the other two with sixteen barrels of
whiskey, "in about that proportion the two articles are used in Lecompton."[22] Kenekuk, near the Kickapoo Agency, was described in 1860 as a
thriving town where "whiskey was all the business," [23] and the announce-
ment that same year that a large distillery was to be constructed on the
Santa Fe Trail between the Missouri River and Council Grove prompted
a Kansas City reporter to caution, "Nice time then when they get that fire
water manufactory in full blast! It is our opinion that with the scarcity of
corn in Kansas, our neighbors would do better to make what they have
into bread rather than tangle-foot."[24] And as evidence that Indians took
advantage of such manufactories with not a little encouragement from the
white invader, there is the recollection of a thirsty Leavenworth reporter
who in 1858 encountered a beautiful Indian girl just outside the Quindaro
brewery, in Indian country just across the river from Kansas City:

The bright eyes of a [Delaware] girl attracted me in. Bareheaded, her
long black hair was somewhat disleveled; but she seemed none the
less attractive for that. Her person was not scrupulously clean, but
she was a child of nature, and cleanliness belongs to civilization.
Observing that I was admiring her, she came up, slapped me on the
back, and said in good English, 'You treat me?' Who could resist such
an appeal? I treated![25]

Less congenial but certainly no less committed to supplying Indians with alcohol was Perry Fuller, field agent for the Kansas City firm of Northrup and Chick. Orphaned at an early age and determined to make his mark in Indian country, Fuller followed Benton's advice and in the mid-1850s established himself at Centropolis, a few miles north of the Sauk and Fox reservation. In one year alone he sold forty thousand dollars worth of goods from his consignment store there, underwritten by Northrup and Chick and patronized by tribal leaders fearful that taking their business elsewhere would lead to cancellation of their annuities. Sauk and Fox Agent Francis Tymany complained of being "terrorized" by Fuller, whose principal business at Centropolis was whiskey and who hired ruffians to threaten him at annuity payment times. When several Sauks and Foxes died with symptoms of bleeding from the mouth, Agent Tymany reported to territorial officials that the alcohol dispensed at Centropolis was laced with strychnine—which if administered sparingly could enhance the inebriating force of alcohol dramatically and, in excess, cause fatality. Territorial Governor James W. Denver's response was that to obtain convictions in such instances was difficult at best, and in any case, legal responsibility for such matters rested not with him but with the Indian Office in Washington. Soon thereafter, Tymany was fired for having challenged the authority of federal marshals to arrest a man on the Sauk and Fox reservation, on what Tymany termed "trumped-up charges." His replacement was Perry Fuller.[26]

While infighting and administrative disarray at the agency level thus emboldened the whiskey merchants, Governor Denver's contention that the problem was not his but that of the Indian Office was consistent with his and his predecessor's failure to exert executive leadership in apprehending illicit liquor vendors in Kansas Territory.[27] In its first session in 1855, the territorial legislature passed a law authorizing a penalty of two hundred to five hundred dollars, and a prison sentence of one to six months, for the sale of spirituous liquors and wine to Indians in Kansas. Sheriffs and other civil officials were empowered to search for and destroy ardent spirits found on Indian reservations or in such places indicating a clear intent to sell to Indians. But unlike under the federal law of 1847, which called for larger fines and more extended periods of imprisonment, Indians could serve as competent witnesses at the pleasure of judges or juries in Kansas Territory.[28] More often than not, Indian testimony was thus squelched, and the results belied any serious effort at enforcement. Yet as a British traveler through Kansas wrote in 1855, there was no lack of raw data to consider. Not unaware that the wagon train serving as his host carried twenty-four barrels of alcohol "designed for the Indian trade," he lamented,

> It seems almost impossible that a blind man, retaining the senses of smell, taste and hearing, could remain ignorant of a thing so palpably plain. The alcohol is put into wagons, at Westport or Independence, *in open day-light,* and taken into the territory, *in open day-light,* where it remains a week or more awaiting the arrival of its owners. Two Government agents reside at Westport, while six or eight companies of Dragoons are stationed at Fort Leavenworth, ostensibly for the purpose of protecting Indians and suppressing this infamous traffic,—and yet it suffers no diminution from *their vigilance!* What *faithful* public officers! How prompt in the discharge of their *whole* duty![29]

Only two federal liquor violation cases were filed in Kansas Territory in 1855, followed by twelve in 1856, eleven in 1857 and 1858, twenty-one in 1859, and only six in 1860. One, in 1856, accused the defendant of selling to Indians "without first having been directed by a physician, and contrary to the form of the statute in such cases." Another, in 1855, dealt with liquor sales to the Shawnees in nearby Missouri. The majority of cases involved the annuity-rich Miamis, and the only case involving the Sauks and Foxes was filed five years after the Centropolis whiskey operation was first reported by Agent Tymany.[30] Convictions were obtained in most cases, but sentences were anything but severe, generally in the range of twenty-five-dollar fines and one day in jail. In the case of Charley Bundrem, the jury assessed a fine of only one dollar, on the promise that the defendant would quit selling. "There this vexed matter rests," reported a local paper, "and it remains only with those who persist in forcing the traffic to decide whether it shall stay so."[31] And to compound the problem, Indian agents were often ill informed regarding the proper court in which to file a liquor violation case. If, for example, the vendor was a resident of Missouri (as many were), should he be tried in a Missouri state court or in a federal court in Kansas Territory where the violation took place? As one obviously confused and frustrated agent put it, "I simply want to be informed to whom the complaint is to be made." No less assuring for enforcement was a denial by the secretary of the interior in 1855 to provide agents in the Southern Superintendency with legal assistance in cases they had turned over to the State of Missouri for prosecution.[32]

The failure of the courts to provide any significant obstacle to illicit sales thus indicated only lukewarm public support for the government's antialcohol policy. If federal Indian policy insisted on reshaping native culture on the model of prevailing white norms, as was the case since the days of Jefferson, why single out the vendor as a particularly nefarious player in the increasingly dynamic arena of westward expansion? Distillers and retailers routinely satisfied the needs of white imbibers, it should be remembered, so why not Indians? Once the goals of detribalization and incorporation had been realized, surely the natives would consume alcohol in a more civilized way, as opposed to the frenzied and excessive manner supposedly consequent to their savage state. Important also in the laxity of enforcement was that alcohol for native consumption was obtained with funds authorized by treaties negotiated in good faith by the government, funds that judges and jurors responsible for enforcement in Indian country viewed as fair game for traders whose licenses were issued by a corrupt federal bureaucracy working in league with rapacious attorneys and contractors determined to fleece Indians of their annuity entitlement. As one irate senator lambasted the Indian Office leadership during a heated debate on the Indian appropriation bill of 1855,

> I would do no wrong to the red man; and I would, least of all, while I was pretending to civilize, to Christianize, and to elevate him to the standard of the white man, teach him first to be a robber, a knave, a swindler, and an ingrate, as our government does by its policy. . . . You speak to them with the voice of Jacob while you give to them the hairy hand of Esau. Sir what morals can you expect from such teachers?[33]

Given these views and circumstances, then, Commissioner Manypenny's almost wistful hope "that something efficient will yet be done toward aiding the government in relieving the poor Indian from the evils arising from the use of ardent spirits" was a veiled but nevertheless resolute indictment of the judicial approach toward halting alcohol sales in Indian country.[34]

The fact is that Indian country as defined two decades earlier was being dismantled under Manypenny's very eyes. Responding to the demands of land-jobbers, railroad promoters, and a host of squatters urged on by the slavery issue in the trans-Missouri West, Congress assured the demise of Indian county when, on July 22, 1854, it legalized preemption privileges to settlers on the *unsurveyed* public lands in Kansas Territory to which Indian title had been surrendered.[35] Portions of the Sauk and Fox of Missouri, Kickapoo, Potawatomi, Delaware, and Shawnee lands had already been cleared of title by the time this dramatic change in public domain policy went into effect, and pressure for more cessions became the order of the day. "By alternate pressure and force," wrote a disillusioned Manypenny, "these tribes have been removed . . . until they have been pushed halfway across the continent. They can go no farther; on the ground they now occupy the crisis must be met, and their future determined."[36]

Responding to the congressional mandate over which he had no control, Manypenny negotiated nine land cession treaties with the tribes of the trans-Missouri West in the spring of 1854, including six in Kansas Territory alone.[37] In Kansas the treaties were delivered to the Senate in less than a month, and in one manner or another included provisions for diminished reservations, sales of ceded land to squatters and/or white corporations, and allotment to individual tribal members, thus indicating the government's determination to amalgamate Indians with the white population there. But there was more. For the first time the problem of Indian drinking was addressed in a direct and unambiguous manner. Up to 1854, only five treaties dating back to 1778—specifically, the Choctaw treaties of 1820 and 1830, the Comanche-Caddoan treaty of 1846, and the Sioux treaties of 1851—called attention to the alcohol problem, and these had simply insisted on compliance with the alcohol code as stipulated in the federal statutes then in effect.[38] By contrast, the Manypenny treaties of 1854 were so worded as to place responsibility for deterring consumption on the Indians themselves. Not atypical was the Otoe-Missouria treaty of March 15, 1854:

ARTICLE 10: The Ottoes [sic] are desirous to exclude from their country the use of ardent spirits, and to prevent their people from drinking the same; and therefore it is provided that any one who is guilty of bringing liquor into their country, or who drinks liquor, may have his or her proportion of the annuities withheld from him or her for such time, as the President may determine.[39]

And the Delawares, in somewhat more urbane, but nevertheless effusive, words:

ARTICLE 10: The Delawares promise to renew their efforts to suppress the introduction and the use of ardent spirits in their country and among their people, and to encourage industry, integrity, and virtue, so that every one may become civilized, and, as many are now, competent to manage their business affairs; but should some of them unfortunately continue to refuse to labor, and remain or become dissipated and worthless [i.e., drunken], it shall be discretionary with the President to give such direction to that portion of funds, from time to time, due to such persons, as will prevent them from squandering the same, and secure the benefit thereof to their families.[40]

As for the Miamis, they vowed "to prevent the introduction and use of ardent spirits in their country." Under the signature of Indian Commissioner George W. Manypenny, their promise was certified on June 5, 1854, in a land cession treaty providing the Miamis an additional annuity of two hundred thousand dollars, to be distributed over a twenty-year period.[41] It was the largest per capita annuity of any tribe in the United States, reported Indian Office officials from Indian country, but promises and exertions on their part to the contrary, the Miamis remained a "hopelessly drunken and lazy set of human beings."[42] So too were the Kansas, with an annuity of ten thousand dollars and much more to come from land sales at Council Grove in 1859.[43] Indeed, so appealing was the wicked water that to supplement their annuities the Kansas resorted to stealing not only from anyone whom by happenstance they encountered but from each other as well. "I believe," wrote their agent in 1855, "that they have lost all confidence in themselves."[44] So had certain Indian women regarding their male counterparts on the Wyandot reserve across the river from Kansas City. "Indian girls here of any ambition sim-ply will not marry Indians," reported a correspondent to the *Cincinnati Gazette* from White Cloud in Indian country, "for most of the tribe have become drunken and totally worthless."[45] Clearly, the strategy of deter-ring Indian drinking by treaty fiat was no more successful than the courts. With a non-Indian population approaching one hundred thou-sand and a dizzying array of cession, trust, and allotment treaties avail-able to accommodate the invading horde, Indian country west of Missouri was a fiction by 1860.[46] More to the point, however, it was an arena of profit, a place where money flowed freely from Washington to squatters and entrepreneurs in the border country, with Indians serving as the conduit. As a Kansas City editor unabashedly emphasized in 1859, "We learn that Mr. [Benjamin J.] Newsom, agent for the Shawnees, will pay the Indians this week $100,000, this being the fifth annuity payment since the treaty [of 1854]. This money as usual will circulate freely on the border, and very freely in Kansas City and Westport. Go to the pay-ment if you want to see the mediums of circulation. An Indian payment is a greater treat than the best written narrative of Indian legend or tra-dition ever produced!"[47]

Chapter 7

The Demise of Locus in Quo

Tribal drinking in Indian country continued unabated in the late 1850s and early 1860s, and in some instances increased dramatically due to supplemental annuities provided by additional land cession treaties.[1] At the same time, a strong temperance movement took hold among the non-Indian population in Kansas Territory. The dire physical, economic, and social suffering resulting from chronic inebriety among both Indians and non-Indians doubtless played a part in this, but the principal impetus for temperance in Kansas came from outside influences, principally New England and the Old Northwest.

In 1851 a law prohibiting the manufacture and sale of all intoxicants save the amount deemed essential for medical and mechanical purposes went into effect in Maine; by 1855 it had spread over the rest of New England as well as New York, Indiana, Michigan, and Iowa. Strong support for the "Maine Law" could also be found in Pennsylvania, Wisconsin, Ohio, and Illinois—all Free States that in the aggregate provided nearly 75 percent of the native-born white Americans who came to Kansas in the nineteenth century. Not surprisingly, then, the public mind identified the growing temperance movement in Kansas with the Free State cause, while conversely styling squatters and town promoters from Missouri and other Southern states as unprincipled slavemongers whose thirst for alcohol could not be contained. New Englander and avowed Republican Sara T. D. Robinson, whose husband became the first state governor of Kansas in 1861, described Missourians as "whiskey-drinking, degraded, foul-mouthed marauders," while a composite portrait prepared by the *New York Tribune* in 1857 asserted that their only interest was "to loaf around whiskey shops" and "to drink whiskey for a living."[2] From the Free State perspective also, territorial officials of Democratic party persuasion and especially Indian Office appointees at the agency level often were viewed as bungling bureaucrats or profit-minded members of an "Indian Ring" beholden to

President Buchanan and Southern politicos for their federal sinecures, and, because of their own addiction to the pleasures of the keg, either unwilling or simply incapable of enforcing a prohibition code designed unilaterally for Indians.[3]

In fact, drinking in territorial Kansas crossed political and ideological lines, as did efforts to put in place so-called dramshop laws. In August 1855 the pro-slave legislature passed a law providing a local-option vote every two years to determine who would be issued licenses to sell alcohol. If a request received a majority vote of an incorporated town or rural township, the successful applicant was obliged to present a petition signed by a majority of householders of the town or township, recommending the said applicant. Violators could be fined two to five hundred dollars and be sentenced to a term of one to six months for "selling or attempting to sell" alcohol. The act applied to Indians also, who at the discretion of the court could serve as competent witnesses but who were subject to only one-fourth the penalties specified for non-Indians. The military were excluded from all provisions of the act, as was alcohol prescribed by a physician for individual use. Less stringent for Indians was the law enacted by the Free State legislature in 1859, which reduced the minimum fine to five dollars, allowed the court to substitute a fine for imprisonment, and, unlike the 1855 law, contained no prohibition against the introduction of liquor into Indian reservations. Neither law was rigidly enforced, and the few cases that were filed resulted in either trivial penalties or simply the dismissal of charges for lack of witnesses.[4] Indicative of even greater laxity under Free State control was the legislative action of February 27, 1860, which, having affirmed the penalties of the 1859 law, went a step further by explicitly *exempting* from arrest and conviction all persons selling liquor to Indians who were "citizens of the United States or of the Territory of Kansas."[5]

Since Kansas was, according to the most recent and comprehensive study of drinking and prohibition in the Jayhawker State, seemingly "awash with liquor" well into the 1870s,[6] it is perhaps understandable that her founding fathers welcomed "citizen" Indians into its taverns and doggeries as proof that acculturation was alive and well. Obviously flaunting the federal alcohol code dating back to the days of removal, even a full-blood Indian who might still be drawing annuities could legally drink to his heart's content under the 1860 legislation, so long as he was a United States citizen and his vendor was licensed by the community wherein the transaction took place. Or, like so many of his white counterparts, he might feign illness and claim that his consumption of alcohol was strictly for medical reasons.

As treaty after treaty altered the boundaries of Indian county in an erratic and confusing manner, the 1860 Kansas law bore evidence that Indian identity was becoming cloudy as well. A bewildering array of land cessions, diminished reserves, trust lands, allotments, and special concessions to individual Indians and whites made it difficult to know precisely where Indian country was at a given time, or to determine Indian identity for enforcement of the various federal laws then in effect. Legally, the issue of who an Indian was had come up before, although in a different context. In 1846 the United States Supreme Court ruled that for an Indian to be an Indian, he or she must have some Indian blood and be accepted by the tribe of claimed affiliation,[7] but not until 1870 (supplemented by decisions extending into the early twentieth century) did Indians remain Indians in the eyes of the courts, even though they held allotments, were no longer under the control or immediate supervision of the federal government, and were citizens of the United States and the state wherein they resided.[8] In the meantime, Indian drinking and identity, and the *locus in quo* of Indian country became explosive issues on the Wyandot reserve just west of Kansas City, issues that led to violence and provided an important backdrop for renewed congressional interest in closing the loopholes of prohibition in Indian country.

In 1842 the Wyandots relinquished their lands in Ohio and Michigan in return for a 148,000-acre reservation west of the Mississippi River for their "permanent" home. But the United States reneged on the agreement and the following year negotiated a treaty whereby the Delawares sold the Wyandots 24,960 acres of the Delaware reservation at the confluence of the Missouri and Kansas Rivers. Not until 1850 did the United States compensate the Wyandots for their losses with a cash payment of $185,000 and an agreement that they relinquish all land claims under the 1842 treaty.[9] Numbering less than six hundred at the time of their arrival in West, the Wyandots brought with them a taste for alcohol derived from their previous residence in Ohio and Michigan; but once in Indian country, and especially following the 1850 government payment, their consumption of whiskey increased dramatically. In 1851 it was reported that nearly a dozen had died of drunkenness and another thirteen of cholera aggravated by chronic drinking. "Thus the fate of quite a portion of my charges seems doomed," wrote their subagent, "and before many years will lead to inevitable ruin and destruction." Three years later, the Wyandots were characterized by the Indian Office as a Christian people in principle but "habitual drunkards" in practice.[10]

With such earthly needs and as owners of some of the most valuable tracts in all of Indian country, it was inevitable that the Wyandots would once again reel under the federal treaty hammer. It mattered not that their close proximity to the Missouri merchants had demoralized them, that the bulk of their 1850 financial settlement had gone for alcohol, or that their orphaned children were sick and starving. With land values skyrocketing west of Kansas City and transcontinental railroad talk in the air, it was with little difficulty that the Wyandot leadership was persuaded the time had come to dissolve tribal organization, partition the reservation in severalty for individual Wyandots to dispose of as they might choose, and accept United States citizenship as a bonus for their efforts. Following an introductory affirmation that the Wyandots were "sufficiently advanced in civilization" to terminate tribal affiliation and communal land ownership, the treaty of 1855 provided for the allotment of the Wyandot reservation in fee simple and the granting of United States citizenship to all individual members of the tribe. The inducement was $350,000 for relinquishing all claims under all previous treaties, to be distributed equally in three annual payments to tribal members on a per capita basis, and, in the same manner, an additional $100,000 plus interest under the treaty of 1850. Including "orphans, idiots, or the insane," whose funds were to be overseen by guardians designated by the tribal council, the three-year award came to nearly $2,500 for each member of the tribe—payments that in the aggregate amount and rapidity of disbursement were unprecedented in the trans-Missouri West to that time.[11]

If consumption of alcohol were evidence that the Wyandots were "sufficiently" civilized to assume the responsibilities of United States citizenship, those who negotiated the 1855 treaty were not disappointed. In the spring of 1856 the majority of the chiefs were described by Indian Agent William Gay as "drunken sots" and so obstructive that land office personnel were unable to survey the boundaries of the recently authorized allotments. No less deplorable was drinking among the rank and file, whose "frolics" led to intratribal fighting and the burning of the Methodist mission church and several houses on Wyandot land—including the home of a white widow and her young daughter. The ultimate culprit, reported Gay, was a white man who brazenly operated a rum and whiskey store on the very grounds of the Wyandot reservation. When Gay threatened to arrest the trader and withhold all annuity payments to Indians who had purchased alcohol, the Wyandot chiefs informed him that the vendor had every right to operate his business and that "as citizens of the United States they had as good a right to have liquor as any one else." Accompanying Gay's letter to the Indian Office was a dispatch he had received from Kansas Attorney General Andrew J. Isaacs, authorizing legal action against the merchant and his Indian customers, and requesting witnesses of good character for a formal hearing in Leavenworth. None were found, no indictments were issued, and the Wyandot alcohol trade continued at a brisk pace—even though Gay withheld payment from those he "suspected of mischief." One year later, the Shawnee agent was murdered by unknown assailants while en route from Westport to Indian country with annuity monies for his agency. Some white observers suspected the murder was the act of pro-slave fanatics or simply highway robbers who frequented the area, but those more informed regarding the mounting uncertainty of Indian country believed Gay had died at the hands of those Wyandots whom he had refused payment under the 1855 treaty.[12]

The Wyandot incident illustrates well the difficulties of administering federal liquor law in Indian country at midcentury. While lip service was given to the attendant horrors of Indian drinking, land acquisition and detribalization remained central to government policy in Indian country. As the Wyandots understood the 1855 agreement, they were citizens of the United States, their lands were no longer part of Indian country, and how they spent their money was as much their own business as that of their white neighbors. Distillers, liquor retailers, and even the courts took this view as well. But as in most agreements contemplating the reshaping of Indian culture on white standards, the government reserved the right to determine who would qualify as a "civilized" Indian. In a carefully worded rejoinder, Article 1 of the 1855 treaty stated that those Wyandots who requested exemption from citizenship status could enjoy the continued assistance and protection of the United States and their Indian agent for a period of time to be determined by the commissioner of Indian affairs, and that on the expiration of such period of time the assistance and protection would cease and the said Wyandots would become citizens of the United States.[13] Twelve years later, in a treaty admitting that the citizenship and allotment experiment of 1855 had proven unsuccessful, the Wyandots were moved to future Oklahoma and reconstituted as a formal Indian tribe. Those individuals who in the meantime were impoverished following sale of their allotments could once again become official Wyandot Indians—and hence non–United States citizens—if their agent determined they were "unfit to exercise the responsibilities of United States citizenship and likely to become a public charge."[14]

Treaties with the Potawatomis in 1861, and the Ottawas and Kickapoos in 1862,[15] provided for citizenship and land cessions not unlike that of the Wyandots in 1855, and by the time the Civil War had thrown tribal loyalties into a state of turmoil, particularly in eastern Kansas and among the Five Civilized Tribes to the south, it was virtually impossible to determine who an Indian was or, for that matter, where Indian country was for purposes of enforcing the Indian alcohol statutes. Moreover, as pressure mounted for the removal of all Indians, the federal bench in Kansas became increasingly contemptuous of liquor laws dictated from distant Washington and consequently more permissive regarding the legality of Indian drinking. Judge John Pettit of the First District in Kansas Territory, for example, an "ill-natured, petulant, profane, and abusive jurist . . . for whom it was nothing unusual to go to Kansas City and play poker and drink whiskey all night," ruled in 1860 that it was perfectly legal for mixed-blood A. A. Bertrand to sell all the liquor he wanted to his fellow Potawatomis so long as he had even a minuscule amount of Indian blood flowing through his veins;[16] and in 1863 the Kansas City press ranked Kansas District Judge Mark W. Delahay "with [Joseph] Story, [John] Marshall, and the noted judges of all time for his humane and just opinion that the Indians ought to be killed off as fast as possible by bad whiskey."[17] Surely one of the most straightforward assertions that moral deficiency and a natural propensity for alcohol were reasons enough to divest Indians of their realty was the report of Indian Agent James B. Abbot, pleading for a land cession treaty in 1862 that would allow his Shawnee wards to flee the wicked water and seek refuge among their Wyandot brethren in the area south of Kansas:

> It a well known fact that there are between thirty and forty places within and near the Shawnee settlements where spirituous liquors can be obtained, and it is also a well established fact that the moral development of the Indians is not sufficient to protect them against the temptations and sources which are set for them by the unscrupulous liquor vendors, and being possessive with a natural appetite for strong drinks, the consequences are that a very large portion of the Shawnees are either habitual or occasional drunkards, and they and their families have to suffer the ruinous effects, which naturally follow.[18]

Not until after the Civil War did the Shawnees received an additional twelve thousand dollars by treaty;[19] in the meantime, "[T]owns were laid out all over the reservation, and in every town from one to ten liquor shops were opened."[20] Under revised military regulations also, Indians who served in the Union army were issued free whiskey rations whenever they experienced or claimed to experience fatigue or exposure.[21] They displayed arrogance regarding their newly acquired right to consume alcohol on the model of their Great Father's own soldiers, and were not unaware of the hypocrisy implicit in the government's dual standard. Thus with pride in their hearts and military-issued revolvers in their hands, they drank heavily when on leave, served as role models for their fellow tribesmen, and were feared by non-Indians as a violent threat to the white settlements in Indian country.[22]

As report after report told of unabated drinking,[23] it was clear that unless some radical changes in the liquor code were effected, it would be better to leave the matter to the Indians themselves. Such was the view of one disillusioned Indian agent, who wrote, "This liquor business is so well understood between the vendors and the Indians who use it, that it is simply out of the question to reach the evil by law."[24] But the temperance and self-help efforts of the Indians were not at all encouraging. The marshall of the Cherokee Cold Water Army reported in 1857 that while the theory of temperance was still good, he would like to have it better carried out in practice.[25] Others agreed, including one agent who insisted that the mental stamina of the Indians simply was insufficient to resist the temptation of intoxication.[26] Still others, including Indian Commissioner William P. Dole, believed the solution was to reform existing Indian law.

Appointed to head the Indian Office by President Lincoln on March 8, 1861, Dole was a strong advocate of concentrated reservations, with proceeds from the sale of excess Indian lands placed in trust for Indian education and moral improvement. It was his view also that the era of Indian treaties was rapidly drawing to a close and that treaties must be negotiated with all tribes not covered by binding legal agreements, so that Indian land claims enrolled in the public documents could not be ignored by Congress or the courts in the future. In office Dole sent a flurry of circulars to field agents and superintendents, requesting information regarding employees, agency operations, progress in civilization, and suggestions for reform.[27] The responses were many, including pointed criticisms of the Indian liquor laws in general and, in particular, the absurdity of allowing a person to vend whiskey within a few yards of an Indian reservation and still not come within the purview of the law.[28] Not unaware of the implications these reports had on his strategy for compressing the Indian land base, Dole lost little time in calling for a "radical reform" of the trade and intercourse laws in his first annual report to the secretary of the interior.[29]

To Commissioner Dole and Indian agents in the field, the overriding issue was what lawyers and judges termed *locus in quo*—that is, the locale where alcohol sales could or could not take place by law. Every law dealing with regulation and/or prohibition dating back to the Jefferson administration included "Indian country" as the place of enforcement. But the creation of new territories, states, and a host of diminished reservations, as well as a confusing array of trusteeships, special allotments, and citizenship to selected Indians in the meantime, suggested that this supposed inviolate entity had become amorphous at best. Congress, however, presumed that the definition provided in Section 1 of the Trade and Intercourse Act of 1834[30] was perfectly adequate for purposes of enforcement, and in 1862 focused on individual competency as the proper approach for revising the Indian alcohol code. In the debate that ensued, attitudes regarding drinking by Indians as well as non-Indians came to the fore and insisted that whatever else might be accomplished, bringing Indian drinking under control was a matter of acculturation on the white model, and that failing in this, an intractably drunken Indian—like the *locus* of Indian country—was the responsibility of the courts.

On January 17, 1862, Representative Thomas M. Edwards from the House Committee on Indian Affairs reported an amendment (H.R. 186) to the Trade and Intercourse Act of 1834, to insert after the word "Indian" in Section 20 of that act the phrase "under the charge of an Indian superintendent or Indian agent appointed by the United States." The only purpose of the amendment, said Edwards, was to describe the Indian in respect to whom the bill should apply, to which Representative Samuel S. Cox of Ohio responded that there existed a very stringent law against selling liquor to the Indians and that unless some reasons were presented for the failure of that law, he saw no need for additional legislation. Emphasizing also that the amendment provided no prohibition against the military taking liquor into the Indian country, Cox proposed an amendment that would allow anyone in the service of the United States and any Indian to seize and destroy "any ardent spirits or wine" brought into Indian country "with the intent to dispose of it to the Indians." This was unacceptable to Edwards, who warned that the Cox amendment would also "punish" miners for taking alcohol into Indian country "for their own peculiar purposes," and in his defense Representative Cyrus Aldrich of Minnesota reminded his fellow solons that under the 1834 law the secretary of war was empowered to permit liquor to pass into Indian country, and that the only change proposed was to prevent the Indians from obtaining spirituous liquors outside their reservations.[31]

Edwards and Aldrich pushed hard for a quick vote on the proposal, but the exemption of the military delayed such action and prompted a lively, even jocular, exchange indicative of the sacred cow alcohol rights the War Department enjoyed in Indian country:

MR. [OWEN] LOVEJOY [ILLINOIS]: Do I understand that this bill allows liquor to be taken into the Indian reservations, under the direction, by permission of the Secretary of War?

MR. ALDRICH: The present law does the same.

MR. LOVEJOY: The question then comes back whether the War Department intends to monopolize the liquor business with the Indians, or to allow free trade. (Laughter.)

MR. ALDRICH: In answer to the gentlemen's question, I will state that I have never known the War Department to grant permission to take any liquor into the Indian country.

MR. LOVEJOY: Why not, then, prohibit it altogether?

MR. ALDRICH: I will state that there are military posts in the Indian country; and it may become necessary, occasionally, for medicinal purposes, to take a little there. (Laughter.)[32]

A week later, Representative Anson P. Morrill of Maine picked up where Lovejoy left off. "If it be good medicine for the white man," asked Morrill, "why not also for the red man? We find that liquor demoralizes the one as well as the other." Delegate John S. Watts of New Mexico Territory, who unsuccessfully proposed that the Pueblo Indians be excluded from the original amendment, continued the attack:

I am ready to go as far as any member of the Committee on Indian Affairs for striking down this traffic among the Indian, or anybody else. But, at the same time, I do not see why, when thirty thousand white people are permitted to kill themselves by the inordinate use of intoxicating liquors annually, the poor, ignorant savage might not be permitted to enjoy the same glorious luxury. (Laughter.) If it is an easy and pleasant way to die, why not permit the poor Indian, for whom our sympathies run out in uninterrupted stream, to enjoy the privilege of dying in that glorious manner? (Laughter.)[33]

Additional debate focused on the transfer of Indian administration back to the War Department and a vitriolic counterattack accusing the military of murdering most of the Indians the Interior Department had been unable to civilize. In the final analysis, however, the debate came down to federal versus states rights regarding authority over what Representative Edwards termed "a class of Indians within the old States to whom this bill ought not to apply."[34] Insisting that federal authority over Indians who no longer resided on reservations or in Indian country was now under the protection of the states (and presumably well on the road to assimilation), and that it was inadvisable to extend federal law within the states for the purpose of protecting the morals or habits of the people any further than was absolutely necessary. It was a brilliant tactic, for Edwards had struck a chord that most members of the House could understand and support. As in previous legislation, however, no attempt was made to define Indian country beyond the guidelines of 1834, and nothing was said regarding Indians who claimed to be legal residents of the states wherein they resided. On January 24, 1862, the amendment was passed in its original form by the House; the Senate quickly concurred, and three weeks later it was enrolled in the statute books.[35]

Responding to the challenge served up by Congressman Edwards, the fledgling Kansas legislature passed a blanket Indian prohibition law less than a month after the federal law went into effect. Any person, including numerous but indeterminate numbers of Indians of varying degrees of tribal membership and/or acculturation in Kansas, who sold, bartered, or gave intoxicating liquor to any Indian would, upon conviction, be imprisoned in the state's county jails "for not less than three months nor more than one year or by fine not less than fifty nor more than five hundred dollars, or both such fine and imprisonment."[36] The unwary student of alcohol regulation and control in the trans-Missouri West might well conclude that here was the rock-bottom foundation of constitutional prohibition in the Jayhawker State two decades later, the first to do so in the nation. To the contrary, the 1862 Kansas law, with strong roots in the territorial period[37] and not unlike that of other states in or adjacent to Indian country,[38] was more an assertion of state power over Indians and a strong complaint that federal liquor policy for Indians was not working. Not surprisingly, then, the problem was thrown back to the courts. In the meantime, the majority of Indians continued to drink.

Chapter 8

Legislative Adversity and Back to the Bench

The cardinal feature of the 1862 law was that only Indians under the legal charge of an Indian Office official would be protected from the liquor vendors, whether Indian or white. Opting for the new restriction was thus tantamount to the government's admission that the locus of Indian country was an obstacle to enforcement, and that a more effective measure was the Indians' progress toward civilization—that is, assimilation and qualification for citizenship in the majority white culture. Congressman Edwards insisted in the 1862 debate that the principal purpose was to describe the Indians with respect to whom the bill applied, as opposed to where liquor law infractions took place. True, he admitted, there might be drunkards among those Indians designated as civilized by the secretary of the interior, but in such instances the laws of the states were fully capable of protecting them.[1] Whether in fact these laws were enforced or whether white drinkers saw themselves as models for Indian improvement were issues not addressed by Congressman Edwards. As chairman of the House Committee on Indian Affairs, it was his job to provide a resolution to the failure of federal Indian prohibition dating back more than a quarter of a century.

Commissioner William Dole's initial response was optimistic. He reported to the secretary of the interior in the fall of 1862 that the more "intelligent Indians" and "respectable whites" approved of the amended law, and that in general it was having a salutary effect.[2] A year later he changed his mind. "In Kansas, and indeed everywhere," he wrote, "are drunkenness and gambling. It seems impossible to prevent the demoralizing effects of these vices while they are fostered and encouraged by vicious and unprincipled whites who collect around the Indian settlements."[3] Agents in Kansas and Nebraska agreed. Whiskey could be had by anyone who had the money with which to buy, reported one;[4] another was amazed and embarrassed by the ease with which the Indians could obtain whiskey;[5] still another reported that every trader in his agency had violated the Indian alcohol code.[6] And at more distant Fort Laramie, in response to a suggestion by the Board of Indian Commissioners that the Sioux locate their agency in their own country where white men and soldiers dared not go, Chief Red Cloud's retort was that white men went everywhere, and "every place a white man goes, whiskey goes. You can see them here drinking day and night."[7]

In Colorado, Territorial Delegate H. P. Bennet flatly asserted that it was impossible to prevent the Indians from "obtaining whiskey and demoralizing their women" at military installations in his jurisdiction,[8] while from the area between Fort Larned and Fort Dodge in western Kansas, the Kiowa-Comanche agent reported being threatened with lawsuits for having seized whiskey sold to the Indians.[9] Certainly there was an ample supply.[10] With intoxication in the military running five to six times the norm for civilian society in the post–Civil War years,[11] and an increasing number of military posts serving as the principal points of contact between Indians and whites in the plains and the mountain West, the failure to place the military-Indian alcohol trade under some form of civilian control severely compromised the 1862 law.

More divisive were laws in the Indian country states banning alcohol sales to Indians. In the larger picture, these laws were symptomatic of the belief that the federal government was dragging its feet in clearing title to undeveloped land, and that it was coddling a native population whose inherent deficiencies augured against any early amalgamation with more civilized white society. So suggested a resolution sent by the Kansas legislature to Congress in 1868, accompanying a request that the southern boundary of the state be moved one degree south to take over land occupied by unproductive Indians: "The government of the United States should cease to use its bayonets to turn back the process of civilization. . . . There is an irrepressible conflict between civilization and barbarism. The government should not try to uphold both."[12] Clearly, the laxity of state enforcement indicated less concern for putting the whiskey merchants out of business than contempt for the federal government's ability to turn the Indians away from alcohol, as well as frustration regarding its failure to secure the white settlements from violence too often prompted by Indian drunkenness.[13] Yet the net result was continued Indian drinking, regardless of jurisdictional squabbling between the states and the federal government.

Indeed, reported one federal agent in 1866, the paucity of convictions and the triviality of sentences at all levels actually served as *inducements* to engage in the liquor traffic,[14] while in Washington that same year the Interior Department was informed that convictions were so rare as to discourage *all* appeals to the law.[15] Under such circumstances, and urged on by the 1862 amendment to the Trade and Intercourse Act of 1834, it was inevitable that the issue of a state's jurisdiction over Indian drinking within its own boundaries would ultimately find its way to the highest court of the land.

Although a separate ruling would subsequently be rendered in the federal court of Kansas, the issue was addressed in a consolidation of cases appealed on a division of opinion from the circuit courts of Minnesota and Michigan to the United States Supreme Court in 1865, on grounds that the sale of alcohol by one Mr. Haas and one Mr. Holliday to the two Indians, respectively, not on their reservations nor in Indian country, and both citizens of and landowners in their states of residence, but who still were entitled to annuities under treaties with the United States, were nonindictable under the federal law of 1862 and hence exclusively cognizable under the alcohol laws of Minnesota and Michigan. Attorneys for the Indians argued that the whole subject of the regulation and sale of liquors "within the states and away from Indian Reservations" was a matter for the states in the exercise of their police powers; that the acts were committed neither against the "limited sovereignty" nor against the public rights, justice, peace, trade, or policies of the United States; and that the 1862 amendment to the act of 1834 "was not in any way, a regulation of commercial intercourse."[16]

With the prefatory comment that it was difficult to perceive why Indians should not be protected from the "destructive poison" of alcohol, whether they were inside a reservation or not, or in Indian country or not, the high court noted that in consequence of the 1862 revision of Section 20 of the 1834 law, it could not be doubted the purpose was to remove the restriction of Indian country as written into the 1834 law, "and to make parties liable if they sold to Indians under the charge of a superintendent or agent, wherever they might be." This much was certain. But what of the argument that the police power to protect the morals of its citizens was a power reserved to the states, that the states of Minnesota and Michigan had a right to exercise such power over Indians within their own boundaries, regardless of additional stipulations imposed by the federal government?[17]

Conceding that the federal law in question might partake of some aspects of the acts of the state legislatures, the ruling nevertheless was that the police power as presented by the defense was inapplicable, and that the federal act of 1862 clearly fell under the powers of the national government to regulate commerce. Quoting *Gibbons v. Ogden* (1824), in which Chief Justice John Marshall had ruled that "commerce undoubtedly is traffic, but it is something more; it is intercourse," the act of 1862 described this kind of commerce or traffic, and therefore came well within the terms of the constitutional provision. Continued the court,

> It follows from these propositions, which seem to be incontrovertible, that if commerce, or traffic, or intercourse, is carried on with an Indian tribe, or with a member of such tribe, it is subject to be regulated by Congress, although within the limits of a State. The locality of the traffic can have nothing to do with the power. The right to exercise it in reference to any Indian tribe, or any person who is a member of such tribe, is absolute, without reference to the locality of the traffic, or the locality of the tribe or the member of the tribe with whom it is carried on.[18]

A modern authority on Indian law has written that, while Congress has not always exercised sweeping regulation over Indian tribes, "its power has been completely demonstrated in the Indian liquor laws."[19] *Holliday and Haas* corroborates this and to that time constituted a capstone of federal power over Indians at the expense of the states dating back to *Johnson v. McIntosh*[20] and *Cherokee Nation v. Georgia*.[21] Moreover, in conjunction with *U.S. v. Ward*,[22] which in 1863 abrogated state authority over reservations established by treaty, *Holliday and Haas* announced the death knell of Indian country dating back to 1834 and created an obstacle to enforcement of the various state Indian alcohol laws—unless, of course, Indians who purchased or bartered for liquor were no longer Indians as defined by the 1862 federal statute.

Or so it seemed. By dismissing Indian country as a place of enforcement, the Supreme Court failed to take notice of that entity's once grandiose dimensions, and the fact that most of the highly mobile Plains tribes located mainly west of the hundredth meridian were not then confined to treaty reservations. Moreover, the majority of these Indians were not under a degree of federal trusteeship that would stand up in court under the 1862 law, and of the few whose reservation boundaries had been delineated, more often than not their members obtained alcohol at locations other than their own reservations. Certain Indians acknowledged no legal restraint beyond the laws of their own tribe, insisting that selling to other Indians or even non-Indians on their reservations was their own business,[23] and, of course, the ubiquitous Indian-military trade was unaffected by the 1865 Supreme Court ruling.

A series of congressional enactments and executive orders not long after the 1865 court ruling actually encouraged the availability of alcohol among the Plains tribes. On March 19, 1866, Senator James W. Grimes of Iowa submitted an amendment to the Indian appropriation bill, providing that "any loyal citizen of good moral character" should be permitted to trade with any Indian tribe, so long as he executed the bond required by law.[24] Over the objections of both the Indian Office[25] and certain other senators,[26] who insisted the change would encourage the alcohol trade with Indians, the amendment become law on July 26, 1866[27]—largely on grounds that more traders and thus more competition allegedly would be to the benefit of the Indians. Two days later, the office of military sutler was abolished by Congress, and on May 24, 1867, in response to the Grimes amendment and the departure of the sutler, a general War Department order provided that any person, without limit or number, was allowed to engage in the post trade business at any military post situated between the hundredth meridian and the eastern boundary of California. Since it was never legally determined whether or not the act of March 19, 1862, prohibiting the sale of intoxicants by sutlers, applied to post traders as well, these frontier entrepreneurs lost no time in offering a wide assortment of spirits to the military, to white emigrants and freighters, and to the Indians.[28] Little wonder, then, that at Fort Larned just prior to the Medicine Lodge Treaty of 1867 General John B. Sanborn of the United States Peace Commission plied Kiowa Chief Satanta with whiskey, that the nine gallons of brandy Sanborn had purchased ran dry before the Medicine Lodge negotiations could be consummated,[29] that four barrels of whiskey were issued to the Osages as a "positive inducement" at the Drum Creek Treaty of 1868,[30] or that in 1871 a Special Government Liquor Commission established to investigate the illegal smuggling of alcohol to the Five Civilized Tribes by construction crews of the Missouri, Kansas, and Texas Railroad reported that military authorities—abetted by inaction of the U.S. marshall for the Western District of Arkansas—were negligent in providing support requested by the Indian Office for enforcement of the alcohol laws among the Five Tribes.[31] Prohibiting alcohol sales to Indians or establishing fine distinctions between what was or was not Indian country were the responsibilities of the civilian branch of government and the courts, not the military.

As the Indian liquor trade continued to flourish, pressure in Washington mounted for a major revision of the 1862 law and the inclusion of the Indians themselves in the federal alcohol code, if for no other reason than the competition they presented to non-Indian vendors. One white trader complained bitterly to the Indian Office that most of the whiskey purchased by the Plains tribes was sold by Indians from eastern and central Kansas,[32] while another reported that Indian middlemen—including the politically powerful Bent mixed-blood clan of the Southern Cheyennes—so dominated the traffic as to constitute "the moral ulcer of the body politic."[33] To further complicate matters, tribal leaders insisted that the federal government had no legal jurisdiction over alcohol transactions consummated by Indian vendors, so long as barter or sales took place within the boundaries of reservations where tribal law was alleged to be supreme. More important justifications for change were the need to include beer, hard cider, and wine in the list of spirits to be interdicted[34] and a curt demand from the civilian Board of Indian Commissioners that a major alteration of the 1862 alcohol code was essential to remedy the difficulties of apprehending and convicting offenders, including Indians.[35]

Following three years of inaction, Chairman John T. Averill of the House Committee on Indian Affairs finally offered a bill calling for the placement of all Indians engaged in the liquor trade under authority of federal law and the resurrection of Indian country as an instrument of legal enforcement.[36] But other than Indian Commissioner Edwin P. Smith's whining complaint, seconded by Interior Secretary Columbus Delano, that the 1862 law "was no terror to evil-doers" and that the government was losing money attempting to prosecute the occasional whiskey vendor arrested,[37] Averill's proposal prompted little controversy and no debate in either the House or the Senate. As finally enrolled, and in view of the dramatic changes that had taken place in Indian country since 1834, Section 2139 of the Revised Statutes of 1874 had all the trappings of a litigious nightmare:

> No ardent spirits shall be introduced, under any pretense, into the Indian country. Every person, except an Indian, in the Indian country, who shall sell, exchange, give, barter, or dispose of any spirituous liquors or wine to any Indian under the charge of any Indian superintendent or agent, or introduce or attempt to introduce any spirituous liquor into the Indian country, shall be punishable by imprisonment for not more than two years, and by a fine of not more than three hundred dollars. But it shall be deemed sufficient defense to any charge of introducing or attempting to introduce liquor into the Indian country, that the acts charged were done by order or under authority of the War Department, or any officer duly authorized unto by the War Department.[38]

The phrase "Indian country" was thus returned to the federal alcohol code, but with no clarification regarding its boundaries other than that provided in Section 20 of the Trade and Intercourse Act of 1834. Yet from the time of the 1862 exclusion to the return of "Indian country" by the 1874 revision, virtually all of the tribes west of Missouri and Iowa had been removed to lands purchased from the Five Tribes in future Oklahoma or allotted in severalty leading to the abrogation of reservations and the granting of United States citizenship at some future date. Indeed, by 1874 there remained in Kansas only the Prairie Band Potawatomis, a small band of Kickapoos, and even smaller bands of Iowas and Sauks and Foxes of Missouri. Similar removals and/or detribalization had taken place in Nebraska as well. While the 1874 revision clearly prohibited all ardent spirits from being "introduced" into Indian country, Indians nevertheless were allowed to sell or exchange with Indians so long as such transactions were consummated in Indian country—an apparent concession to tribal authority within reservation boundaries and presumably beyond either state or federal jurisdiction. But what of sales to Indians who resided on a reservation but who purchased alcohol outside the reservation boundaries—the actual locus of the majority of alcohol transactions?

Did a modicum of Indian country go with the Indian as he or she left the reservation, particularly if the reservation in question had not been specifically excluded from state authority by a federal treaty or statute at the time the state was created by an act of Congress? In short, *where* was Indian country in 1874?

A crossroads on alcohol control in Indian country had been reached, and it came in 1876, in the courtroom of the Honorable Casius Gaius Foster, United States Judge for the District of Kansas. Foster, who publicly chastised prohibition-minded Kansans as "an army of softhanded non-producers, who live by looking after the morals and habits of their neighbors,"[39] was no friend of law as a deterrent to excessive indulgence, and he made the most of the abstruse and convoluted wording in the 1874 law. As he put it, "This law is wonderfully and fearfully made, and like the grace of God 'it passeth all understanding.' "[40]

Sometime prior to 1876, it was admitted in Judge Foster's court, one Mr. Downing "did, within the District of Kansas, sell, exchange, give and barter one pint of spirituous liquor to Richard Rice and Peter Burdeaus, both Indians of the tribe and nation of Potawatomis, and being under the charge of M. H. Newlon, an Indian agent duly appointed, etc." G. C. Clements, attorney for the defendant, moved to quash on grounds that the indictment, under the second and third lines of Section 2139 of the 1874 federal law, charged no offense against his client. Those lines, it will be recalled, included the phrase "except an Indian, in the Indian country," which Judge Foster considered the fundamental question at issue. Did the words "in the Indian country" refer to the residence of the Indian excepted from the operation of the law, or did they define the *locus in quo* of the act prohibited? In other words, queried Foster, did the law only prohibit the traffic in liquor in Indian country, by any person except an Indian, or did it prohibit the traffic with any Indian under the charge of a superintendent or agent, whether in the Indian country or not?[41]

Here Judge Foster's penchant for unfettered logic came to the fore and is best told in his own words:

It was evidently the intention of the [federal] legislature [in 1862] to prevent not only the introduction of liquor into the Indian country, but also the selling or giving it to the Indian after it had been introduced, by every person except an Indian. The exception prevents the application of the law to an Indian. . . . So it would seem the "untu-tored child of the forest" might traffic in liquor without limit, sub-ject only to the inconvenience of seizure and confiscation. If the other view of this law is taken, and the words "in the Indian coun-try" be applied to the domicile of the Indian excepted, it would result in a special privilege granted to an Indian in the Indian country, over an Indian in any other locality. The former could carry on this traf-fic with all the tribes and nations of Indians, while the latter would be prohibited. And this further question would arise: Would the Indian in the Indian country be limited to traffic in that country, or would he carry his privilege about him, and have a roving commis-sion to deal in whiskey anywhere he pleased, provided the Indian country was his domicile? In brief, would it except an Indian living in the Indian country, or an Indian selling in the Indian country from operation of the law? Or must the excepted Indian both reside and carry on the traffic in the Indian country?[42]

In his decision allowing the indictment against Downing to be quashed on grounds that the liquor transaction with Rice and Burdeaus had not taken place in Indian country, Judge Foster recognized that his ruling allowed vendors to set up traffic on the borders of Indian country with impunity. But against this, he noted, stood two safeguards: (1) if the trader's business was to *introduce or attempt to introduce* liquor into Indian country, the penalty of the law would reach the malefactor (with the caveat "Whether selling a drink of liquor to an Indian who crossed the border for that purpose would be introducing liquor into Indian country is a question in metaphysics too abstruse for me to solve"); and (2) the State of Kansas had a statute fully capable of reaching malefac-tors who sold to Indians beyond the limits of Indian reservations. Hav-ing thrown the bottle back to Kansas, Foster fired a final salvo for benefit of the Jayhawk Judiciary: "The great body of Indian tribes have been removed to the Indian country and there is but little reason to appre-hend that the state of Kansas can not amply protect herself from the few remnants of tribes still remaining within her borders."[43]

Judge Foster's ruling was felt far beyond the borders of Kansas, for in the 1876 revision of the federal statutes, the phrase "except an Indian, in the Indian country" was deleted, and it was conceded that the conviction of off-reservation vendors was simply impossible under federal law.[44] While Indian Commissioner John Quincy Smith immediately demanded that Congress enact a sweeping law making it a penal offense to sell alcohol to any Indian anywhere,[45] Central Superintendent William Nicholson, whose jurisdiction included all of the Kansas and Indian Territory agencies, reported that the consequences of Foster's ruling were truly alarming: "The Indians gave loose rein to their appetites, drunkenness and brawls were common, and industry seemed suddenly paralyzed. This evil is the greatest obstacle to civilization that exists," wrote Nicholson, "and it is of paramount importance to the welfare of the Indian that such laws be enacted as will prevent the sale of all intoxicating drinks to them."[46]

But such a law was not immediately forthcoming, due in large measure to the first alcohol case to reach the Supreme Court, one year after the Foster ruling in Kansas. In *Bates v. Clark*[47] the issue involved whether an off-reservation seizure of liquor in Dakota Territory by an army officer under Section 20 of the 1834 law, amended by the 1862 act and construed by *Downing*, had or had not taken place in Indian country. The Court ruled that it had, and that notwithstanding the immense changes which had taken place in that vast region since 1834, Indian country remained Indian country so long as the Indians retained their original title to the soil, and ceased to be Indian country wherever they lost that title, in the absence of any different provision by treaty or act of Congress. Thus the 1862 law, which had sought to overcome the conflict and divided jurisdictions between the federal and state government over enforcement of the alcohol code, was brushed aside. Wrote Mr. Justice Miller in support of the high Court's opinion:

Congress has not thought it necessary to make any new definition of Indian country. Yet during all this time a large body of laws has been in existence, whose operation was confined to Indian country, whatever that might be. And men have been punished by death, by fine, and by imprisonment, of which the courts who so punished them had no jurisdiction, if the offences were not committed in the Indian country as established by law. These facts afford the strongest presumption that the Congress of the United States, and the judges who administered those laws, must have found in the definition of Indian country, in the act of 1834, such an adaptability to the altered circumstances of what was then Indian country as to enable them to ascertain what it was *at any time since then* [emphasis added].[48]

Advocates of general tribal allotment who gained favor in the late 1870s, and who achieved their objective by the General Allotment Act[49] (or Dawes Act, after Senator Henry L. Dawes of Massachusetts, its principal sponsor) by 1887, presented a no less important stumbling block to enforcement of the Indian alcohol code. The argument was that by granting 160 acres of land to heads of families, 80 acres to single persons over eighteen and orphans under eighteen, and 40 acres to single persons under eighteen—all of which were to be held in trust by the government for twenty-five years—tribal organization and traditional culture would fall by the wayside. As one federal official put it as early as 1876, "It will encourage them to enlarge and beautify their farms, rendering their titles more secure to themselves individually and their children after them, and bring them a step nearer to citizenship, and equality with the whites."[50] But this being the case, how was it possible to reconcile prohibition for Indians, presumably on the right road to civilization after 1887, with no such restriction for whites? True, the state of Kansas had broken new ground by implementing prohibition for all of its citizens in 1881. But widespread evasion by means of alcoholic prescriptions (mainly whiskey, beer, wine, and gin) written for colds, debility, cramps, rheumatism, nervousness, diarrhea, biliousness, colic, asthma, chills, dyspepsia, and the flu—not to mention numerous "mechanical purposes" which were perfectly legal under the Kansas prohibition amendment—belied any serious concern for the letter of the law.[51] Like the nation at large, which annually consumed an average of two gallons of ethyl alcohol per person in the mid-1880s,[52] supposed teetotaler Kansans were not far off the mark. And in an ironical twist they could, perhaps, empathize with Indians whose adaptation to the wicked water required the surmounting of numerous legal obstacles placed in their way.

In the wake of *Downing* and *Bates v. Clark*, "Indian country" was dropped in the 1877 revision of the statutes,[53] thus casting aside that elusive phrase once and for all. But it was a decade and a half before

Congress finally passed an absolute prohibition law, one that enjoyed the support of the Indian Office and the various "Friends of the Indians" organizations, including the Indian Rights Association, which lauded the new measure as a moral victory "in which every friend of the red race will rejoice."[54] As enrolled in the statutes on July 23, 1892, the law made it illegal for any person to

> sell, give away, dispose of, exchange, or barter any malt, spirituous, vinous liquor, including beer, ale, and wine, or any ardent or other intoxicating liquor of any kind whatsoever, or any essence, extract, bitters, preparation, compound, composition, or any article whatsoever, under any label, or brand, which produces intoxication to any Indian to whom an allotment of land has been made while under charge of any Indian superintendent or agent, or to any Indian, including mixed bloods, over whom the Government, through its departments, exercises guardianship.

Allottees whose land titles were held in trust and thus inalienable without consent of the government were also included, and penalties were imprisonment for not more than one year and a fine of not more than five hundred dollars for the first offense, and not more than five years and two thousand dollars for all subsequent convictions, with the stipulation in both instances that violators be committed until all fines and costs were paid. Jurisdiction, whether on or off Indian reservations, was the prerogative of the federal government.[55] The revised statute of January 30, 1897, provided that first convictions would result in a fine of not less than one hundred dollars and imprisonment of not less than sixty days, thus assuring that every person found guilty would spend at least two months in confinement.[56]

Ostensibly, then, the champions of Indian prohibition had finally carried the day. For Indians to drink legally the test was their ability to satisfy the property requirements of the Dawes Act[57] and/or to convince the federal government they had reached that rarefied realm of assimilation whereby they no longer were Indians in the legal sense. Property as an instrument of control was one thing, but as Frederick E. Hoxie has pointed out,[58] what of the Indians' personal rights? This was the issue addressed by the Supreme Court in 1905, in *Matter of Heff*, which was frustrating in the extreme to Washington policy makers determined to hold the Indians in check. Responding to the prosecution's argument that Heff's sale of whiskey to a citizen Indian in Kansas was illegal, and that acceptance of the lower court's ruling would relegate Indians to the status of permanent government guardianship, the high court ruled that the Heff sale was no infraction of the 1897 law. Since the legal status of citizen allottees had been determined by Congress, that august body was under no constitutional obligation "to perpetually continue the relationship of guardian and ward."[59]

But the *Heff* decision was disregarded by the Supreme Court in 1911[60] and expressly overruled five years later on grounds that the constitutional power to regulate commerce with Indian tribes was the very foundation of legislative control over the liquor traffic.[61] In the meantime, Indians continued to obtain alcohol, generally at bootleg costs far in excess of prices paid under the annuity–land cession system underlying the liquor business in the nineteenth century, and, as was the case during national prohibition of the twenties, too often accompanied by intimidation, violence, and murder.[62]

In 1876, posing the question as to why Indians so readily accepted what they themselves called the wicked water, an Indian superintendent's answer was simply, "They have not the moral force to resist temptation."[63] His view was not unlike that of virtually every politician, government official, liquor vendor, or philanthropist who dealt with American Indians and alcohol in the nineteenth century. But whatever the level of deficiency, the temptress was clearly bad environment, especially that of hard-drinking whites who heroically pushed back the yeoman frontier and who profited enormously by supplying the tribes through the annuity subsidy. Here the words of Bernard W. Sheehan for the formative period of Indian philanthropy, but valid nonetheless for the later years of the nineteenth century, are worth recalling: "The ironies were rich," concluded Sheehan. "Ultimately, the white man's sympathy was more deadly than his animosity. . . . Although philanthropists [including Congress and the Indian Department] condemned the unbridled behavior of the western settlers, they continued to instill in the native population values similar to those celebrated on the frontier."[64] But all was not lost. Bad environment would surely give way to good, for moral improvement of the natives was the very cornerstone of

Indian policy in general, and prohibition laws in particular. Thus, continued the superintendent in his recommendation to Washington officialdom,

> I am convinced that the practice of paying moneyed annuities to Indians is fraught with evil consequences, tending to encourage idleness and improvidence by causing them to depend too much upon that source for subsistence, without putting forth their energies in improving and cultivating their lands. I would therefore call attention to the [Indian] Department to the propriety of . . . allotment of their lands, which will greatly facilitate their improvement by doing away with the tribal relations, and throwing each individual as far as practicable on his own resources.[65]

Insofar as alcohol was concerned, this is precisely what was not done. Allotments were granted and then lost, cohesion for many tribes fell by the wayside until energized by federal law in 1934, and citizenship was finally granted to all Indians in 1924. But until August 15, 1953, when Congress finally ended Indian prohibition,[66] Indians were obliged to live as marginal Americans. Whether consumption of the wicked water in the meantime constituted a form of protest against this special status and an attempt to validate their Indianness[67] is suggestive but not at all certain. Summarizing the record from the first Jefferson administration to the capstone law of 1892, it may at least be said that drinking for most Indians was a learning experience, that Indians drank because non-Indians drank, that the postremoval liquor trade was socially and economically devastating to most western Indians while at the same providing considerable economic resources for the white invasion of the trans-Missouri West, and that, with few exceptions, prohibition failed to discourage either Indian drinking or the interdiction of alcohol in Indian country.

Chapter 9

Epilogue

The conclusion that American Indians drank because non-Indians drank warrants some additional comment, if for no other reason than Indian drinking viewed as a matter of learning may appear too simplistic. But if we keep in mind that, with a few exceptions, the first Americans had no experience with alcohol prior to the Columbian invasion,[1] and that savage instinct, moral deficiency, or some innate craving for the product of grain distillation offered as reasons for Indian drinking—temperate or otherwise—are racist constructions and thus provide no sensible insights into the problem, we are left with the possibility of one culture accommodating another with significant and, perhaps, lasting results.

But how lasting? Some readers may regard the termination of this account in the decade of the 1890s as abrupt and, perhaps, begging for extension into the twentieth century. If so, they are not alone. In numerous and sometimes lively discussions with students and professional colleagues during the course of preparing this study, I detected far greater interest in Indian drinking today than in the past. In these discussions it was generally conceded that the irony, or better yet the contradiction, of a technologically advanced and numerically superior culture committed to the highest ideals of democracy and free expression insisting that a few thousand Indians in a remote social laboratory called Indian country be legally denied a commodity that the majority culture produced and consumed with little restraint was a topic of more than passing interest. But what of the *continuity* of Indian drinking from the initial white contact to the present? Even conceding that Indian prohibition in the nineteenth century failed on a scale comparable to the debacle of national prohibition in the twentieth, and the profits from illicit alcohol vending in both instances were enormous, did not individual Indian deficiency and/or collective tribal dysfunction over the long haul provide some important clue regarding excessive Indian drinking today, whether on an isolated reservation in South Dakota or in an urban ghetto in Los

Angeles? Like a beleaguered Egyptologist attempting to solve the riddle of the Sphinx while surrounded by a host of impatient journalists, I was most often asked whether or not my study of the wicked water in Indian country over a century ago pointed to some groundbreaking theorem regarding "problem" Indian drinking in our own time.

There are, of course, sound and compelling reasons for concern regarding contemporary Indian drinking. The National Institutes of Health and the United States Department of Health and Human Resources report that alcohol-related deaths for American Indians in the final quarter of the twentieth century are three to four times higher than for the general population, and that more than half of these deaths are caused by cirrhosis of the liver. Alcohol is also an important factor in higher rates of homicide, suicide, road and off-road accidents, and family abuse. One recent study, based on interviews of Indian people at the Juel Fairbanks Aftercare Residence in St. Paul, Minnesota, concludes that nearly half of the American Indian population is chemically dependent and that an additional 40 percent are affected as families and friends. And for sheer gut response there is Michael Dorris's recent, devastating commentary on the addictive and even life-threatening consequences of chronic alcohol ingestion by pregnant Indian women on their unborn children.[2]

But such data have little meaning for the nineteenth century, when Indian people for the first time encountered prohibition as part of the Great Father's watchful benevolence, while at the same time confronted with the full force of capitalistic enterprise and a concerted program of tribal dispossession. During the days of Presidents Jefferson and Jackson, or Hayes, Garfield, and Arthur, there was no knowledge or awareness of fetal alcohol syndrome, nor were statistics compiled by federal agencies to indicate that because of excessive alcohol consumption minorities suffered disproportionate levels of malnutrition, morbidity, and premature death. There was no AA, no twelve steps toward serenity and a Higher Power, and certainly no recognition (or debate) regarding the disease theory of alcoholism. Immoderate, antisocial consumption was then viewed more as evidence of savage deficiency than as an individual malady or community pathology afflicting humans irrespective of social, ethnic, or racial boundaries.

What is important to avoid is a monolithic view of Indian drinking or some comparable cultural phenomenon, what Richard White in a much broader context involving Indian-white relations between 1650 and 1815 has termed "upstreaming"—the technique of using ethnographic data of the present to interpret and draw firm conclusions regarding social and cultural practices of the past. If, as White suggests, "accommodation" is preferable to "assimilation" or "acculturation" for understanding a "middle ground" where competing people adjusted their differences through sometimes creative and sometimes expedient misunderstandings, a place where interactive people sought to induce persons different from themselves by deploying a solicitous approach to the values and behavior of the others, then we can see, perhaps, the weakness of judging nineteenth-century Indian drinking by twentieth-century standards and the difficulty of demonstrating a necessary continuity between the two.[3]

White's "middle ground" is what the French called the *pays d'en haut*, the central and western Great Lakes watershed where in the century and a half after 1650 neither the French nor the English could dictate to Indians, a region of cultural diversity where new systems of meaning and exchange existed and, on occasion, even thrived. Trade goods, diplomacy, and other avenues of accommodation were, for the most part, mutually satisfactory. But White notes also that by the late eighteenth century the white man's alcohol was "shifting the meaning of exchange on the middle ground toward a commodity transfer whose end was private profit," with the result that the time-consuming process of constructing and maintaining a common world of meaning was undermined and in the process of being destroyed. That destruction was completed by the end of the War of 1812, when land-hungry Americans with the support of the federal government obliterated the middle ground, and when accommodation and creative exchange became relics of the past.[4]

While acknowledging the destructive impact of alcohol during the closing years of the colonial period, White's middle ground is essentially pre-Revolutionary, and to extrapolate his findings into the future might well be termed "downstreaming"—the converse technique of judging later tribal societies on data of the past. It is more helpful to look at nineteenth-century America as it in fact was—acquisitive, expansive, and, insofar as Indians were concerned, mindful of the profits that could be derived from taking their peltry and land while providing them with alcohol. The fur trade was the logical place of beginning, for there is no question that alcohol exchanged for skins and robes in a remote setting where enforcement of the prohibition code was virtually impossible presented a setting for accommodation that was attractive on both sides of the cultural divide. The hypothetical—but nevertheless penetrating statement of Sir George Simpson of the Hudson's Bay Company—"It is not for your Cloth and Blankets that we undergo all this labor . . . but it is the prospect of a Drink in the Spring . . . that carries us through the Winter and induces us to work so hard"—was matched on the American side by the Swiss traveler Rudolph Friederich Kurz (quoting Edward Denig, married to an Indian woman and for years a resident of the upper Missouri country), who reported only one ill effect of the liquor-fur trade: a slight increase in the number of killings (for which the Indians supposedly were prepared psychologically), but more than offset by the fur-harvesting Indians working harder, living more industriously, dressing better, and in general enjoying a more prosperous life.[5]

Here, then, was a latter-day middle ground of sorts. Even so, the liquor-fur trade of the upper Missouri and mountain West was in irreversible decline by the mid-1840s and in fact had been less pervasive from the start than the alcohol disbursements of vendors operating in the *pays d'en haut* and among the removal tribes of the lower Missouri, Platte, Kansas, and Arkansas watersheds—that vast region where, according to Lewis O. Saum, "the liquor-laden trader had more time to play upon the red man's unfortunate weakness and, thus, to defile him."[6] And here it was also that Indian people for the first time experienced the full force of alcohol in concert with land greed, what James Axtell has termed the ultimate "white man's contaminants."[7]

Whether "contaminants" is the proper designation, there is no question that within the framework of federal removal and land compression policy the two were inextricably entwined. Moving Indian people from one place to another and reducing their landholdings coincided with the demise of old trade patterns and the government's insistence that Indians once and for all abandon hunting and trapping for the life of the garden and the plow. The failure of such strategy, of course, is an all too familiar theme in nineteenth-century United States Indian policy. What is forgotten, sometimes, is that land cession treaty after land cession treaty placed a regular supply of federal dollars in the hands of Indians, who, taking a cue from the hard-drinking and supposedly more civilized non-Indians who surrounded them, invested not a little of these funds in alcohol at the expense of the agricultural enterprise supposedly guaranteed by their treaties. Whatever might be offered as a medium of exchange—a buffalo robe or a stolen horse—vendors preferred dollars, and alcohol for Indians was expensive, very expensive.

The Kansa tribe provides a vivid example of the alcohol business in practice. Residing on the eastern flank of future Indian country a century before it became a part of the United States, the Kansas engaged in trade with the French and Spanish prior to the American Revolution and with American traders at Fort Osage prior to the demise of the factory system in the early 1820s. During the next half century the Kansas signed three major land cession treaties with the United States: in 1825, in 1846, and in 1859.[8] In the aggregate these treaties provided the tribe of approximately fifteen hundred individuals with $272,000 in annuities, plus the proceeds, at a minimum of $1.25 per acre, from the sale of 256,000 acres of their last reservation lands in Kansas[9]—a total of more than half a million dollars by the time all payments had been made in the early twentieth century. But throughout the treaty period the Kansas were described by white observers as a slovenly, lazy, and poverty-stricken people who simply would not (or could not) adjust to the new dispensation.

The Kansas were introduced to alcohol prior to the treaty period by Franco-Spanish traders west of the Mississippi River in the early eighteenth century. But European tools, textiles, weapons, and utensils were the mainstays of exchange for the peltry offered by the Kansas, and although more alcohol was available during and following the French and Indian War, by no means was it central to the pre-American trade. After the 1825 treaty and the annuities thereby authorized, however, consumption increased dramatically, and for the next half century the reports of traders, travelers, and government agents document the centrality of alcohol in the daily lives and economy of the Kansas. Baronet Vasquez, their first government agent appointed in 1825, was a "hard drinker" and trusted friend of White Plume, principal chief and signer of the 1825 treaty. Determined to walk the white man's way, White Plume flirted with Catholicism, accepted missionary alcohol with pride, and eventually died of whiskey and exposure while on a buffalo hunt in 1834. One of his successors, Fool Chief, killed a fellow tribesman in a drunken brawl while on a "begging mission" to Westport a few years later, and in 1867 still another Kansa chief was stripped of his authority by both the tribe and his Indian agent for having killed a warrior in a drinking bout following the annual annuity distribution. In the mid-1830s the Kansa town of Indianola near modern Topeka was deemed "a den of whiskey smugglers," and it was reported that the Kansas were engaged in a lively alcohol trade with the neighboring Osages. By mid-century the Kansas were regular suppliers of alcohol to Indians along the Santa Fe Trail and the upper Arkansas, prompting the Indian Office to characterize them as some of the greatest "dealers and drinkers" west of Missouri, and in 1859 an Indian country paper reported that the entire tribe was drunk following their annual government payment. Urgent requests for emergency provisions in the post–Civil War years and subsequent reports that the Kansas were destitute and starving suggest that hunting, trapping, and garden farming were little more than memories, and that the double-edged sword of annuities and alcohol had played an important role in this revolutionary change.[10]

Precisely *how* important alcohol was in the decline of the Kansas is difficult to determine. The tribe suffered two major smallpox epidemics and several cholera outbreaks between 1825 and 1875. Graft in the procurement and distribution of government flour and other basic commodities plagued the Kansas during this period as well, while natural disasters such as droughts and the great flood of 1844 either discouraged or obliterated their otherwise meager farming endeavors.[11] And it should be emphasized that because of the prohibition laws, clandestine sales or bartering of alcohol to individuals on a regular basis went unrecorded, and we are essentially left with the accounts of those few bootleggers who were apprehended, the even fewer who were brought to trial, the generalized reports of an occasional white observer or government agent, the drinking profiles of tribal leaders who enjoyed better access to annuity funds, and, of course, the more spectacular accounts of communal Kansa drinking at the time of treaty deliberations or the distribution of annuities. The same may be said for most of the other removal tribes in Indian country.

It is worth remembering also that national prohibition applied only to Indians in the nineteenth century, and here, perhaps, may be found a key for understanding the origins and full flowering of the "drunken

Indian/sober white" stereotype that continues to this day. "[N]o stereotype has been so long-lasting and so thoroughly ensconced in our social
fabric as that of the 'drunken Indian,'" reports Joseph Westermeyer on
the basis of careful investigation. In fact, says Westermeyer, "[The] federal government gave it official recognition by prohibiting the sale of
beverage alcohol to Indian people for over a century."[12] His conclusions
are based on studies of the Chippewas of the upper Great Lakes and
Minnesota in the twentieth century and include a direct challenge to
the notion that Indians who drink excessively do so by virtue of some
inherent racial trait, for example, a deficient vasomotor response to alcohol metabolization as opposed to that of non-Indians. In addition to the
absence of several variables critical to the support of such an argument,
Westermeyer argues that the underlying logic for such studies is faulty,
since Oriental's physiological response to alcohol has been used to
explain why Orientals have less alcoholism than whites, while a like
argument has been used to explain why Indians with certain indisputable
Oriental genetic characteristics suffer more alcoholism.[13]

Nancy Oesterich Lurie offers a different dimension to the dynamics
of tribal drinking and attempts to address the nuts-and-bolts question of
why Indians do in fact drink. Basing her conclusions on studies among
the Winnebagos of Wisconsin and the Dogribs of northern Canada, she
concludes that "Indian drinking is an established means of asserting and
validating Indianness and will be either a managed and culturally pat-
terned recreational activity or else not engaged in at all in direct proportion to the availability of other effective means of validating
Indianness."[14] Applied to conditions in nineteenth-century Indian
country, her analysis suggests that an Indian binge here and there might
be viewed as a logical protest against the interposition of a prohibitory
code for Indians only, while in the meantime—with no fear of legal
sanction—non-Indians could drink themselves into oblivion. Happily,
such analysis may be exempted from Richard White's foreboding
"upstreaming" by turning, in 1862, to New Mexico Territorial Delegate
John S. Watts's comment on the occasion of a congressional attempt to
close certain loopholes in Indian prohibition: " I do not see why, when
thirty thousand white people are permitted to kill themselves by the
inordinate use of intoxicating liquors annually, the poor, ignorant savage might not be permitted to enjoy the same glorious luxury."[15]

This is essentially what Craig MacAndrew and Robert B. Edgerton concluded just over a hundred years later: "It [is] . . . our contention that the Indians of this continent took as their exemplars of alcohol's effects on the comportment the drunken doings of the very white men who introduced alcohol to them."[16] An unidentified Indian visiting Fort Larned in the heart of Indian country in 1864 doubtless comprehended this, when, after "wistfully and longingly" admiring the indulgence and satisfaction of a white man draining an entire bottle of whiskey in one swig, the white man hit the Indian in his face with the empty bottle, while in the meantime white citizens and soldiers alike were allowed "to enter their [the Cheyennes'] villages with whisky in day time & night; to make the men drunk & cohabit with the squaws, disseminating venerial [sic] diseases among them; while the Commanding Officer at the Post [Fort Larned] continues to get drunk every day & insult and abuse the leading men of the Tribes, & make prostitutes of their women."[17] And surely the Reverend William H. Goode, with ten years of experience ministering to Indians in the "Outposts of Zion," understood this as well while recalling his sojourn in Indian country from the Choctaw and Cherokee lands north to future Kansas:

> Our guide informed us that . . . about thirty barrels and several jugs of whiskey had been discovered in the vicinity of the Council Ground . . . a large portion of it the property of a white man. I have seen, I feel, the deep degradation of our Indian tribes; but often I have been compelled to ask myself, "Who is the civilized and who is the savage?" Their principal vices are emphatically our vices. If they get drunk it is upon *our* whiskey. . . . [A]nd yet we claim to be "civilized" and freely deal out to them the epithet "savage."[18]

NOTES

Preface

1. "Report on the Hygiene of the United States Army," *Report of the Surgeon General of the United States for 1875* (Washington, D.C.: Government Printing Office, 1875), 273. See also "Report on Barracks and Hospitals," *Report of the Surgeon General for 1868* (Washington, D.C.: Government Printing Office, 1870), 300.

2. William E. Unrau, ed., *Tending the Talking Wire: A Buck Soldier's View of Indian Country, 1863–1866* (Salt Lake City: University of Utah Press, 1979), 103.

3. David K. Strate, *Sentinel to the Cimarron: The Frontier Experience of Fort Dodge, Kansas* (Dodge City, Kans.: Cultural Heritage and Arts Center, 1970), 63.

4. Craig Miner and William E. Unrau, *The End of Indian Kansas: A Study of Cultural Revolution, 1854–1871* (Lawrence: Regents Press of Kansas, 1978).

5. Otto Frovin Frederickson, *The Liquor Question among the Indian Tribes in Kansas, 1804–1881*, Bulletin of the University of Kansas, Humanistic Studies, vol. 4, no. 4 (Lawrence: University of Kansas, 1932).

1. Setting the Standard

1. Among the more important studies of Indian addiction to alcohol, here listed alphabetically by author or authors, are Joan Baker, "Alcoholism and the American Indian," *Alcoholism: Development, Consequences, and Interventions*, ed. Nada J. Estes and M. Edith Heinemann (St. Louis: C. V. Mosby, 1977), 194–207; Thomas M. Brod, "Alcoholism as a Mental Health Problem of Native Americans: A Review of the Literature," *Archives of General Psychiatry* 32 (1975): 1385–91; Edward P. Dozier, "Problem Drinking among the American Indians," *Quarterly Journal of Studies on Alcohol* 27 (1966): 72–87; Laurence French and Jim Hornbuckle, "Alcoholism among Native Americans: An Analysis," *Social Work* 25 (1980): 275–80; Joy Lealand, *Firewater Myths: North American Indian Drinking and Alcohol Addiction* (New Brunswick, N.J.: Rutgers Center for Alcohol Studies, 1976); Nancy Oesterich Lurie, "The World's Oldest On-Going Protest Demonstration: North American Indian Drinking Patterns," *Pacific Historical Review* 40 (August 1971): 311–32; Craig MacAndrew and

126 White Man's Wicked Water

Robert B. Edgerton, *Drunken Comportment: A Social Explanation* (New York: Aldine, 1969); Peter C. Mancall, *Deadly Medicine: Indians and Alcohol in Early America* (Ithaca, N.Y.: Cornell University Press, 1995); Philip A. May, "The Epidemiology of Alcohol Abuse among American Indians: The Mythical and Real Properties," *American Indian Culture and Research Journal* 18 (1994): 121–44; Joan Weibel-Orlando, "Indians, Ethnicity, and Alcohol: Contrasting Perceptions of the Ethic Self and Alcohol Use," in *The American Experience with Alcohol: Contrasting Cultural Perspectives*, ed. Linda A. Bennett and Genevieve M. Ames (New York: Plenum, 1985): 201–26; Joseph Westermeyer, "The Drunken Indian: Myths and Realities," *Psychiatric Annals* 4 (November 1974): 29–36; and A. M. Winkler, "Drinking on the American Frontier," *Quarterly Journal of Studies on Alcohol* 29 (1968): 413–45.

2. One of the most frequently cited studies regarding Indian acculturation to abusive alcohol consumption concludes that the first inhabitants of North America "took as their exemplars of alcohol's effects on comportment the drunken doings of the very white men who introduced alcohol to them." See MacAndrew and Edgerton, *Drunken Comportment*, 136.

3. W. J. Rorabaugh, *The Alcoholic Republic: An American Tradition* (New York: Oxford University Press, 1979), 6–7.

4. William Cobbett, *A Year's Residence in the United States of America, Treating of the Face of the Country, the Climate, the Soil, the Products, the Mode of Cultivating the Land, the Prices of Land, of Labour, of Food, of Raiment; of the Expenses of Housekeeping, and of the Usual Manner of Living; of the Manners and Customs of the People; and of the Institutions of the Country, Civil, Political and Religious* (Carbondale: Southern Illinois University Press, 1964), 197.

5. Rorabaugh, *The Alcoholic Republic*, 7.

6. J. G. Adams and E. H. Chapin, eds., *The Temperance Fountain, or, Jettings from the Town Pump* (New York: H. Dayton, Publisher, 1860), 11.

7. Rorabaugh, *The Alcoholic Republic*, Table A1.1, 233.

8. Winkler, "Drinking on the American Frontier," 421.

9. Nathaniel Hawthorne, "A Rill from the Town-Pump" (1835), in *The Centenary Edition of the Works of Nathaniel Hawthorne*, vol. 9, ed. William Charvat, Roy Harvey Pearce, and Claude M. Simpson (Columbus: Ohio State University Press, 1974), 146.

10. Rorabaugh, *The Alcoholic Republic*, 77–89; 95–99. See also William L. Downard, *Dictionary of the History of the American Brewing and Distilling Industry* (Westport, Conn.: Greenwood Press, 1980), xxi–xxii.

11. Ibid., 90–91.

12. Ibid., 140–44.

13. Peter Way, "Evil Humors and Ardent Spirits: The Rough Culture of Canal Construction Workers," *Journal of American History* 79 (March 1993): 1412–13.

14. Francis Paul Prucha, *American Indian Policy in the Formative Years: The Indian Trade and Intercourse Acts, 1790–1834* (Cambridge, Mass.: Harvard University Press, 1962), 115; Henry L. Ellsworth to Elbert Herring, November 4, 1833, Letters Received by the Office of Indian Affairs (hereafter LROIA), Record Group (hereafter RG) 75, Microfilm (hereafter M) 234, Fort Leavenworth Agency, Roll (hereafter R) 300, National Archives (hereafter NA).

15. David Michael Delo, *Peddlers and Post Traders: The Army Sutler on the Frontier* (Salt Lake City: University of Utah Press, 1992), 11.

16. William E. Johnson, *The Federal Government and the Liquor Traffic*, rev. ed., (Westerville, Ohio: American Issue Publishing Company, 1917), 146–47.

17. Ibid., 148–50.

18. Ibid., 151–52.

19. U.S., Congress, House, *Spirituous Liquors to the Army: Letter from the Secretary of War, in Reply to a Resolution of the House of Representatives Inquiring What Beneficial Effects, If Any, Have Arisen from the Daily Use of Spirituous Liquors by the Army, &c. &c.,* 20th Cong., 2d sess., February 3, 1829, H. Doc. 103, serial 186, 1–7.

20. Ibid., 1.

21. Ibid., 4–6.

22. Ibid., 2.

23. Johnson, *The Federal Government and the Liquor Traffic*, 152–55.

24. Delo, *Peddlers and Post Traders*, 48–49.

25. Ibid., 65; Johnson, *The Federal Government and the Liquor Traffic*, 156–58.

26. Captain Eugene F. Ware, *The Indian War of 1864* (Lincoln: University of Nebraska Press, 1960), 33, 92–93.

27. Johnson, *The Federal Government and the Liquor Traffic*, 159–62.

28. Ibid., 163–65; Delo, *Peddlers and Post Traders*, 141–42, 148–153.

29. House, *Spirituous Liquors to the Army* (ser. 186), 3.

30. Prucha, *American Indian Policy in the Formative Years*, 52-56.

31. Frederickson, *The Liquor Question*, 45.

32. Lawrence Taliaferro to Wright Prescott, September 25, 1825, LROIA, RG 75, M 234, St. Louis Superintendency, R 748, NA.

33. Lewis Cass, "Remarks on the Policy and Practices of the United States and Great Britain in Their Treatment of the Indians," *North American Review* 24 (April 1827): 404.

34. Bernard C. Peters, "Hypocrisy on the Great Lakes Frontier: The Use of Whiskey by the Michigan Department of Indians Affairs," *Michigan Historical Review* 18 (Fall 1992): 4–8.

35. Ibid., 12.

36. Francis Tymany to Charles Mix, November 4, June 13, and April 11, 1858, LROIA, RG 75, M 234, Sac and Fox Agency, R 733, NA.

37. Major Garland to Acting Secretary of War, July 31, 1832, LROIA, RG 75, M 234, St. Louis Superintendency, R 750, NA.

38. Lawrence Taliaferro to William Clark, May 18, 1830, LROIA, RG 75, M 234, St. Louis Superintendency, R 749, NA.

39. John Dougherty to William Clark, November 10, 1831, LROIA, RG 75, M 234, St. Louis Superintendency, R 749, NA.

40. William Armstrong to C. A. Harris, July 31, 1837, LROIA, RG 75, M 234, Western Superintendency, R 922, NA.

41. John Montgomery to George Manypenny, January 18 and March 19, 1856, Letters Sent by the Office of Indian Affairs (hereafter LSOIA), RG 75, M 234, R 53, NA; Samuel G. Colley to John Evans, LROIA, RG 75, M 234, Colorado Superintendency, R 197, NA; Strate, *Sentinel to the Cimarron*, 66.

42. *U.S. Statutes at Large 2:* 146; ibid., 3: 682–83.

43. Prucha, *American Indian Policy,* 115.

44. Ibid.; Clark to Elbert Herring, December 3, 1831, LROIA, RG 75, M 234, St. Louis Superintendency, R 749, NA.

45. Prucha, *American Indian Policy in the Formative Years,* 107–8.

46. Thomas Forsyth to William Clark, April 9, 1924, LROIA, RG 75, M 234, St. Louis Superintendency, R 747, NA.

47. *Western Journal of Commerce* (Kansas City), March 26, 1859.

2. Father's Milk East, Wicked Water West

1. Wilbur R. Jacobs, *Diplomacy and Indian Gifts: Anglo-French Rivalry along the Ohio and Northwestern Frontiers, 1743–1763* (Palo Alto, Calif.: Stanford University Press, 1950), 53.

2. Paul Chrisler Phillips, *The Fur Trade,* vol. 1 (Norman: University of Oklahoma Press, 1961), 89, 109, 122, 139, 144–45, 211–13.

3. Bernard W. Sheehan, *Seeds of Extinction: Jeffersonian Philanthropy and the American Indian* (Chapel Hill: University of North Carolina Press, 1973), 232–33; Randall Craig Davis, "Firewater Myths: Alcohol and Portrayals of Native Americans in American Literature" (Ph.D. diss., Ohio State University, 1991), 29.

4. Francis Jennings, *The Invasion of America: Indians, Colonialism, and the Cant of Conquest* (New York: W. W. Norton, 1976), 39–40; Mancall, *Deadly Medicine*, 31–61, 155–67 passim.

5. James A. Clifton, *The Prairie People: Continuity and Change in Potawatomi Indian Culture, 1665–1965* (Lawrence: Regents Press of Kansas, 1977), 94–95.

6. Charles J. Kappler, comp., *Indian Affairs: Law and Treaties*, vol. 2, *Treaties* (Washington, D.C.: Government Printing Office, 1904), 270; Thomas L. McKenney, *Sketches of a Tour to the Lakes, of the Character and Customs of the Chippeway Indians, and of Incidents with the Treaty of Fond Du Lac* (Baltimore: Fielding Lucas, 1827), 286–88, 299–300.

7. Davis, "Firewater Myths," 33–39. See also Yasuhide Kawashima, *Puritan Justice and the Indian: White Man's Laws in Massachusetts, 1630–1763* (Middletown, Conn.: Wesleyan University Press, 1986), 82–88.

8. C. S. Weslager, *The Delaware Indians: A History* (New Brunswick, N.J.: Rutgers University Press, 1972), 139.

9. William E. Unrau and H. Craig Miner, *Tribal Dispossession and the Ottawa Indian University Fraud* (Norman: University of Oklahoma Press, 1985), 18.

10. Bert Anson, *The Miami Indians* (Norman: University of Oklahoma Press, 1970), 33, 151, 188, 226.

11. R. David Edmunds, *The Potawatomis: Keepers of the Fire* (Norman: University of Oklahoma Press, 1978), 160.

12. William T. Hagan, *The Sac and Fox Indians* (Norman: University of Oklahoma Press, 1958), 206.

13. Thomas Forsyth to Superintendent of Indian Affairs, April 9, 1824, and Statement of Joseph Ojae, April 19, 1824, LROIA, RG 75, M 234, St. Louis Superintendency, R 747, NA.

14. Russell Thorton, *American Indian Holocaust and Survival: A Population History Since 1492* (Norman: University of Oklahoma Press, 1987), 69.

15. Thomas Nuttall, *A Journal of Travels into the Arkansas Territory during the Year 1819*, ed. Savoie Lottinville (Norman: University of Oklahoma Press, 1979), 65.

16. Arthur H. DeRosier Jr., *The Removal of the Choctaw Indians* (Knoxville: University of Tennessee Press, 1970), 61; Kappler, *Treaties*, 193.

17. Herman J. Viola, *Thomas L. McKenney, Architect of America's Early Indian Policy: 1816–1830* (Chicago: Swallow Press, 1974), 197.

18. Sheehan, *Seeds of Extinction*, 152.

19. Ibid., 153.

20. Francis Paul Prucha, *The Great Father: The United States Government and the American Indian*, vol. 1 (Lincoln: University of Nebraska Press, 1984), ii.

21. Peters, "Hypocrisy on the Great Lakes Frontier," 7–8.

22. McKenney, *Sketches*, 462, 468.

23. James Wilkinson, Benjamin Hawkins, Andrew Pickens to Hon. Henry Dearborn, December 18, 1801, *American State Papers: Indian Affairs*, vol. 1 (Washington, D.C.: Gales and Seaton, 1832), 659.

24. Taliaferro to Wright Prescott, September 24, 1825, and Clark to Secretary of War, June 16, 1827, LROIA, RG 75, M 234, St. Louis Superintendency, R 748, NA.

25. Extract of a talk delivered by Little Turtle to the President of the United States, January 4, 1802, *Indian Affairs*, 1: 655.

26. Th. Jefferson to Gentlemen of the Senate and of the House of Representatives, January 28, 1802, ibid., 653.

27. *U.S. Statutes at Large* 2: 146.

28. Prucha, *American Indian Policy in the Formative Years*, 104–5.

29. Ibid., 105–8.

30. *U.S. Statutes at Large* 3: 243–44.

31. Richard E. Oglesby, *Manuel Lisa and the Opening of the Missouri Fur Trade* (Norman: University of Oklahoma Press, 1963), 173–75.

32. Th. Jefferson to Gentlemen of the Senate and House of Representatives, January 18, 1803, *Indian Affairs*, 1: 684–85.

33. William H. Goetzmann, *Exploration and Empire: The Explorer and Scientist in the Winning of the American West* (New York: Alfred A. Knopf, 1966), 5.

34. James P. Ronda, *Lewis and Clark among the Indians* (Lincoln: University of Nebraska Press, 1984), 1, 8–9.

35. *Original Journals of the Lewis and Clark Expedition, 1804–1806*, vol. 1, ed. Reuben Gold Thwaites (New York: Arno Press, 1969), 26, 67, 98, 114, 131, 133; Ronda, *Lewis and Clark*, 31–33, 57–58. The Pawnee rejection of alcohol was in large measure a consequence of the control that their several chiefs exercised over trade relations with Euro-Americans. There was growing intemperance among the Pawnees in the early 1840s, but by the 1850s the chiefs had decreed a total ban on liquor in their villages, which lasted through the 1860s. See Richard White, *The Roots of Dependency: Subsistence, Environment, and Social Change among the Choctaws, Pawnees, and Navajos* (Lincoln: University of Nebraska Press, 1983), 191–92.

36. Herbert T. Hoover, "Whiskey Trade in the History of Sioux Country since 1802," *Platte Valley Review* 19 (Winter 1991): 8.

37. *James' Account of S. H. Long's Expedition, 1819–1820*, pt. 2, *Early Western Travels, 1748–1846*, vol. 15, ed. Reuben Gold Thwaites (Cleveland: Arthur H. Clark, 1905), 49–50.

38. *U.S. Statutes at Large* 3: 243–44.

39. John W. Steiger, "Benjamin O'Fallon," in *The Mountain Men of the Fur Trade of the Far West*, vol. 5, ed. LeRoy R. Hafen (Glendale, Calif.: Arthur H. Clark, 1968), 263.

40. Deposition of John McCorkle, State of Missouri, County of Chariton, n.d., 1824, LROIA, RG 75, M 234, St. Louis Superintendency, R 747, NA.

41. Prucha, *American Indian Policy in the Formative Years*, 115–16.

42. The end of the factory system, which dated to 1795, resulted from enormous pressure exerted by the private fur trade lobby, as well economic problems consequent to the Panic of 1819, inadequate government funding in general, and problems with the British during the War of 1812. During the period that Thomas L. McKenney served as superintendent of the Indian trade, 1816–1822, alcohol was scrupulously prohibited as a trade item at the government factories, thus discouraging Indians in quest of alcohol from trading with the government. Such was especially the case at the Fort Osage factory on the lower Missouri, as reported by Indian Agent Benjamin O'Fallon in 1819. See Steiger, "Benjamin O'Fallon," 263. The most perceptive analysis of the factory system's demise is in Viola, *Thomas L. McKenney*, 47–70.

43. *U.S. Statutes at Large* 3: 682–83.

44. Prucha, *American Indian Policy in the Formative Years*, 111–17.

45. George A. Schultz, *An Indian Canaan: Isaac McCoy and the Vision of an Indian State* (Norman: University of Oklahoma Press, 1972), 49–50.

46. Isaac McCoy, *History of Baptist Indian Missions: Embracing Remarks on the Former and Present Condition of the Aboriginal Tribes: Their Former Settlement within the Indian Territory, and Their Future Prospects* (Washington, D.C.: William M. Morrison, 1840), 143.

47. Colonel J. Snelling to Secretary of War, August 23, 1825, *American State Papers: Indian Affairs*, vol. 2 (Washington, D.C.: Gales and Seaton, 1834), 661.

48. Ibid.

49. Schultz, *An Indian Canaan*, 49; McCoy, *History of Baptist Indian Missions*, 144.

50. Joseph B. Herring, *Kenekuk, the Kickapoo Prophet* (Lawrence: University Press of Kansas, 1988), 26–36.

51. Kappler, *Treaties*, 365–67.

52. Kickapoo Statement to Commissioner Ellsworth, September (?), 1833, LROIA, RG 75, M 234, Western Superintendency, R 921, NA.

53. Ellsworth Talk with Kickapoos, ibid.

3. Respite and Resolve

1. *U.S. Statutes at Large* 4: 411–12.

2. Prucha, *American Indian Policy in the Formative Years*, 231–49, and *The Great Father*, 1: 191–208. See also DeRosier, *The Removal of the Choctaw Indians*, 108–12, and Mary E. Young, "Indian Removal and Land Allotment: The

Civilized Tribes and Jacksonian Justice," *American Historical Review* 64 (October 1958): 34–45.

3. *Natchez Gazette*, February 3, 1830; quoted in DeRosier, *The Removal of the Choctaw Indians*, 107.

4. Extract of a letter received of the Chiefs and principal men of the Stockbridge or Muh-he-cennewee Indians, January 8, 1827, Committee on Indian Affairs, Sen. 19A-D7, RG 46, NA.

5. John Tipton to Col. Thomas McKenney, January 31, 1830, and Journal of the Proceedings of the Council held with the Miami Nation of Indians at the Fork of the Wabash, in the state of Indiana, by Governor George B. Porter of Michigan, General William Marshall of Indiana, and the Reverend J. F. Schermehorn, Commissioner appointed by the President of the United States to negotiate with said Nation for the purchase of their lands, n.d., 1830, LROIA, RG 75, M 234, Miami Agency, R 416, NA.

6. Winkler, "Drinking on the American Frontier," 421.

7. John Dougherty to William Clark, November 10, 1831, LROIA, RG 75, M 234, St. Louis Superintendency, R 749, NA.

8. Prucha, *American Indian Policy in the Formative Years*, 117.

9. William Clark to James Barbour, Secretary of War, June 11, 1825, Documents Relating to the Negotiation of Ratified and Unratified Treaties, Treaties, RG 75, Target 494, NA.

10. *U.S. Statutes at Large* 12: 628; *John Brown and Jane Brown v. Adel (Clement) Belmarde*, 3 Kan. 35. For a careful analysis of the Kansa mixed-blood tracts, see Robert Joseph Keckeisen, "The Kansa 'Half-Breed' Lands: Contravention and Transformation of United States Indian Policy in Kansas (master's thesis, Wichita State University, 1982).

11. Prucha, *American Indian Policy in the Formative Years*, 119–20.

12. John Jacob Astor to the Hon. Col. Benton, January 29, 1829, Committee on Indian Affairs, Sen. 20A-D6, Folder 1, RG 46, NA.

13. *Sundry Goods, Wares, and Merchandises v. United States*, 2 Pet. 357.

14. Prucha, *American Indian Policy in the Formative Years*, 121–26.

15. Isaac McCoy, *Remarks on Indian Reform*, 47, Indian Pamphlets, Library Division, Kansas State Historical Society, cited in Frederickson, *The Liquor Question*, 48.

16. Kappler, *Treaties*, 246–50.

17. There is no evidence that the Kansa hunters who signed the Running Turkey Creek treaty were aware of the land cession agreement concluded three months earlier by Clark in St. Louis. See William E. Unrau, *Mixed-Bloods and Tribal Dissolution: Charles Curtis and the Quest for Indian Identity* (Lawrence: University Press of Kansas, 1989), 27–28.

18. Kappler, *Treaties*, 217–25, 246–50.

19. William E. Foley and C. David Rice, *The First Chouteaus: River Barons of Early St. Louis* (Urbana: University of Illinois Press, 1983), 82.

20. Ibid., 184 n. 48; *Missouri Gazette* (St. Louis), March 22, 1821.

21. See chap. 2, n. 32.

22. Kappler, *Treaties*, 95–99.

23. By the time of Missouri statehood in 1821, Howard County, midway between St. Louis and the western state line, had a population of 13,427—the most populous of Missouri's fifteen counties. The Franklin land office, which opened in 1819, reported land selling at an average of $4.00 an acre in 1820, as opposed to the average of $2.84 at the St. Louis office. See Walter A. Schroeder, "Spread of Settlement in Howard County, Missouri, 1810–1859," *Missouri Historical Review* 58 (October 1969): 9–12, and Floyd Calvin Shoemaker, *Missouri's Struggle for Statehood, 1804–1821* (Jefferson City, Mo.: n.p., 1916), 68–69.

24. Kappler, *Treaties*, 207–9, 217–21.

25. *History of Clay and Platte Counties* (St. Louis: National Historical Company, 1885), 100.

26. "Cyrus Curtis," Kansas City Biographies, Native Sons Collection, vol. 1, R 17, Department of Special Collections, Kansas City Public Library.

27. Charles P. Deatherage, *Early History of Greater Kansas City Missouri and Kansas*, vol. I (Kansas City: Charles P. Deatherage, 1927), 218.

28. Five years prior to the Removal Act of 1830, the Missouri Shawnees agreed to relinquish their lands near Cape Girardeau in exchange for an immediate payment of fourteen thousand dollars and "an equal quantity of land, to be selected on the Kansas River, and laid off either south or north of that river, and west of the boundary of Missouri, not reserved or ceded to any other tribe." Under the treaty also, members of the same tribe then residing in Ohio were allowed to emigrate to the same reservation, if they so chose. See Kappler, *Treaties*, 262–64.

29. "James Hyatt McGee," Kansas City Biographies, Native Sons Collection, vol. 1, R 12, Department of Special Collections, Kansas City Public Library; *A Memorial and Biographical Record of Kansas City and Jackson County, Missouri* (Chicago: Lewis Publishing Company, 1896), 197–98; R. Richard Wohl, "Three Generations of Business Enterprise in a Midwestern City: The McGees of Kansas City," *Journal of Economic History* 16 (1956): 516–27; Richard Cummins to Thomas H. Crawford, October 20, 1843, LROIA, RG 75, M 234, Fort Leavenworth Agency, R 302, NA.

30. George C. Sibley to Senator David Barton, January 10, 1824, George C. Sibley Papers, Missouri Historical Society.

31. Louise Barry, comp., *The Beginning of the West: Annals of the Kansas Gateway to the American West, 1540–1854* (Topeka: Kansas State Historical Society,

1972), 165; Otis E. Young, *The First Military Escort on the Santa Fe Trail, 1829* (Glendale, Calif.: Arthur H. Clark, 1952), 84.

32. David J. Weber, *The Taos Trappers: The Fur Trade in the Far Southwest, 1540–1846* (Norman: University of Oklahoma Press, 1971), 72–73.

33. Janet Lecompte, "Mathew Kinkade," in *The Mountain Men of the Fur Trade of the Far West*, vol. 2, ed. LeRoy R. Hafen, (Glendale, Calif.: Arthur H. Clark, 1965), 192.

34. George Bird Grinnell, "Bent's Old Fort and Its Builders," *Collections of the Kansas State Historical Society* 15 (1919–1922): 45, 58–59.

35. Ibid., 59.

36. Janet Lecompte, "Simeon Turley," in *The Mountain Men of the Fur Trade of the Far West*, vol. 7, ed. Leroy R. Hafen. In 1847 Turley was killed and his distillery burned to the ground by Indians of the Taos region (ibid., 310–13).

37. John Dougherty to William Clark, November 10, 1831, LROIA, RG 75, M 234, St. Louis Superintendency, R 749, NA; A. G. Morgan (Fort Leavenworth Sutler) to Clark, October 5, 1832, LROIA, RG 75, M 234, St. Louis Superintendency, R 750, NA; *Report of the Commissioner of Indian Affairs* (hereafter *RCIA*), 1834, 97.

38. Chouteau to Cass, September 19, 1832, LROIA, RG 75, M 234, Osage Subagency, R 631, NA.

39. Clark to Cass, November 10, 1831, LROIA, RG 75, M 234, St. Louis Superintendency, R 749, NA.

40. Ronald N. Satz, "Elbert Herring," in *The Commissioners of Indian Affairs, 1824–1977*, ed. Robert M. Kvasnicka and Herman J. Viola (Lincoln: University of Nebraska Press, 1979), 13.

41. Ibid., 13–14.

42. Clark to Elbert Herring, December 3, 1831, LROIA, RG 75, M 234, St. Louis Superintendency, R 749, NA.

43. Hiram Martin Chittenden and Alfred Talbot Richardson, eds., *Life, Letters, and Travels of Father Pierre-Jean DeSmet, S.J.*, vol. 1 (New York: Francis P. Harper, 1905), 1214. A twentieth-century study of Indian drinking presents a striking similarity to the conclusions of DeSmet: "The cheap and vile quality of the spirituous liquors supplied to the Indians, combined with the lack of inhibition in these undisciplined barbarians, made their drinking revels so brutal and terrible as to defy adequate description"; see Frederickson, *The Liquor Question*, 5. A more recent and comprehensive treatment of Indian-white relations in general describes Frederickson's monograph as a "thorough discussion of the evils of the liquor traffic among the Indians"; see Prucha, *The Great Father*, vol. 1, 313 n. 48.

44. Cass, "Remarks on the Policy and Practices," 404.

45. Gary C. Stein, "A Fearful Drunkenness: The Liquor Trade to the Western Indians as Seen by European Travellers in America, 1800–1860," *Red River Valley Historical Review* 1 (Summer 1974): 110–11.

46. Sheehan, *Seeds of Extinction*, 239.

47. *U.S. Statutes at Large*, 4: 564.

48. *Register of Debates in Congress*, 21 Cong., 1st sess., VIII (Washington, D.C.: Gales and Seaton, 1833), 988–89.

49. The best discussion of the debate is in Prucha, *American Indian Policy in the Formative Years*, 250–73.

50. Ibid., 272.

51. *U.S. Statutes at Large* 4: 729–35.

52. Ibid., 733.

53. RCIA, 1835, 263.

54. Private Council with the Delaware and Shawnee Chiefs, n.d., 1834, LROIA, RG 75, M 234, Western Superintendency, R 921, NA.

55. Ibid.

56. Ibid.

4. Annuities and Alcohol in Indian Country

1. *The United States Magazine and Democratic Review* 14 (February 1844): 183.

2. Report of the Senate Committee on Indian Affairs, March 15, 1836, Sen. 24 A-D7, RG 46, NA; Schultz, *An Indian Canaan*, 177–79.

3. See, for example, the Byrd and Belding claim for supplying rations for the Choctaws, which the government's principal disbursement agent termed "perfectly absurd"; J. Brown to General George Gibson, March, 10, 1833, U.S. Congress, Senate, *United States Subsistence Department, The Indian Removals, Furnished in Answer to a Resolution of the Senate of 27th December, 1833, by the Commissary of General Subsistence*, 23 Cong., 1st Sess., S. Doc. 512, vol. 1, serial 244, 502–3.

4. James B. Gardiner to Lewis Cass, June 20, 1832, ibid.

5. Gardiner to General George Gibson, October 3, 1832, ibid.

6. William Armstrong to Gibson, October 11, 1833, ibid.

7. Perry McCandless, *A History of Missouri*, vol. 2 (Columbia: University of Missouri Press, 1972), 56.

8. Captain John Stuart to General R. Jones, June 9, 1838, LROIA, RG 75, M 234, Western Superintendency, R 922, NA.

9. Waldo R. Wedel, ed., *The Dunbar-Allis Letters on the Pawnee* (New York: Garland, 1985), 587–89, 699, 718, 733.

10. Chittenden and Richardson, *Life, Letters, and Travels*, 1: 172–74.

11. Isaac McCoy to John C. Spencer, Secretary of War, October 25, 1841; cited in Schultz, *An Indian Canaan*, 196.

12. A Missouri newspaper reported that "the Oregon emigrants know no better than to sell whiskey to Indians"; *St. Joseph Gazette* (St. Joseph Missouri), June 27, 1849. At the Blue River crossing of the Oregon Trail whiskey was sold at a "private post office" to anyone for twenty-five cents a glass; Barry, *The Beginning of the West*, 1068. In 1848 Fort Leavenworth Agent Richard Cummins reported that the Sante Fe traders "contend that the road from [the Missouri River] to Santa Fe is a public highway" and that they had the right to carry spirits so long as "they did not leave the road and go into Indian country"; Cummins to Thomas H. Harvey, January 20, 1848, LROIA, RG 75, M 234, St. Louis Superintendency, R 301, NA.

13. For a compilation of the land cessions leading to these reservations, including abstracts of the various treaties and detailed maps, state by state, see Charles C. Royce, comp., *Indian Land Cessions in the United States: Eighth Annual Report of the Bureau of American Ethnology* (1896–1897), pt. 2 (Washington, D.C.: Government Printing Office, 1899).

14. Marston G. Clark to William Clark, September 30, 1833, LROIA, RG 75, M 234, St. Louis Superintendency, R 750, NA; Elvid Hunt, *History of Fort Leavenworth, 1827–1927* (Fort Leavenworth, Kans.: General Services Press, 1927), 67–68; Merril J. Mattes, "John Dougherty," in Hafen, ed., *The Mountain Men of the Fur Trade of the Far West*, vol. 8, ed. Leroy R. Hafen (Glendale, Calif.: Arthur H. Clark, 1971), 130.

15. *History of Clay and Platte Counties*, 111, 119, 596.

16. Deatherage, *Early History of Greater Kansas City*, 260, 355.

17. Workers of the Writers' Program of the Works Progress Administration in the State of Missouri, *The WPA Guide to the 1930s Missouri* (Lawrence: University Press of Kansas, 1986), 76; A. Theodore Brown, *Frontier Community: Kansas City to 1870* (Columbia: University of Missouri Press, 1963), 152; Theodore S. Case, *History of Kansas City, Missouri* (Syracuse, N.Y.: D. Mason, 1888), 46.

18. Deatherage, *Early History of Greater Kansas City*, 334.

19. William E. Miller, *History of Jackson County* (Kansas City, Mo.: Birdsall and Williams, 1881), 70.

20. Kappler, *Treaties*, 145–626, passim.

21. *U.S. Statutes at Large*, 4: 730.

22. *RCIA*, 1843, 388.

23. Richard Cummins to Thomas Harvey, December 12, 1847, LROIA, RG 75, M 234, Fort Leavenworth Agency, R 302, NA.

24. Charles Bent to David D. Mitchell, May 1, 1843, LROIA, RG 75, M 234, St. Louis Superintendency, R 753, NA.

25. Jesse H. Leavenworth to Dennis W. Cooley, May 8, 1866, LROIA, RG 75, M 234, Kiowa-Comanche Agency, R 375, NA.

26. Edward W. Wynkoop to Dennis W. Cooley, August 11, 1866, and J. L. Butterfield to Thomas Murphy, February 5, 1868, LROIA, RG 75, M 234, Upper Arkansas Agency, R 879 and 880, NA; Special Orders no. 229, Adjutant General's Office, July 7, 1864, cited in August W. Burton Papers, Manuscript Division, Kansas State Historical Society; Records of the War Department, Letters Sent, Fort Dodge, Kansas, January 13, 1867 and January 24, 1868, cited in Strate, *Sentinel to the Cimarron*, 32, 61; George Manypenny to Alexander Cumming, January 18 and March 19, 1856, LSOIA, RG 75, M 21, R 53, NA.

27. Frederickson, *The Liquor Question*, 74; Thomas Goodrich, *Bloody Dawn: The Story of the Lawrence Massacre* (Kent, Ohio: Kent State University Press, 1991), 10; William E. Unrau, *The Kansa Indians: A History of the Wind People, 1673–1873* (Norman: University of Oklahoma Press, 1971), 198; Sondra Van Meter, *Marion County Kansas: Past and Present* (Marion, Kans.: Marion County Historical Society, 1972), 24, 225–26; *Wichita Eagle* (Wichita, Kansas), November 11, 1992; "Peketon County, K.T.," George H. Brown Papers, Manuscript Division, Kansas State Historical Society; William E. Unrau, "Investigation or Probity? Investigations into the Affairs of the Kiowa-Comanche Indian Agency, 1867," *Chronicles of Oklahoma* 42 (Autumn 1964): 313–15; *Smoky Hill and Republican Union* (Junction City, Kansas), July 9, 1864.

28. Kappler, *Treaties*, 595, 601.

29. J. L. Butterfield to Thomas Murphy, February 5, 1868, LROIA, RG 75, M 234, Upper Arkansas Agency, R 880, NA.

30. William E. Murphy to Alfred Cumming, November 12, 1868, LROIA, RG 75, M 234, Potawatomi Agency, R 681, NA.

31. *Council Grove Press* (Council Grove, Kansas), May 4, 1861.

32. *St. Joseph Gazette* (St. Joseph, Missouri), June 22, 1849.

33. J. Hayden to Headquarters, Department of Kansas, May 14, 1862, *The War of the Rebellion: A Compilation of the Official Records of the Union and Confederate Armies*, series 1, vol. 13 (Washington, D.C.: Government Printing Office, 128 vols., 1880–1901), 382; D. D. Mitchell to Orlando Brown, LROIA, RG 75, M 234, St. Louis Superintendency, R 755, NA.

34. Royce, *Indian Land Cessions*, plates 26–27.

35. Kappler, *Treaties*, 222–25.

36. Clark to James Barbour, June 11, 1825, Documents Relating to the Negotiation of Ratified and Unratified Treaties, Ratified Treaties, RG 75, Target 494, NA.

37. Ibid.

38. Clark to James Barbour, October 19, 1825, LROIA, RG 75, M 234, St. Louis Superintendency, R 747, NA.

39. Marston Clark to William Clark, September 30, 1833, LROIA, RG 75, M 234, Kansas Agency, R 750, NA.

40. McCoy to John Tipton, July 20, 1837, Isaac McCoy Papers, R 9, Manuscript Division, Kansas State Historical Society.

41. Barry, *Beginning of the West*, 456–57.

42. Mitchell to Orlando Brown, October 13, 1849, LROIA, RG 75, M 234, St. Louis Superintendency, R 755, NA.

43. Keckeisen, "The Kansa 'Half-Breed' Lands."

44. Barry, *Beginning of the West*, 357, 534.

45. Mitchell to T. Hartley Crawford, October 25, 1841, LROIA, RG 75, M 234, St. Louis Superintendency, R 752, NA.

46. William Hamilton, "Autobiography of Reverend William Hamilton," *Transactions and Reports of the Nebraska State Historical Society* 1 (1885): 64.

47. Mitchell to T. Hartley Crawford, September 12, 1842, *RCIA*, 1842, 425–26.

48. A trader named Goldstein accompanying the westward movment of troops in July 1846 sold pints of whiskey at 400 percent above the price for the same amount in St. Louis; Captain William Pelzer, a company commander in the Indian Battalion enlisted in Missouri for service in New Mexico, was chronically drunk and eventually resigned to escape court-martial. See William Y. Chalphant, *Dangerous Passage: The Santa Fe Trail and the Mexican War* (Norman: University of Oklahoma Press, 1994), 74, 253.

49. Cass, "Remarks on the Policy and Practices," 404–5.

50. Stokes, Schermerhorn, and Ellsworth to Lewis Cass, February 10, 1834, *RCIA*, 1834, 103.

51. *RCIA*, 1844, 10.

52. *RCIA*, 1846, 16–17.

53. *Missouri Democrat* (St. Louis), December 12, 1853.

54. *Council Grove Press* (Council Grove, Kansas), June 22, 1861.

55. Stein, "A Fearful Drunkeness," 110, 112.

56. Frederickson, *The Liquor Question*, 5. A contemporary authority on Indian-white relations has uncritically termed Frederickson's study "a thorough discussion of the evils of the liquor traffic among the Indians." See Prucha, *The Great Father*, 1: 313 n. 48.

57. For the failure of the Western Indian Territory proposal, see Annie Heloise Abel, "Proposals for an Indian State, 1778–1878," *Annual Report of the American Historical Association for the Year 1907*, 1 (May 1846): 89–102; Schultz,

An *Indian Canaan*, 177–79; and especially Reports of the Senate Committee on Indian Affairs, January 11, March 16, 1836, January 13, 1838, Sen. 24A-D7, RG 46, NA.

58. McCoy to Secretary of War John G. Spencer, May 17, 1842, and McCoy to Department of Indian Affairs and President of the United States, May (?), 1842, McCoy Papers, Correspondence, 1839–1842, R 10.

59. T. H. Crawford to William Wilkins, November 25, 1844, *RCIA*, 1844, 4–5.

60. Francis Paul Prucha, "American Indian Policy in the 1840s: Visions of Reform," in *The Frontier Challenge: Responses to the Trans-Mississippi West*, ed. John G. Clark (Lawrence: University Press of Kansas, 1971), 96–97; Ronald N. Satz, "Thomas Hartley Crawford," in Kvasnicka and Viola, *The Commissioners of Indian Affairs, 1824–1877*, ed. Robert M. Kvasnicka and Herman J. Viola (Lincoln: University of Nebraska Press, 1979), 24.

61. Prucha, "American Indian Policy in the 1840s," 97.

62. Writing to Commissioner Medill in 1846, federal liquor inspector Thomas P. Moore (himself described by Charles Larpenteur as "a great drunkard") reported "that the Indian country was soggy with illicit alcohol, that spies [for the traders] watched his every move, and that only a detachment of dragoons could keep the liquor out." See John E. Sunder, *The Fur Trade on the Upper Missouri, 1840–1865* (Norman: University of Oklahoma Press, 1965), 84–85.

63. Robert A. Trennert, "William Medill," in *The Commissioners of Indian Affairs, 1824–1877*, ed. Robert M. Kvasnicka and Herman J. Viola, (Lincoln: University of Nebraska Press, 1979), 29–31.

64. As early as 1834, Senator John Tipton of Indiana asserted, "The Chiefs, most generally, are traders, and will pay the people in goods and whiskey, and keep the money, and the poor Indians never see a dollar," *Congressional Globe* (May 22, 1834), 400.

65. Trennert, "William Medill," 31.

66. *Congressional Globe* (May 18, 1836), 469.

67. Harvey to Medill, September 5, 1846, *RCIA*, 1846, 71.

68. Richard S. Elliott to Thomas H. Crawford, July 24, 1845, *RCIA*, 1845, 553.

69. "Administration of Indian Affairs," *United States Magazine and Democratic Review* 18 (May 1846): 334.

70. See, for example, the Otoe-Missouria and Omaha treaties of March 15 and 16, 1854, Kappler, *Treaties*, 610, 613.

71. Henry Dodge to Medill, October 8, 1846, *RCIA*, 1846, 39.

72. *RCIA*, 1844, 10.

73. Harvey to Medill, September 5, 1846, *RCIA*, 1846, 71.

74. McCoy to President of the United States, April 6, 1846, McCoy Papers, Correspondence, 1843–1878, R 11.

75. Medill to Secretary of War William L. Marcy, November 30, 1846, *RCIA*, 1846, 17.

76. *U.S. Statutes at Large*, 9: 203.

77. Ibid.

78. Ibid.

79. Cummins to Harvey, January 20, 1848, LROIA, RG 75, M 234, Fort Leavenworth Agency, R 301, NA.

80. William L. Marcy, "Regulations, April 13, 1847," *RCIA*, 1847, 33–36.

81. Marcy to Governors of Arkansas, Missouri, and Iowa, July 14, 1847, cited in Prucha, "American Indian Policy in the 1840s," 100–101.

82. United States District Attorney Reports-Returns, Entry 145, Vol. 3, Missouri-North Carolina (1851–1856), Records of the Solicitor of the Treasury of the United States, RG 206, NA.

5. Courting Disaster

1. United States District Attorney Reports-Returns, Entry 145, vol. 2, Missouri (1845–1850), and vol. 3, Missouri-North Carolina (1851–1856), RG 206, NA.

2. Wohl, "Three Generations of Business Enterprise," 516–27.

3. Cummins to T. Hartley Crawford, October 20, 1843, LROIA, RG 75, M 234, Fort Leavenworth Agency, R 302, NA; Barry, *Beginning of the West*, 500; Brown, *Frontier Community*, 49–50, 210.

4. Entry, April 16, 1846, Jotham Meeker Journal, typed copy, Manuscript Division, Kansas State Historical Society.

5. Ibid., Entries, April 8–September 5, 1848.

6. Unrau and Miner, *Tribal Dispossession*, 66.

7. B. A. James to Commanding Officer, Fort Leavenworth, Indian Territory, August 8, 1853, LROIA, RG 75, M 234, Sac and Fox Agency, R 733, NA.

8. Unrau and Miner, *Tribal Dispossession*, 67; Eleanor Meeker to Sister, n.d., 1855, Jotham Meeker Papers, Manuscript Division, Kansas State Historical Society, R 2.

9. *United States v. See See Sah Mah & Eschatiah* (1850), Records of the District Courts of the United States, District of Missouri, Circuit Court, vol. 4 (1845–1853), RG 21, Federal Records Center, NA, Kansas City, Missouri.

10. Ida M. Ferris, "The Sauks and Foxes of Franklin and Osage Counties, Kansas," *Collections of the Kansas State Historical Society* 11 (1909–1910): 344.

11. *United States v. See See Sah Mah & Eschatiah.*

12. Ibid.

13. Ibid.

14. Frederickson, *The Liquor Question*, 62.

15. W. George Ewing Jr. to Charles E. Mix, Acting Commissioner of Indian Affairs, July 28, 1851, LROIA, RG 75, M 234, Potawatomi Agency, R 678, NA; Depositions of E. B. Horner and George Huffaker, accompanying Ewing to Commissioner of Indian Affairs Luke Lea, August 26, 1852, LROIA, RG 75 M 234, Central Superintendency, R 55, NA. Contracts awarded to Boone and Bernard are provided in Barry, *Beginning of the West*, 979, 1016; appointments and administrative changes in the Indian agencies are listed in Edward E. Hill, *The Office of Indian Affairs, 1824–1880: Historical Sketches* (New York: Clearwater, 1974), 130–33, 150–53. Albert G. Boone, senior partner in the firm of Boone and Bernard, was the grandson of the celebrated Daniel Boone of Kentucky, and had been licensed to trade with the emigrant Indians west of Missouri for nearly two decades. Recounting his travels through the interior in the late 1830s, Francis Parkman observed "many drunk Indians" at Boone's commercial establishment in Westport; see Nicholas P. Hademan, "Albert Gallatin Boone," in *The Mountain Men of the Fur Trade of the Far West*, ed. Leroy R. Hafen (Glendale, Calif.: Arthur H. Clark, 1987), 39–40.

16. Sunder, *The Fur Trade*, 48.

17. Pierre Chouteau to David D. Mitchell, August 23, 1842, LROIA, RG 75, M 234, St. Louis Superintendency, R 753, NA.

18. Andrew Drips to David D. Mitchell, July 2, 1843, ibid.

19. Sunder, *The Fur Trade*, 49–51, 69–72; "Andrew Drips," Kansas City Biographies, Native Sons Collection, vol. 1, R 17, Department of Special Collections, Kansas City Public Library.

20. Sunder, *The Fur Trade*, 90–91.

21. During the April 1848 term of the circuit court, for example, John A. Sire's deposition stated that John Durock of St. Louis, an important material witness subpoenaed by the prosecution in one of the American Fur Company cases, "had for a temporary purpose gone to New Orleans out of this [Judicial] District, and that his purpose to leave St. Louis was not known"; see "John A. Sire Deposition," in *United States v. Alexander Culbertson*, United States Circuit Court for the District of Missouri, April 1848 Term, LROIA, RG 75, M 234, St. Louis Superintendency, R 755, NA.

22. In May 1848 Benton acknowledged receiving a letter from Indian Commissioner William Medill and promised to communicate with Chouteau on the judicial matter, what Benton called "a request both natural and just considering the part I had in the arrangement in April, 1846"; Benton to Medill, May

11, 1848, LROIA, RG 75, M 234, St. Louis Superintendency, R 755, NA. Another prominent Missourian who assisted in the continuance strategy was Lewis Vital Bogy, prominent St. Louis businessman and Missouri state legislator, who signed on as Chouteau's personal attorney and who was appointed commissioner of Indian affairs on October 8, 1866; see Bogy to Chouteau, May 23, 1848, ibid., and William E. Unrau, "Lewis Vital Bogy," in *The Commissioners of Indian Affairs, 1824–1877*, ed. Robert M. Kvasnicka and Herman J. Viola (Lincoln: University of Nebraska Press, 1979), 109–14.

23. Unrau, "Lewis Vital Bogy," 113–17. Sunder's summary of the American Fur Company suits is based on United States District Attorney Reports-Returns, and Cases Decided, RG 206, NA; Complete and Final Record, United States Circuit Court, District of Missouri, vol. 3, RG 21, Federal Records Center, Kansas City, NA; and Chouteau Family Papers and Andrew Drips Papers, Manuscript Division, Missouri Historical Society.

24. Ibid., 90.

25. See, for example, Richard Cummins to Thomas A. Harvey, September 26, 1848; Jotham Meeker to Harvey, September 22, 1848; J. E. Fletcher to Harvey, October 4, 1848; and S. M. Irwin and William Hamilton to A. J. Vaughan, September 25, 1848, RCIA 1848, 445–49, 458, 460, 485; and Richard Cummins to Harvey, September 16, 1848, LROIA, RG 75, M 234, Fort Leavenworth Agency, R 302, NA.

26. U.S. Congress, Senate, *Report of the Secretary of War Transmitting in Compliance with a Resolution of the Senate, Documents in Relation to the Difficulties Which Took Place at the Payment of the Sac and Fox Annuities Last Fall*, 30th Cong., 1st sess., August 9, 1848, S. Exec. Doc. 70, serial 510, 1–128; Barry, *Beginning of the West*, 579–80, 718–19.

27. *RCIA*, 1849, 5.

28. Ibid.

29. *RCIA*, 1848, 402.

30. The literature on temperance in white antebellum America is substantial. Among the more comprehensive studies are Rorabaugh, *The Alcoholic Republic*; Ian R. Tyrrell, *Sobering Up: From Temperance to Prohibition in Antebellum America* (Westport, Conn.: Greenwood Press, 1979); John A. Krout, *The Origins of Prohibition* (New York: Alfred A. Knopf, 1925); Mark Edward Leader and James Kirby Martin, *Drinking in America: A History* (New York: Free Press, 1982); Barbara L. Epstein, *The Politics of Domesticity: Women, Evangelism and Temperance in Nineteenth-Century America* (Middletown, Conn.: Wesleyan University Press, 1981); and Norman H. Clark, *Deliver Us from Evil: An Interpretation of American Prohibition* (New York: W. W. Norton, 1976).

31. Frederickson, *The Liquor Question*, 28–31.

32. Unrau and Miner, *Tribal Dispossession*, 67; Meeker to Burton A. James, September 4, 1854, Meeker Papers, R 2.

33. Burton A. James to Alexander Cumming, September 1, 1854, *RCIA*, 1854, 104.

34. Herring, *Kenekuk*, 28–32; Frederickson, *The Liquor Question*, 31–33.

35. William Armstrong to T. Hartley Crawford, September 10, 1842, and W. D. Collins to James Logan, September 18, 1845, LROIA, RG 75, M 234, Western Superintendency, R 923, NA; Frederickson, *The Liquor Question*, 19–44.

36. Petition from Persons of Jasper County, Missouri, to President John Tyler wishing the removal of Robert Callaway, Testimony in Jasper County, Missouri, regarding Callaway's Destruction of their Whiskey, (?) McBride to T. Hartley Crawford, Petition to His Excellency John Tyler, President of the United States, September n.d., 1842; Statements of Principal Chiefs, with Two of the Little Chiefs and a few of the Headmen of the Osage Nation, June 14, 1843, LROIA, RG 75, M 234, Osage Agency, R 632, NA.

37. Ramsay D. Potts to William Armstrong, August 31, 1843, Samuel Worcester to Armstrong, September 5, 1843, Cyrus Byington to Armstrong, September 22, 1843, and Ebenezer Hotchkin to Armstrong, October 10, 1843, *RCIA*, 1843, 335–40.

38. William Armstrong to T. Hartley Crawford, March 12, 1842, LROIA, RG 75, M 234, Western Superintendency, R 923, NA.

39. C. Kingsbury to Armstrong, October 18, 1843, *RCIA*, 1843, 338.

40. A. M. M. Upshaw to T. Hartley Crawford, September 4, 1843, ibid., 411–12.

41. Upshaw to Samuel M. Rutherford, August 22, 1848, *RCIA*, 1848, 532.

42. Memorial of the Chiefs, & Members of the General Council, of the Choctaw and Chickasaw Districts, To the Honorable, the Senate and House of Representatives of the State of Texas in Legislature Assembled, November 9, 1851; copy of the original, private collection of Michael D. Heaston.

43. Ibid.

44. *Digest of the Laws of Missouri Territory, 1818*, 231; *Laws of the State of Missouri, 1818–1839*, 66–67; *Revised Statutes of Missouri, 1845*, 576–77; cited in Frederickson, *The Liquor Question*, 62–64.

45. John M. Richardson to Samuel M. Rutherford, *RCIA*, 1848, 541–42.

46. John Richardson to William Medill, May 22, 1848, LROIA, RG 75, M 234, Osage Agency, R 633, NA.

47. Michael D. Heaston, "Whiskey Regulation and Indian Land Titles in New Mexico Territory, 1851–1861," *Journal of the West* 10 (1971): 473–83.

48. Alexander Ramsey to Luke Lea, October 21, 1850, *RCIA*, 1850, 46, 50.

49. Luke Lea to Secretary of the Interior, November 27, 1850, ibid., 4–6; Lea to Alexander Ramsey, August 6, 1851, ibid., 1851, 22; Kappler, *Treaties*, 592.

50. Robert A. Trennert, "Luke Lea," in *The Commissioners of Indian Affairs, 1824–1877*, ed. Robert M. Kvasnicka and Herman J. Viola (Lincoln: University of Nebraska Press, 1979), 54.

51. *United States v. Cisna*, 25 Fed. Cas. No. 14795 (C. C. Ohio 1835).

6. Alcohol and Indian Country

1. *U.S. Statutes at Large*, 2: 139–46.

2. *United States v. Cisna*, 25 Fed. Cas. no . 14795 (C. C. Ohio 1835).

3. Kappler, *Treaties*, 18–23, 39–45, 66, 77–78, 92–95, 99–100, 105–7, 117–19, 145–55, 162–63, 164, 339–41.

4. U.S. Congress, House, 23d Cong., 1st sess., May 20, 1834, H. R. 464, serial 263, 10. In reference to the 1834 law also, the House Committee recommended that white citizens, as opposed to foreigners, need not have passports "to pass into Indian country." But to trade or reside in Indian country required a federal license. This stipulation was included in the 1834 law, ibid., 11; *U.S. Statutes at Large*, 4: 730.

5. *U.S. Statutes at Large* 4: 729.

6. Kappler, *Treaties*, 460–61, 534–37.

7. *McCracken v. Todd*, 1 Kans. 146–65 (1862). The district court's decision to deny appointment of the Leavenworth County sheriff on grounds that his bond had not been properly processed by the probate court and that Leavenworth County at the time of the appointment in 1854 was still a part of the Delaware reservation to which title had not been ceded, was overruled by the Kansas high court on grounds that the organization of Kansas Territory "by implication" had repealed the Trade and Intercourse Act of 1834. Laws and treaties only prohibited settlement and survey, said the court, "not the passage to and fro by persons over these lands, nor do they prohibit the government . . . from establishing its offices, holding courts and issuing and executing its processes at any place upon them." The only exceptions were reservations specifically excluded from territorial jurisdiction by treaty, or by treaty provisions in force at the date of the admission of Kansas into the union.

8. Ibid.

9. See Roy F. Nichols, "The Kansas-Nebraska Act: A Century of Historiography," *Mississippi Valley Historical Review* 43 (September 1956): 187–212; Gerald D. Wolff, *The Kansas-Nebraska Bill: Party, Section, and the Coming of the Civil War* (New York: Revisionist Press, 1977).

10. Annie H. Abel, "Indian Reservations in, Kansas and the Extinguishment

of Their Title," *Transactions of the Kansas State Historical Society* 8 (1903–1904): 72–109; James C. Malin, *Indian Policy and Westward Expansion*, Bulletin of the University of Kansas, *Humanistic Studies*, vol. 2, no. 3 (Lawrence: University of Kansas, 1921); James C. Malin, *The Nebraska Question, 1852–1854* (Ann Arbor: Edwards Brothers, 1953); Paul Wallace Gates, *Fifty Million Acres: Conflicts over Kansas Land Policy, 1854–1890* (Ithaca, N.Y.: Cornell University Press, 1954); and Miner and Unrau, *The End of Indian Kansas.*

11. *Congressional Globe*, March 3, 1853, p. 359; *U.S. Statutes at Large*, 10: 238.

12. Malin, *The Nebraska Question*, 135–37; Miner and Unrau, *The End of Indian Kansas,*7–9.

13. Ibid., 133; Thomas H. Benton to Charles E. Mix, July 2, 1853, printed in *Liberty Weekly Tribune* (Liberty, Missouri), September 16, 1853; Malin, *The Nebraska Question*, 133, 152. One western Missouri newspaper reported receiving one hundred copies of the Benton map for benefit of potential setters in Indian country; see *St. Joseph Gazette* (St. Joseph, Missouri), September 21, 1853.

14. Malin, *The Nebraska Question*, 132.

15. *Independence Reporter* (Independence, Missouri), September 7, 1853; Malin, *The Nebraska Question*, 133–34; George W. Manypenny, *Our Indian Wards* (Cincinnati: Robert Clarke, 1880; reprint, New York: Da Capo Press, 1972), 117; Gates, *Fifty Million Acres*, 21–22; *U.S. Statutes at Large* 10: 310. Since Benton's request to the Indian Office was actually addressed to Charles E. Mix, head clerk in the Indian Office, it is possible that Manypenny was unaware of the map's existence until he obtained a copy from a white "explorer" in Indian country. Certainly it was there that he first saw the Benton version; see Benton to Mix, July 2, 1853, printed in the *Liberty Weekly Tribune*, September 16, 1853.

16. Miner and Unrau, *The End of Indian Kanas*, 8–9.

17. Gates, *Fifty Million Acres*, 3,19.

18. *White Cloud Kansas Chief* (White Cloud, Kansas Territory), June 11, 1857.

19. *Weekly Western Argus* (Kansas City, Kansas Territory), June 4, 1859.

20. Printed in the *Emporia News* (Emporia, Kansas Territory), April 17, 1858.

21. *Liberty Weekly Tribune*, March 23, 1855.

22. *White Cloud Kansas Chief*, June 11, 1857.

23. William Badger to A. B. Greenwood, February 7, 1860, LROIA, RG 75, M 234, Sac and Fox Agency, R 733, NA.

24. *Western Journal of Commerce* (Kansas City, Missouri), August 23, 1860; *Emporia News*, September 1, 1860.

25. *Kansas Weekly Herald* (Leavenworth, Kansas), July 31, 1858.

26. Ferris, "The Sacs and Foxes in Franklin and Osage Counties, Kansas," 352; Francis Tymany to Charles E. Mix, November 4, June 13, and April 11, 1858, LROIA, RG 75, M 234, Sac and Fox Agency, R 733, NA; Tymany to James W. Denver, February, 28, 1859, ibid., R 734.

27. In 1855 Kansas Attorney General Andrew J. Isaacs advised the Treasury Department that he was dismissing two suits for selling liquor to Indians on grounds that the indictments had been filed under the Trade and Intercourse Act of 1834. Passage of the March 3, 1847, law, asserted Isaacs, had negated the original indictments on grounds that, contrary to the 1834 law, the 1847 enactment authorized prison sentences for convicted defendants. See Isaacs to Solicitor of the Treasury, July 1, 1855, Letters Received from U.S. Attorneys, Clerks of Courts, and Marshalls, United States District Attorney Reports-Returns, Records of the Solicitor of the Treasury, RG 206, Entry 42, Box 33, NA.

28. *Statutes of the Territory of Kansas* (1855), 417–19.

29. George F. Ruxton, *Life in the Far West* (Edinburgh: William Blackwood and Sons,1868), 28.

30. Boxes 8–20, Criminal Case Files, U.S. District Court, Kansas Territory, 1855–1860, Archives Division, Kansas State Historical Society.

31. *Emporia News*, February 25, 1860; *Kansas State Record* (Topeka, Kansas), November 12, 1862.

32. Maxwell McCaslin to Alexander Cumming, July 22, 1855, LROIA, RG 75, M 234, Osage River Agency, R 645, NA; George Manypenny to Thomas S. Drew, February 5, 1855, LSOIA, RG 75, M 21, R 50, NA.

33. *Congressional Globe*, February 12, 1855, 703. For an analysis of the so-called "Indian Ring" in Kansas Territory, which at minimum involved those in control in the Indian Office in Washington and in Indian country, opinion leaders in Congress, the agent of the particular tribe involved, businessmen and attorneys who stood to benefit from a certain set of actions, and at least a part of the tribal leadership, see Miner and Unrau, *The End of Indian Kansas*, 55–80.

34. RCIA, 1854, 18.

35. *U.S. Statutes at Large*, 10: 310. Under the Pre-Emption Act of 1841 only *surveyed* lands of the public domain were open to preemption rights. Kansas Territorial Governor Andrew H. Reeder went further by insisting in 1855 that "the act of 1841, being generally applicable to all the public lands wheresoever situate, did not need the act of 1854 to extend it to this territory"; see Reeder to B. H. Twombly, January 22, 1855, "Governor Reeder's Administration," *Transactions of the Kansas State Historical Society* 5 (1896): 167.

36. RCIA, 1854, 218.

37. Kappler, *Treaties*, 608–46.

38. Ibid., 193, 312, 556, 589, 592.

39. Ibid., 610.

40. Ibid., 616–17.

41. Ibid., 641–46.

42. R. Campbell and Baptiste Peoria to Commissioner of Indian Affairs, October 28, 1854, LROIA, RG 75, M 234, Osage River Agency, R 644, NA.

43. Kappler, *Treaties*, 800–803.

44. John Montgomery to Alexander Cumming, August 31, 1855, LROIA, RG 75, M 234, Kansas Agency, R 364, NA.

45. *White Cloud Kansas Chief*, December 23, 1859.

46. One immigrant guide to Kansas Territory advised potential settlers to have copies of Indian treaties with them so that they could "squat intelligently." Another expressed doubt that the government would prohibit squatters from securing titles to Indian trust lands by selling them at public auction; see Gates, *Fifty Million Acres*, 23–24.

47. *Western Journal of Commerce*, September 15, 1859.

7. The Demise of *Locus in Quo*

1. In 1856 the Osage River agent reported that "the temperance movement which promised so healthily a reformation in point of morality and general well being has since failed with many of the tribes"; M. McCaslin to Alexander Cumming, September 12, 1856, RCIA, 1856, 123. A year later, the marshall of the Cherokee Cold Water Army—a native detachment empowered to enforce the federal liquor code—advised the Indian Office, "The laws against the sale of intoxicating liquors are good. It is a matter of surprise, however, that they are so frequently evaded. Still, among us, the popular sentiment is in favor of temperance; the *theory* is good, but we would like it better carried out in *practice*"; D. D. Hitchcock to George Butler, September 14, 1857, ibid., 1857, 213. The Ottawa tribe made some progress toward temperance in the 1850s, but on the very day their 1862 treaty went into effect and provided new funds from tribal land sales they, like their Sac and Fox neighbors, "began to relapse into old habits of drunkenness and laziness with very few exceptions. All their money and lands are gone from them by waste and prodigality," lamented their agent, "and they now are a squandering people"; J. Jones to Secretary of the Interior, March 11, 1872, LROIA, RG 75, M 234, Ottawa Agency, R 658, NA. The Kansas agent reported, "I am willing to admit that about one-half [of their annuities] is expended for flour, bacon, sugar, and coffee . . . whilst at almost every side and corner of the Indian reservations are the little whiskey shops, supplied,

open, and ready to catch the remaining half of their money, *which they never fail to do*"; John Montgomery to John Haverty, September 26, 1857, *RCIA*, 1857, 187. And from distant New Mexico, the Taos agent reported that intoxicated Indians "are daily witnessed in a state of intoxication in our plaza. . . . Both the Apaches and Pueblos in this agency will part with everything they have to gratify their appetites for whiskey"; Christopher Carson to J. L. Collins, ibid., 1860, 164.

2. Robert Smith Bader, *Prohibition in Kansas: A History* (Lawrence: University Press of Kansas, 1986), 13–14, 18–19.

3. In 1857 the Indian Office was advised that Kansas Attorney General Andrew J. Isaacs supplemented monetary bribes with alcohol while negotiating personal land transactions with the Delawares, and prior to his appointment as Sac and Fox agent in 1859, Perry Fuller was partner in a firm whose main business was selling whiskey to Indians. See Gottlieb F. Oehler to Commissioner of Indian Affairs, June 20, 1857, LROIA, RG 75, M 234, Delaware Agency, R 274, NA; and Miner and Unrau, *The End of Indian Kansas*, 64–65.

4. Frederickson, *The Liquor Question*, 81–82; Bader, *Prohibition in Kansas*, 20–21.

5. *General Laws of the State of Kansas in Force at the Close of the Session of the Legislature Ending March 6th, 1862, to Which Is Appended the Constitution of the United States, Treaty of Cession, Organic Act, Constitution of the State of Kansas, and the Act of Admission* (Topeka: J. H. Bennet, State Printer, 1862), 601.

6. Bader, *Prohibition in Kansas*, 22. One government agent reported in 1857 that "as the Territory of Kansas becomes populated, drunkenness and other vices become more prevalent"; John Montgomery to John Haverty, Superintendent of Indian Affairs, *RCIA*, 1857, 186.

7. *United States v. Rogers*, 4 How. 567 (1846). In this case the court ruled that an adult white man did not become an Indian even though he had been adopted by the Cherokee tribe.

8. Felix S. Cohen, *Handbook of Federal Indian Law* (1941; reprint, Buffalo, N.Y.: William S. Hein, 1988), 2. For a general discussion of the problem of Indian identity, see William E. Hagan, "Full Blood, Mixed Blood, Generic, and Ersatz: The Problem of Indian Identity," *Arizona and the West* 27 (Winter 1985): 309–26.

9. Kappler, *Treaties*, 534–37, 587–88, 1048.

10. Frederickson, *The Liquor Question*, 17; Thomas Mosley to Colonel D. D. Mitchell, September 4, 1850, *RCIA*, 1850, 34; George W. Manypenny to Secretary of the Interior, November 26, 1853, ibid., 1853, 7.

11. Kappler, *Treaties*, 677–81.

12. William Gay to A. Cumming, May 3, 1856, enclosing Andrew J. Isaacs to William Gay, n.d., 1856; Report (unsigned) to Commissioner of Indian

Affairs, June 9, 1857, LROIA, RG 75, M 234, Shawnee Agency, R 809, NA; Miner and Unrau, *The End of Indian Kansas*, 59–60.

13. Kappler, *Treaties*, 677–78.

14. Ibid., 960, 963.

15. Ibid., 825, 830, 836.

16. William Murphy to Superintendent of Indian Affairs, January 20, 1860, LROIA, RG 75, M 234, Potawatomi Agency, R 682, NA; *Wyandotte County and Kansas City, Kansas* (Chicago: The Goodspeed Company, 1890), 254–55.

17. *Western Journal of Commerce*, December 5, 1863.

18. James B. Abbot to William B. Dole, Commissioner of Indian Affairs, April 10, 1862, LROIA, RG 75, M 234, Shawnee Agency, R 812, NA.

19. Kappler, *Treaties*, 960–62.

20. James B. Abbot to H. B. Branch, September 15, 1862, *RCIA*, 1962, 112.

21. The Revised Army Regulations issued by Secretary of War Simon Cameron on August 10, 1861, authorized a one-gill ration of whiskey per man daily, in cases of excessive fatigue or severe exposure. In practice, however, this so-called fatigue ration meant whatever a company or regimental commander wished it to mean. So widespread was the abuse that on March 19, 1862, Congress passed a joint resolution providing that officers (but not enlisted men) found guilty of "habitual drunkenness" should be immediately dismissed from the service. Included also in the act of 1862 was a stipulation prohibiting army sutlers from selling liquor, which in effect turned the lucrative military alcohol business over to the private sector; see Johnson, *The Federal Government and the Liquor Traffic*, 158–61.

22. John G. Pratt to Thomas Murphy, August 8, 1865, *RCIA*, 1865, 362.

23. In addition to continued drinking among the emigrant tribes of Kansas and the Five Civilized Tribes, and the introduction of alcohol among the Wichita and Affiliated Tribes who fled from Confederate agents in the Canadian River valley to south-central Kansas during the Civil War, headmen of the Southern Cheyennes and Arapahos complained bitterly in 1861 that traders and the military at Fort Lyon in Colorado Territory openly peddled whiskey for sexual favors that "debauched" their women. One year earlier, Christopher Carson reported that as a result of their daily associations with the Pueblos, who by a territorial statute were exempted from prosecution under federal liquor law and who thereby were enjoying substantial profits as alcohol brokers, the Apaches and other Indians of the upper Rio Grande valley could be observed in "a daily state of intoxication" at the central plaza in Taos. A lively alcohol trade was reported at Fort Leavenworth, where whiskey worth twenty cents a gallon was sold for up to five dollars a gallon to the Indians in 1862. From Fort Sully deep in Sioux country, it was reported that tribal drunkenness was on the

increase and that whiskey was unloaded there by almost every steamboat pass-ing up the Missouri River, while from Fort Larned on the upper Arkansas, Spe-cial Agent H. T. Ketcham wrote in 1865, "Exclude spirituous liquors from the posts and from this country and prohibit sutlers from trading directly or indi-rectly with the Indians and there will be no inducement for them to bring their women in for prostitution"; see Avis German, "Refugee Indians within and from the Indian Country, 1861–1867" (Master's thesis, Wichita State University, 1987), 123; Edmund Jefferson Danziger Jr., *Indians and Bureaucrats: Administer-ing the Reservation Policy during the Civil War* (Urbana: University of Illinois Press, 1974), 36; Christopher Carson to J. L. Collins, August 29, 1860, RCIA, 1860, 164; W. F. N. Army to J. L. Collins, September 1, 1862, ibid., 1862, 242–46; C. C. Hutchinson to H. B. Branch, September 17, 1862, ibid., 108; J. R. Hanson to D. N. Cooley, May 19, 1866, ibid., 1866, 166; and H. T. Ketcham to John Evans, April 4, 1865, ibid., 1864, 257.

24. Maxwell McCaslin to Superintendent of Indian Affairs, St. Louis, Sep-tember 12, 1856, ibid., 1856, 123.

25. Marshall of the Cherokee Cold Water Army to George Butler, September 14, 1857, ibid., 1857, 212–13.

26. Maxwell McCaslin to A. Cumming, September 12, 1856, ibid., 1856, 123.

27. Harry Kelsey, "William P. Dole," in *The Commissioners of Indian Affairs, 1824–1877*, ed. Robert M. Kvasnicka and Herman J. Viola (Lincoln: Univer-sity of Nebraska Press, 1979), 90–91. Danziger, *Indians and Bureaucrats*, 202–3.

28. William E. Rector to William P. Dole, September 25, 1861, RCIA, 1861, 155.

29. William P. Dole to Caleb B. Smith, November 27, 1861, ibid., 1861, 28–29.

30. See chap. 3, p. 37.

31. *Congressional Globe* (January 17, 1862), 384–85.

32. Ibid., 385.

33. Ibid., 480.

34. Ibid., 478.

35. Ibid., 481; *U.S. Statutes at Large* 12: 338–39.

36. *General Laws of the State of Kansas, in Force at the Close of the Session of the Legislature, Ending March 6th, 1862,* 601–2.

37. *Statutes of the Territory of Kansas* (Shawnee Manual Labor School: Pub-lic Printer, 1855), 417–19.

38. *Revised Statutes of Missouri, 1846* (Jefferson City: Public Printer, 1856), 682–88; Frederickson, *The Liquor Question*, 498–500.

8. Legislative Diversity and Back to the Bench

1. *Congressional Globe*, January 17, 1862, p. 384.

2. Dole to Caleb B. Smith, October 14, 1862, RCIA, 1862, 42.

3. Dole to J. P. Usher, October 31, 1863, ibid., 1863, 6, 29.

4. Potawatomi Agent L. R. Palmer to Thomas Murphy, September 17, 1866, ibid., 1866, 264.

5. Omaha Agent O. H. Irish to H. B. Branch, September 4, 1863, ibid., 1863, 241.

6. Upper Platte Agent John Loree to H. B. Branch, September 1, 1862, ibid., 1862, 131.

7. Report of a Conversation Held at General John E. Smith's Headquarters at Fort Laramie, recorded by Thos. K. Cree, clerk, June 13, 1871, ibid., 1871, 28. See also James C. Olson, *Red Cloud and the Sioux Problem* (Lincoln: University of Nebraska Press, 1965), 145.

8. H. P. Bennet to William P. Dole, January 28, 1864, RCIA, 1864, 245. In 1868 the chaplin at Fort Dodge charged post commander Major Henry E. Douglass and several of his staff with selling whiskey to the Indians. Douglass immediately resigned his commission to escape court-martial and entered the gunpowder business in New York City; see Strate, *Sentinel to the Cimarron*, 66.

9. Jesse H. Leavenworth to Dennis N. Cooley, May 8, 1866, LROIA, RG 75, M 234, Kiowa-Comanche Agency, R 375, NA.

10. In 1863, for example, the army issued eight barrels of whiskey for benefit of the Seventh Iowa Cavalry, whose task it was to construct Fort Cottonwood west of Fort Kearney. On September 18, while headed west from Omaha, it was reported that "about one-third of the boys when we started in the morning were more or less intoxicated"; see Ware, *The Indian War of 1864*, 12, 33.

11. Delo, *Peddlers and Post Traders*, 186.

12. Concurrent Resolution of the Kansas Legislature, February 5, 1868, File 40A-H 8.2, Records of the United States House of Representatives, RG 233, NA.

13. In late summer 1864 a Kansas newspaper reported: "Every evening our town is filled with drunken Indians. . . . They ride backward and forward at full speed, through our streets, threatening, cursing, whooping, and firing pistols. They even enter the stores, and places of business, and threaten and curse the inmates. Assaults have been committed on several of our citizens. . . . Some of the farmers in the neighborhood are complaining of having their stock slaughtered and stolen. Unless some changes take place soon, the citizens will be compelled to take active measures, for the protection of life and property"; see *White Cloud Kansas Chief*, September 14, 1864.

14. H. W. Farnsworth to Thomas Murphy, September 10, 1866, *RCIA*, 1866, 275.

15. D. N. Cooley to Secretary of the Interior, October 22, 1866, ibid., 51.

16. *United States v. Lorton Holliday and U.S. v. Joseph Haas*, 3 Wall. 497–20 (1865).

17. Ibid.

18. Ibid.

19. Cohen, *Handbook of Federal Indian Law*, 91.

20. *Johnson v. McIntosh*, 8 Wheat. 543 (1823).

21. *Cherokee Nation v. Georgia*, 5 Pet. 1 (1831).

22. *United States v. Ward*, 28 Fed. Cas. No. 16639 (C. C. Kan. 1863).

23. Saloons and wholesale jobbers located on the Kansa mixed-blood reservations directly across the Kansas River from Topeka served as major sources of supply for the Indians of eastern Kansas and southern Nebraska in the mid-1860s. The Antietam Saloon on mixed-blood Reservation No. Four (the future sight of North Topeka) posted sales of twenty-five hundred dollars in just five days in 1866, with most of the patrons reported as "camped out Indians"; see Unrau, *Mixed-Bloods and Tribal Dissolution*, 52.

24. *Congressional Globe* (March 19, 1866) 1491.

25. Dennis N. Cooley to James Harlan, March 19, 1866, Records (Letters Received), Office of the Secretary of Interior, Indian Division, RG 48, Box 15, NA.

26. *Congressional Globe* (March 19, 1866), 1491–92.

27. *U.S. Statutes at Large* 14: 230.

28. Johnson, *The Federal Government and the Liquor Traffic*, 162–63.

29. Douglas C. Jones, *The Treaty of Medicine Lodge* (Norman: University of Oklahoma Press, 1966), 41, 49, 52, 54.

30. Miner and Unrau, *The End of Indian Kansas*, 124.

31. R. S. Stevens to D. Stewart, April 15, 1871; E. C. Baufield, Solicitor of the Treasury, to J. H. Huckleberry, October 18, 1871; Attorney General of the United States to C. Delano, Secretary of the Interior, April 10, 1872; George H. Williams, Attorney General for the United States to Logan A. Roots, U.S. Marshall for the Western District of Arkansas, April 1, 1872; and Report of the Special Liquor Commission, by Henry E. Alvord, October, n.d., 1872, LROIA, RG 75, M 234, Central Superintendency, R 60, NA.

32. W. R. Irwin to Commissioner of Indian Affairs, November 3, 1866, LROIA, RG 75, M 234, Upper Arkansas Agency, R 880, NA.

33. J. Hayden to Headquarters, Department of Kansas, May 14, 1862, *The War of the Rebellion*, 382; Jesse H. Leavenworth to Dennis N. Cooley, May 8, 1866, LROIA, RG 75, M 234, Kiowa-Comanche Agency, R 375, NA.

34. N. G. Taylor to O. H. Browning, November 23, 1868, *RCIA*, 1868, 21. An example of the increasing popularity of beer among the military and Indians was the large brewery established in the late 1860s by former Fort Larned sutler Theodore Weichselbaum at Ogden, near Fort Riley. In his reminiscences Weichselbaum recalled selling up to one thousand dollars worth of beer per month to the Indians and military forts of western Kansas; see "Statement of Theodore Weichselbaum, of Ogden, Riley County, July 17, 1908," *Collections of the Kansas State Historical Society* 11 (1909–1910): 568–69.

35. Vincent Colyer, Secretary, Board of Indian Commissioners to Honorable Columbus Delano, Secretary of the Interior, December 12, 1871, *RCIA*, 1871, 17.

36. *Congressional Record*, May 4, 1874, 3580.

37. Edwin P. Smith to Secretary of the Interior, March 5, 1874, and Columbus Delano to Speaker of the House of Representatives, March 9, 1874, U.S. Congress, House, *Penalty for Selling Liquor to Indians*, 45th Cong., 1st sess., March 11, 1874, H. Exec. Doc. 177, serial 1610, 1–2.

38. *Revised Statutes of the United States, Passed at the First Session of the Forty-Third Congress, 1873–'74* (Washington, D.C.: Government Printing Office, 1875), 375. In addition, Section 2141 of the 1874 *Statutes* held that "every person who shall, within the Indian country, set up or continue any distillery for manufacturing ardent spirits, shall be liable to a penalty of one thousand dollars; and the Superintendent of Indian Affairs, Indian Agent, or Sub-Agent, within the limits of whose agency any distillery of ardent spirits is set up or continued, shall forthwith destroy and break up same"; ibid., 375–76.

39. *The United States Biographical Dictionary*, Kansas volume (Chicago: S. Lesis and Co., 1879), 878–79.

40. *United States v. Downing*, Fed. Cas. no.14-903 (Kansas 1876), 3 *Central Law Journal*: 383.

41. Ibid.

42. Ibid.

43. Ibid.

44. *Supplement to the Revised Statutes of the United States*, vol. 1, Legislation of 1874–1881, the 43rd, 44th, 45th, and 46th Congresses, prepared and edited by William A. Richardson (Washington, D.C.: Government Printing Office, 1881), 269. In a letter to the Indian Office in Washington, Central Superintendent William Nicholson stated that statutory revision was the result of "inadvertence or otherwise," but a more reasonable explanation is that the federal alcohol statute was revised to conform with Judge Foster's ruling in *Downing*, which was issued a few months earlier; see Nicholson to John Q. Smith, September 26, 1876, *Eighth Annual Report of the Agents of the Central Superintendency*

(Lawrence, Kans.: Republican Steam Printing Establishment, 1876), RG 75, NA.

45. John Q. Smith, "Recommended Legislation," n.d., 1876, *RCIA*, 1876, 24.

46. William Nicholson to John Q. Smith, September 25, 1876, *Eighth Annual Report of the Agents of the Central Superintendency*.

47. *Bates v. Clark*, 95 U.S. 204 (1877).

48. Ibid.

49. *U.S. Statutes at Large* 27: 794–96.

50. William Nicholson to John Q. Smith, September 25, 1876, *Eighth Annual Report of the Agents of the Central Superintendency*, 30.

51. Bader, *Prohibition in Kansas*, 85.

52. Rorabaugh, *The Alcoholic Republic*, Table A1.2., p. 233

53. *Supplement to the Revised Statutes*, Legislation of 1874–1881, p. 269.

54. Francis Paul Prucha, *American Indian Policy in Crisis: Christian Reformers and the Indian, 1865–1900* (Norman: University of Oklahoma Press, 1976), 222.

55. *U.S. Statutes at Large* 27: 260.

56. *U.S. Statutes at Large* 29: 506.

57. In *U.S. v. Rickert*, 188 U.S. 437 (1903), and *Tiger v. Western Investment Co.*, 221 U.S. 286 (1911), the Supreme Court upheld the property and guardianship restrictions under the Dawes Act.

58. Frederick E. Hoxie, *A Final Promise: The Campaign to Assimilate the Indians, 1880–1920* (Lincoln: University of Nebraska Press, 1984), 219.

59. *Matter of Heff*, 197 U.S. 488 (1905).

60. *Hallowell v. U.S.*, 221 U.S. 381 (1911).

61. *U.S. v. Nice*, 241 U.S. 591 (1916).

62. See, for example, the tragic consequences of the bootlegger business on the Osage reservation in the early twentieth century, as carefully documented in Terry P. Wilson, *The Underground Reservation: Osage Oil* (Lincoln: University of Nebraska Press, 1985), 64–66, 70–71, 133–34.

63. William Nicholson to John Q. Smith, September 25, 1876, *Eighth Annual Report of the Agents of the Central Superintendency*, 30.

64. Sheehan, *Seeds of Extinction*, 278.

65. William Nicholson to John Q. Smith, September 25, 1876, *Eighth Annual Report of the Agents of the Central Superintendency*, 30.

66. *U.S. Statutes at Large* 67: 586–87. This law allowed off-reservation liquor sales to Indians and reservation sales on a local option basis.

67. Lurie, "The World's Oldest On-Going Protest Demonstration," 315. Lurie's "protest" hypothesis appears to conform well with the situation on the Potawatomi reservation in the summer of 1868. "Last fall," reported Central

Superintendent Thomas Murphy, "I paid the Pottawatomies their annuities for the third and fourth quarters of 1867. Not a single drunken Indian was to be seen at that payment. On the 11th last, I went to pay them for the first and second quarters of 1868. Over two-thirds of the Indians present at this payment—among them some of their principal chiefs—got beastly intoxicated on the first night after my arrival. Father Diehl, the missionary, said the cause of their conduct was due to the non-ratification of the treaty"; Thomas Murphy to N. G. Taylor, Commissioner of Indian Affairs, June 23, 1868, *RCIA*, 1868, 59–60.

9. Epilogue

1. MacAndrew and Edgerton, *Drunken Comportment*, 100.

2. Gerald Vizenor, *Crossbloods, Bone Courts, Bingo, and Other Reports* (Minneapolis: University of Minnesota Press, 1976), 306; Thorton, *American Indian Holocaust*, 170; Michael Dorris, *The Broken Cord* (New York: Harper & Row, 1989).

3. Richard White, *The Middle Ground: Indians, Empires, and Republics in the Great Lakes Region, 1650–1815* (Cambridge: Cambridge University Press, 1991), x, xiv. For the "accommodation" thesis applied, with some variation, to a specific Indian group in more recent years, see Melissa L. Meyer, *The White Earth Tragedy: Ethnicity and Dispossession at a Minnesota Anishiaabe Reservation, 1889–1920* (Lincoln: University of Nebraska Press, 1994).

4. White, *The Middle Ground*, 334, 498–517.

5. Lewis O. Saum, *The Fur Trader and the Indian* (Seattle: University of Washington Press, 1965), 168–69.

6. Ibid., 213–14.

7. James Axtell, *The European and the Indian: Essays in the Ethnohistory of Colonial North America* (New York: Oxford University Press, 1981), 98.

8. Kappler, *Treaties*, 222–25; 552–54; 800–803.

9. Unrau, *The Kansa Indians*, 215.

10. Frederickson, *The Liquor Question*, 3, 22; Barry, *Beginning of the West*, 357, 534, 1060; P. L. Chouteau to Lewis Cass, September 19, 1832, LROIA, RG 75, M 234, Osage Agency, R 631, NA; Charles Handy to D. D. Mitchell, September 6, 1850, *RCIA*, 1850, 26; Thomas Murphy to N. G. Taylor, July 29, 1867, LROIA, RG 75, M 234, Kansas Agency, R 637, NA; *Emporia News* (Emporia, Kansas Territory), November 13, 1858; *Kansas Press* (Council Grove, Kansas), October 10, 1859; and William E. Unrau, "The Depopulation of the Dheghia-Siouan Kansas Prior to Removal," *New Mexico Historical Review* 48 (October 1973): 323.

11. Unrau, "The Depopulation of the Dheghia-Siouan Kansas," 316–24.

12. Westermeyer, " 'The Drunken Indian,' " 22.

13. Joseph Westermeyer, "Options Regarding Alcohol Use among the Chippewa," *American Journal of Orthopsychiatry* 43 (1972): 398–403; Westermeyer, " 'The Drunken Indian,' " 22; P .H. Wolff, "Vasomotor Sensitivity to Alcohol in Diverse Mongoloid Populations," *Human Genetics*, 25 (1973): 193–99.

14. Lurie, "The World's Oldest On-Going Protest Demonstration," 315.

15. *Congressional Globe*, January 17, 1862, 480.

16. MacAndrew and Edgerton, *Drunken Comportment*, 136.

17. Special Agent H. T. Ketcham to John Evans, April 4, 1864, LROIA, RG 75, M 234, Colorado Superintendency, R 197, NA.

18. Rev. William H. Goode, *Outposts of Zion, with Limnings of Mission Life* (Cincinnati: Poe & Hitchcock, 1864), 58.

BIBLIOGRAPHY

Manuscripts

National Archives, Washington, D.C.
RG 46, Records of the United States Senate
    Committee on Indian Affairs, Files 19A-D7, 20A-D6, 24A-D7
RG 48, Records of the Secretary of the Interior, Indian Division, Box 15
RG 75, Letters Received by the Office of Indians Affairs (M 234)
    Central Superintendency
    Colorado Superintendency
    Delaware Agency
    Documents Relating to the Negotiation of Ratified and Unratified Treaties,
        Treaties, T 494
    Fort Leavenworth Agency
    Kansas Agency
    Kiowa-Comanche Agency
    Miami Agency
    Osage Agency
    Osage River Agency
    Osage Subagency
    Ottawa Agency
    Potawatomi Agency
    Sauk and Fox Agency
    Shawnee Agency
    St. Louis Superintendency
    Upper Arkansas Agency
    Western Superintendency
    Wyandot Agency
RG 75, Letters Sent by the Office of Indian Affairs (M 21)
RG 206, Records of the Solicitor of the Treasury of the United States
    Letters Received from United States Attorneys, Clerks of Courts, and Mar-
        shalls, Entry 42
    United States District Attorney Reports-Returns, Entry 145

RG 233, Records of the United States House of Representatives File 40 A-H
    8.2

National Archives II, College Park, Md.
RG 11, General Records of the United States Government, Mapa de los Estados
    Unidos de Mejico, Secretary File
RG 77, Records of the Office of Chief of Engineers, Map of the Nebraska and
    Kansas Territories. Showing the Location of Indian Reserves, According
    to Treaties of 1854. Compiled by S. Eastman, Captain, U.S.A. 1854,

Federal Records Center, Kansas City, Mo.
RG 21, Records of the District Courts of the United States
    District of Missouri, Complete and Final Returns, United States Circuit
    Court

Kansas City Public Library, Kansas City, Mo.
Department of Special Collections
    Kansas City Biographies, Native Sons Collection (microfilm)

Kansas State Historical Society, Topeka, Kans.
Archives Division
    Criminal Case Files, United States District Court, Kansas Territory, 1855–
    1860, Boxes 8-20
Manuscript Division
    George H. Brown Papers
    August W. Burton Papers
    Isaac McCoy Papers (microfilm)
    Jotham Meeker Journal

Missouri Historical Society, St. Louis, Mo.
Manuscript Division
    Chouteau Family Papers
    George C. Sibley Papers

Private Collection
Private Collection of Michael Heaston, Austin, Texas
    Memorial of the Chiefs, & Members of the General Council, of the Choctaw
    and Chickasaw Districts, to the Honorable, The Senate and House of
    Representatives of the State of Texas in Legislature Assembled, Novem-
    ber 9, 1851

Published Government Documents

American State Papers: Indian Affairs, 2 vols.

Congressional Globe.

Congressional Record.

Eighth Annual Report of the Agents of the Central Superintendency. Lawrence, Kans.: Republican Steam Printing Establishment, 1876.

General Laws of the State of Kansas in Force at the Close of the Session of the Legislature Ending March 6th, 1862, to Which Is Appended the Constitution of the United States, Treaty of Cession, Organic Act, Constitution of the State of Kansas, and the Act of Admission. Topeka, Kans.: J. H. Bennet, State Printer, 1862.

Indian Affairs: Laws and Treaties. Compiled by Charles J. Kappler. 5 vols. *Treaties*, vol. 2. Washington, D.C.: Government Printing Office, 1904.

Indian Land Cessions in the United States. Eighth Annual Report of the Bureau of American Ethnology (1896–1897), pt. 2. Compiled by Charles C. Royce. Washington, D.C.: Government Printing Office, 1899.

Register of Debates in Congress.

"Report on Barracks and Hospitals." *Report of the Surgeon General of the United States for 1868*. Washington, D.C.: Government Printing Office, 1870.

"Report on the Hygiene of the United States Army." *Report of the Surgeon General of the United States for 1875*. Washington, D.C.: Government Printing Office, 1875.

Reports of the Commissioner of Indian Affairs (Annual).

Revised Statutes of Missouri, 1846. Jefferson City: Public Printer, 1856.

Revised Statutes of the United States, Passed at the First Session of the Forty-Third Congress, 1874–74. Washington, D.C.: Government Printing Office, 1875.

Statutes of the Territory of Kansas. Shawnee Manual Labor School: Public Printer, 1856.

Supplement to the Revised Statutes of the United States. Vol. 1. Legislation of 1874–1881, the 43rd, 44th, 45th, and 46th Congresses. Prepared and edited by William A. Richardson. Washington, D.C.: Goverment Printing Office, 1881.

The War of the Rebellion: A Compilation of the Official Records of the Union and Confederate Armies. Three Series, 128 vols. Series 1, vol. 13. Washington, D.C.: Government Printing Office, 1880–1901.

U.S. Congress. House. 23d Cong., 1st sess., May 20, 1834. H. R. 464. Serial 263.

———. *Spirituous Liquors to the Army. Letter from the Secretary of War, in Reply to a Resolution of the House of Representatives Inquiring What Beneficial Effects, If Any, Have Arisen from the Daily Use of Spirituous Liquors by the Army, &c. &c*. 20th Cong., 2d sess., February 3, 1829. H. Doc. 103. Serial 186.

U.S. Congress. Senate. *Report of the Secretary of War in Compliance with a Resolution of the Senate, Documents in Relation to the Difficulties Which Took Place at the Payment of the Sac and Fox Annuities Last Fall.* 30th Cong., 1st sess., August 9, 1848. *S. Exec. Doc. 70.* Serial 510.

———. *United States Subsistence Department, The Indian Removals, Furnished in Answer to a Resolution of the Senate of 27th December, 1833, by the Commissary of General Subsistence. S. Doc. 512,* vol. 1. Serial 244.

U.S. *Statutes at Large.*

Newspapers

Council Grove Press (Council Grove, Kansas)
Emporia News (Emporia, Kansas Territory)
Independence Reporter (Independence, Missouri)
Kansas Press (Council Grove, Kansas Territory)
Kansas State Record (Topeka)
Kansas Weekly Herald (Leavenworth, Kansas)
Liberty Weekly Tribune (Liberty, Missouri)
Missouri Democrat (St. Louis)
Missouri Gazette (St. Louis)
Smoky Hill and Republican Union (Junction City, Kansas)
St. Joseph Gazette (St. Joseph, Missouri)
Weekly Western Argus (Kansas City, Kansas Territory)
Western Journal of Commerce (Kansas City, Missouri)
White Cloud Kansas Chief (White Cloud, Kansas Territory)
Wichita Eagle (Wichita)

Court Cases

Bates v. Clark, 95 U.S. 204.
Cherokee Nation v. Georgia, 5 Pet. 1.
Hallowell v. United States, 221 U.S. 381.
John Brown and Jane Brown v. Adel (Clement) Belmarde, 3 Kan. 35.
Johnson v. McIntosh, 8 Wheat. 543.
McCracken v. Todd, 1 Kan. 146.
Matter of Heff, 197 U.S. 488.
Sundry Goods, Wares, and Merchandises v. United States, 2 Pet. 257.
Tiger v. Western Investment Co., 221 U.S. 286.
United States v. Alexander Culbertson, United States Circuit Court for the Dis-

trict of Missouri, April (1848) Term, LROIA, RG 75, M 234, St. Louis Superintendency, R 755, NA.

United States v. Cisna, 25 Fed. Cas. No. 14795 (C. C. Ohio 1835).

United States v. Downing, Fed. Cas. No. 14-903 (Kan. 1876), *Central Law Journal*, 383.

United States v. Lorton Holliday and United States v. Joseph Haas, 3 Wall. 497.

United States v. Nice, 241 U.S. 591.

United States v. Rickert, 188 U.S. 437.

United States v. Rogers, 4 How. 567.

United States v. See See Sah Mah & Eschatiah (1850), Records of the District Courts of the United States, District of Missouri, Circuit Court, vol. 4 (1845–1853), RG 21, Federal Records Center, Kansas City, Mo.

United States v. Ward, 28 Fed. Cas. No. 16639 (C. C. Kan. 1863).

Books

Adams, J. G., and E. H. Chapin, eds. *The Temperance Fountain, or, Jettings from the Town Pump.* New York: H. Dayton, Publisher, 1860.

Anson, Bert. *The Miami Indians.* Norman: University of Oklahoma Press, 1970.

Axtell, James. *The European and the Indian: Essays in the Ethnohistory of Colonial North America.* New York: Oxford University Press, 1981.

Bader, Robert Smith. *Prohibition in Kansas: A History.* Lawrence: University Press of Kansas, 1986.

Barry, Louise. *The Beginning of the West: Annals of the Kansas Gateway to the American West, 1540–1854.* Topeka: Kansas State Historical Society, 1972.

Brown, A. Theodore. *Frontier Community: Kansas City to 1870.* Columbia: University of Missouri Press, 1963.

Case, Theodore S. *History of Kansas City, Missouri.* Syracuse, N.Y.: D. Mason, 1888.

Chalphant, William Y. *Dangerous Passage: The Santa Fe Trail and the Mexican War.* Norman: University of Oklahoma Press, 1994.

Chittenden, Hiram Martin, and Alfred Talbot Richardson, eds. *Life, Letters, and Travels of Father Pierre-Jean DeSmet, S.J.* Vol. 1. New York: Francis P. Harper, 1905.

Clark, Norman H. *Deliver Us from Evil: An Interpretation of American Prohibition.* New York: W. W. Norton, 1976.

Clifton, James A. *The Prairie People: Continuity and Change in Potawatomi Indian Culture, 1665–1965.* Lawrence: Regents Press of Kansas, 1977.

Cobbett, William. *A Year's Residence in the United States of America, Treating of the Face of the Country, the Climate, the Soil, the Products, the Mode of Cul-*

tivating the Land, the Prices of Land, of Labour, of Food, of Raiment; of the Expenses of Housekeeping, and of the Usual Manner of Living; of the Manners and Customs of the People; and of the Institutions of the Country, Civil, Political and Religious. Carbondale: Southern Illinois University Press, 1964.

Cohen, Felix S. *Handbook of Federal Indian Law.* 1941. Reprint, Buffalo, N.Y.: William S. Hein, 1988.

Danziger, Edmund Jefferson, Jr. *Indians and Bureaucrats: Administering the Reservation Policy during the Civil War.* Urbana: University of Illinois Press, 1974.

Deatherage, Charles P. *Early History of Greater Kansas City Missouri and Kansas.* Vol. 1. Kansas City: Charles P. Deatherage, 1927.

Delo, David Michael. *Peddlers and Post Traders: The Army Sutler on the Frontier.* Salt Lake City: University of Utah Press, 1992.

DeRosier, Arthur H., Jr. *The Removal of the Choctaw Indians.* Knoxville: University of Tennessee Press, 1970.

Dorris, Michael. *The Broken Cord.* New York: Harper & Row, 1989.

Downard, William L. *Dictionary of the History of the American Brewing and Distilling Industry.* Westport, Conn.: Greenwood Press, 1980.

Edmunds, R. David. *The Potawatomis.* Norman: University of Oklahoma Press, 1978.

Epstein, Barbara L. *The Politics of Domesticity: Women, Evangelism and Temperance in Nineteenth-Century America.* Middletown, Conn.: Wesleyan University Press, 1981.

Foley, William E., and C. David Rice. *The First Chouteaus: River Barons of Early St. Louis.* Urbana: University of Illinois Press, 1983.

Frederickson, Otto Frovin. *The Liquor Question among the Indian Tribes in Kansas, 1804–1881.* Bulletin of the University of Kansas, Humanistic Studies. Vol. 4, no. 4. Lawrence: University of Kansas, 1932.

Gates, Paul Wallace. *Fifty Million Acres: Conflicts over Kansas Land Policy, 1854–1890.* Ithaca, N.Y.: Cornell University Press, 1954.

Goetzmann, William H. *Exploration and Empire: The Explorer and Scientist in the Winning of the American West.* New York: Alfred A. Knopf, 1966.

Goode, Rev. William H. *Outposts of Zion, with Limnings of Mission Life.* Cincinnati, Ohio: Poe & Hitchcock, 1864.

Goodrich, Thomas. *Bloody Dawn: The Story of the Lawrence Massacre.* Kent, Ohio: Kent State University Press, 1991.

Hagan, William T. *The Sac and Fox Indians.* Norman: University of Oklahoma Press, 1958.

Herring, Joseph B. *Kenekuk, the Kickapoo Prophet.* Lawrence: University Press of Kansas, 1988.

Hill, Edward H. *The Office of Indian Affairs, 1824–1880: Historical Sketches.* New York: Clearwater, 1974.

History of Clay and Platte Counties. St. Louis: National Historical Company, 1885.

Hoxie, Frederick E. *A Final Promise: The Campaign to Assimilate the Indians, 1880–1920.* Lincoln: University of Nebraska Press, 1984.

Hunt, Elvid. *History of Fort Leavenworth, 1827–1927.* Fort Leavenworth, Kans.: General Services Press, 1927.

Jacobs, Wilbur R. *Diplomacy and Indian Gifts: Anglo-French Rivalry along the Ohio and Northwestern Frontiers.* Palo Alto, Calif.: Stanford University Press, 1950.

————. *Dispossessing the American Indian: Indians and Whites on the Colonial Frontier.* New York: Charles Scribner's Sons, 1972.

James' Account of S. H. Long's Expedition, 1819–1820. Part 2, *Early Western Travels, 1748–1846.* Vol. 15. Ed. Reuben Gold Thwaites. Cleveland: Arthur H. Clark, 1905.

Jennings, Francis. *The Invasion of America: Indians, Colonialism, and the Cant of Conquest.* New York: W. W. Norton, 1976.

Johnson, William E. *The Federal Government and the Liquor Traffic.* Rev. ed. Westerville, Ohio: American Issue Publishing Company, 1917.

Kawashima, Yasuhide. *Puritan Justice and the Indian: White Man's Laws in Massachusetts, 1630–1763.* Middletown, Conn.: Wesleyan University Press, 1986.

Krout, John A. *The Origins of Prohibition.* New York: Alfred A. Knopf, 1925.

Leader, Mark Edward, and James Kirby Martin. *Drinking in America: A History.* New York: Free Press, 1982.

Lealand, Joy. *Firewater Myths: North American Indian Drinking and Alcohol Addiction.* New Brunswick, N.J.: Rutgers Center for Alcohol Studies, 1976.

MacAndrew, Craig, and Robert B. Edgerton. *Drunken Comportment: A Social Explanation.* New York: Aldine, 1969.

Malin, James C. *Indian Policy and Westward Expansion.* Bulletin of the University of Kansas, Humanistic Studies. Vol. 2, no. 3. Lawrence: University of Kansas, 1921.

————. *The Nebraska Question, 1852–1854.* Ann Arbor, Mich.: Edwards Brothers, 1953.

Mancall, Peter C. *Deadly Medicine: Indians and Alcohol in Early America.* Ithaca, N.Y.: Cornell University Press, 1995.

Manypenny, George W. *Our Indian Wards.* Cincinnati: Robert Clarke, 1880. Reprint. New York: Da Capo Press, 1972.

McCandless, Perry. *A History of Missouri.* Vol. 2. Columbia: University of Missouri Press, 1972.

McCoy, Isaac. *History of Baptist Indian Missions: Embracing Remarks on the Former and Present Condition of the Aboriginal Tribes: Their Former Settlement Within the Indian Territory, and Their Future Prospects*. Washington, D.C.: Wm. M. Morrison, 1840.

McKenney, Thomas L. *Sketches of a Tour to the Lakes, of the Character and Customs of the Chippeway Indians, and of Incidents with the Treaty of Fond Du Lac*. Baltimore: Fielding Lucas, 1827.

Meyer, Melissa L. *The White Earth Tragedy: Ethnicity and Dispossession at a Minnesota Anishiaabe Reservation, 1889–1920*. Lincoln: University of Nebraska Press, 1994.

Miller, William E. *History of Jackson County*. Kansas City, Mo.: Birdsall & Williams, 1881.

Miner, Craig, and William E. Unrau. *The End of Indian Kansas: A Study of Cultural Revolution, 1854–1871*. Lawrence: University Press of Kansas, 1978.

Nuttall, Thomas. *A Journal of Travels into the Arkansas Territory during the Year 1819*. Ed. Savoie Lottinville. Norman: University of Oklahoma Press, 1979.

Oglesby, Richard E. *Manuel Lisa and the Opening of the Missouri Fur Trade*. Norman: University of Oklahoma Press, 1963.

Olson, James C. *Red Cloud and the Sioux Problem*. Lincoln: University of Nebraska Press, 1965.

Original Journals of the Lewis and Clark Expedition, 1804–1806. Vol. 1. Ed. Reuben Gold Thwaites. New York: Arno Press, 1969.

Phillips, Paul Chrisler. *The Fur Trade*. Vol. 1. Norman: University of Oklahoma Press, 1961.

Prucha, Francis Paul. *American Indian Policy in Crisis: Christian Reformers and the Indian, 1865–1900*. Norman: University of Oklahoma Press, 1976.

————. *American Indian Policy in the Formative Years: The Indian Trade and Intercourse Acts, 1790–1834*. Cambridge, Mass.: Harvard University Press, 1962.

————. *The Great Father: The United States Government and the American Indians*. 2 vols. Lincoln: University of Nebraska Press, 1984.

Ronda, James P. *Lewis and Clark among the Indians*. Lincoln: University of Nebraska Press, 1984.

Rorabaugh, W. J. *The Alcoholic Republic: An American Tradition*. New York: Oxford University Press, 1979.

Ruxton, George F. *Life in the Far West*. Edinburgh: William Blackwood and Sons, 1868.

Saum, Lewis, O. *The Fur Trader and the Indian*. Seattle: University of Washington Press, 1965.

Schultz, George A. *An Indian Canaan: Isaac McCoy and the Vision of an Indian State*. Norman: University of Oklahoma Press, 1972.

Sheehan, Bernard W. *Seeds of Extinction: Jeffersonian Philanthropy and the American Indian.* Chapel Hill: University of North Carolina Press, 1973.

Strate, David K. *Sentinel to the Cimarron: The Frontier Experience of Fort Dodge, Kansas.* Dodge City, Kans.: Cultural Heritage and Arts Center, 1970.

Sunder, John E. *The Fur Trade on the Upper Missouri, 1840–1865.* Norman: University of Oklahoma Press, 1965.

Thorton, Russell. *American Indian Holocaust and Survival: A Population History since 1492.* Norman: University of Oklahoma Press, 1987.

Tyrrell, Ian R. *Sobering Up: From Temperance to Prohibition in Antebellum America.* Westport, Conn.: Greenwood Press, 1979.

Unrau, William E. *The Kansa Indians: A History of the Wind People, 1673–1873.* Norman: University of Oklahoma Press, 1971.

_____ . *Mixed-Bloods and Tribal Dissolution: Charles Curtis and the Quest for Indian Identity.* Lawrence: University Press of Kansas, 1989.

_____ . ed., *Tending the Talking Wire: A Buck Soldier's View of Indian Country, 1863–1866.* Salt Lake City: University of Utah Press, 1979.

Unrau, William E., and H. Craig Miner. *Tribal Dispossession and the Ottawa Indian University Fraud.* Norman: University of Oklahoma Press, 1985.

Van Meter, Sondra. *Marion County Kansas: Past and Present.* Marion, Kans.: Marion County Historical Society, 1972.

Viola, Herman J. *Thomas L. McKenney, Architect of America's Early Indian Policy: 1816–1830.* Chicago: Swallow Press, 1974.

Vizenor, Gerald. *Crossbloods: Bone Courts, Bingo, and Other Reports.* Minneapolis: University of Minnesota Press, 1976.

Ware, Captain Eugene F. *The Indian War of 1864.* Introduction and notes by Clyde C. Walton. Topeka, Kans.: Crane and Company, 1911. Reprint, Lincoln: University of Nebraska Press, 1960.

Weber, David J. *The Taos Trappers: The Fur Trade in the Far Southwest, 1540–1846.* Norman: University of Oklahoma Press, 1971.

Wedel, Waldo R., ed. *The Dunbar-Allis Letters on the Pawnee.* New York: Garland, 1985.

Weslager, C. S. *The Delaware Indians: A History.* New Brunswick, N.J.: Rutgers University Press, 1972.

White, Richard. *The Middle Ground: Indians, Empires, and Republics in the Great Lakes Region, 1650–1815.* Cambridge: Cambridge University Press, 1991.

_____ . *The Roots of Dependency: Subsistence, Environment, and Social Change among the Choctaws, Pawnees, and Navajos.* Lincoln: University of Nebraska Press, 1983.

Wilson, Terry P. *The Underground Reservation: Osage Oil.* Lincoln: University of Nebraska Press, 1985.

Wolff, Gerald W. *The Kansas-Nebraska Bill: Party, Section, and the Coming of the Civil War*. New York: Revisionist Press, 1977.

Workers of the Writers' Program of the Work Progress Administration in the State of Missouri. *The WPA Guide to the 1930s Missouri*. Lawrence: University Press of Kansas, 1986.

Young, Otis E. *The First Military Escort on the Santa Fe Trail*. Glendale, Calif.: Arthur H. Clark, 1952.

Articles

Abel, Annie Heloise. "Indian Reservations in Kansas and the Extinguishment of Their Title." *Transactions of the Kansas State Historical Society* 8 (1903–1904): 72–109.

――――― . "Proposals for an Indian State, 1778–1878." *Annual Report of the American Historical Association for the Year 1907* 1 (May 1846): 87–104.

"Administration of Indian Affairs." *United States Magazine and Democratic Review* 18 (May 1846): 333–36.

Baker, Joan. "Alcoholism and the American Indian." In *Alcoholism: Development, Consequences, and Interventions*," edited by Nada J. Estes and M. Edith Heinemann, 194–207. St. Louis: C. V. Mosby, 1977.

Brod, Thomas M. "Alcoholism as a Mental Health Problem of Native Americans: A Review of the Literature." *Archives of General Psychiatry* 32 (1975): 1385–91.

Cass, Lewis. "Remarks on the Policy and Practices of the United States and Great Britain in Their Treatment of the Indian." *North American Review* 24 (April 1827): 365–404.

Dozier, Edward P. "Problem Drinking among the American Indians." *Quarterly Journal of Studies on Alcohol* 27 (1966): 72–87.

Ferris, Ida M. "The Sauks and Foxes of Franklin and Osage Counties, Kansas." *Collections of the Kansas State Historical Society* 11 (1909–1910): 333–95.

French, Laurence, and Jim Hornbuckle. "Alcoholism among Native Americans: An Analysis." *Social Work* 25 (1980): 275–80.

"Governor Reeder's Administration." *Transactions of the Kansas State Historical Society* 5 (1896): 163–234.

Grinnell, George Bird. "Bent's Old Fort and Its Builders." *Collections of the Kansas State Historical Society* 15 (1919–1922): 28–91.

Hademan, Nicholas P. "Albert Gallatin Boone." edited by Leroy R. Hafen, 39–42. *The Mountain Men of the Fur Trade of the Far West*. Vol. 8. Glendale, Calif.: Arthur H. Clark, 1987. pp. 39–42.

Hagan, William E. "Full Blood, Mixed Blood, Generic, and Ersatz: The Problem of Indian Identity." *Arizona and the West* 27 (Winter 1985): 309–26.

Hamilton, William. "Autobiography of Reverend William Hamilton." *Transactions and Reports of the Nebraska State Historical Society* 1 (1885): 61–69.

Hawthorne, Nathaniel. "A Rill from the Town Pump" (1835). In *The Centenary Edition of the Works of Nathaniel Hawthorne*. Vol. 9, edited by William Charvat, Roy Harvey Pearce, and Claude M. Simpson, 146. Columbus: Ohio State University Press, 1974.

Heaston, Michael D. "Whiskey Regulation and Indian Land Titles in New Mexico Territory, 1851–1861." *Journal of the West* 10 (1971): 473–83.

Hoover, Herbert T. "Whiskey Trade in the History of Sioux Country since 1802." *Platte Valley Review* 19 (Winter 1991): 5–24.

Kelsey, Harry. "William P. Dole." In *The Commissioners of Indian Affairs, 1824–1977*, edited by Robert M. Kvasnicka and Herman J. Viola, 89–98. Lincoln: University of Nebraska Press, 1979.

Lecompte, Janet. "Mathew Kinkade." In *The Mountain Men of the Fur Trade of the Far West*. Vol. 2, edited by Leroy R. Hafen, 191–97. Glendale, Calif.: Arthur H. Clark, 1965.

———. "Simeon Turley." In *The Mountain Men of the Fur Trade of the Far West*. Vol. 7, edited by Leroy R. Hafen, 310–13. Glendale, Calif.: Arthur H. Clark, 1969.

Lurie, Nancy Oesterich. "The World's Oldest On-Going Protest Demonstration: North American Indian Drinking Patterns." *Pacific Historical Review* 40 (August 1971): 311–21.

Mattes, Merril J. "John Dougherty." In *The Mountain Men of the Fur Trade of the Far West*. Vol. 8, edited by Leroy R. Hafen, 129–41. Glendale, Calif.: Arthur H. Clark, 1971.

May, Philip A. "The Epidemiology of Alcohol Abuse among American Indians: The Mythical and Real Properties." *American Indian Culture and Research Journal* 18 (1994): 121–44.

Nichols, Roy F. "The Kansas-Nebraska Act: A Century of Historiography." *Mississippi Valley Historical Review* 43 (September 1956): 187–212.

"Our Indian Policy." *United State Magazine and Democratic Review* 14 (February 1844): 169–84.

Peters, Bernard C. "Hypocrisy on the Great Lakes Frontier: The Use of Whiskey by the Michigan Department of Indian Affairs." *Michigan Historical Review* 18 (Fall 1992): 1–13.

Prucha, Francis Paul. "American Indian Policy in the 1840s: Visions of Reform." In *The Frontier Challenge: Responses to the Trans-Mississippi West*, edited by John G. Clark, 81–110. Lawrence: University Press of Kansas, 1971.

Satz, Ronald N. "Elbert Herring." In *The Commissioners of Indian Affairs, 1824–1977*, edited by Robert M. Kvasnicka and Herman J. Viola, 13–16. Lincoln: University of Nebraska Press, 1979.

Schroeder, Walter A. "Spread of Settlement in Howard Country, Missouri, 1810–1859." *Missouri Historical Review* 58 (October 1969): 9–18.

"Statement of Theodore Weichselbaum, of Ogden, Riley County, July 17, 1908." *Collections of the Kansas State Historical Society* 11 (1909–1910): 561–71.

Steiger, John W. "Benjamon O'Fallon." In *The Mountain Men of the Fur Trade of the Far West*. Vol. 5, edited by Leroy R. Hafen, 301–14. Glendale, Calif.: Arthur H. Clark, 1968.

Stein, Gary C. "A Fearful Drunkenness: The Liquor Trade to the Western Indians as Seen by European Travellers in America, 1800–1860." *Red River Valley Historical Review* 1 (Summer 1974): 109–21.

Trennert, Robert A. "Luke Lea." In *The Commissioners of Indian Affairs, 1824–1977*, edited by Robert M. Kvasnicka and Herman J. Viola, 49–55. Lincoln: University of Nebraska Press, 1979.

——— . "William Medill." In *The Commissioners of Indian Affairs, 1824–1977*, edited by Robert M. Kvasnicka and Herman J. Viola, 29–39. Lincoln: University of Nebraska Press, 1979.

Unrau, William E. "The Depopulation of the Dheghia-Siouan Kansa Prior to Removal." *New Mexico Historical Review* 48 (October 1973): 313–28.

——— . "Indian Prohibition and Tribal Disorganization in the Trans-Missouri West, 1802–1862." *Contemporary Drug Problems* 21 (Winter 1994): 519–33.

——— . "Investigation or Probity? Investigations into the Affairs of the Kiowa-Comanche Indian Agency, 1867." *Chronicles of Oklahoma* 42 (Autumn 1964): 300–19.

——— . "Lewis Vital Bogy." In *The Commissioners of Indian Affairs, 1824–1977*, edited by Robert M. Kvasnicka and Herman J. Viola, 109–14. Lincoln: University of Nebraska Press, 1979.

Way, Peter. "Evil Humors and Ardent Spirits: The Rough Culture of Canal Construction Workers." *Journal of American History* 79 (March 1993): 1397–1428.

Weibel-Orlando, Joan. "Indians, Ethnicity, and Alcohol: Contrasting Perceptions of the Ethic Self and Alcohol Use." In *The American Experience with Alcohol: Contrasting Cultural Perspectives*, edited by Linda A. Bennett and Genevieve M. Ames, 201–26. New York: Plenum, 1985. pp. 201-26.

Westermeyer, Joseph. "The Drunken Indian: Myths and Realities." *Psychiatric Annals* 4 (November 1974): 29–36. Reprinted in Steven Unger, ed. *The*

Destruction of Indian Families. New York: Association on American Indian Affairs, 1977, pp. 22–28.

———— . "Options Regarding Alcohol Use among the Chippewa."*American Journal of Orthopsychiatry* 43 (1972): 398–403.

Winkler, A. M. "Drinking on the American Frontier." *Quarterly Journal of Studies on Alcohol* 29 (1968): 413–45.

Wohl, R. Richard. "Three Generations of Business Enterprise in a Midwestern City: The McGees of Kansas City." *Journal of Economic History* 16 (1956): 514–28.

Wolff, P. H. "Vasomotor Sensitivity to Alcohol in Diverse Mongoloid Populations." *Human Genetics* 25 (1973): 193–99.

Young, Mary E. "Indian Removal and Land Allotment: The Civilized Tribes and Jacksonian Justice." *American Historical Review* 64 (October 1959): 34–35.

Theses and Dissertations

Davis, Randall Craig. "Firewater Myths: Alcohol and Portrayals of Native Americans in American Literature." Ph.D. diss., Ohio State University, 1991.

German, Avis. "Refugee Indians within and from the Indian Country, 1861–1867." Master's thesis, Wichita State University, 1987.

Keckeisen, Robert Joseph. "The Kansa 'Half-Breed' Lands: Contravention and Transformation of United States Indian Policy in Kansas." Master's thesis, Wichita State University, 1982.

INDEX